Covenant and Commitments

Covenant and Commitments

Faith, Family, and Economic Life

MAX L. STACKHOUSE

Westminster John Knox Press
Louisville, Kentucky

Book and cover design by Jennifer K. Cox

First edition

Published by Westminster John Knox Press
Louisville, Kentucky

This book is printed on acid-free paper that meets the American National Standards Institute Z39.48 standard. ♾

PRINTED IN THE UNITED STATES OF AMERICA

97 98 99 00 01 02 03 04 05 06 — 10 9 8 7 6 5 4 3 2 1

Library of Congress Cataloging-in-Publication Data

Stackhouse, Max L.
    Covenant and commitments : faith, family, and economic life / Max
L. Stackhouse. — 1st ed.
        p.   cm. — (The family, religion, and culture)
    Includes bibliographical references and index.
    ISBN 0-664-25467-5 (alk. paper)
    1. Family—Religious aspects—Christianity.   2. Covenants—
Religious aspects—Christianity.   3. Sociology, Christian.
I. Title.   II. Series.
BV4526.2.S67   1997
306.85'088'204—dc21   96-40010

Contents

Series Foreword

There is an important debate going on today over the present health and future well-being of families in American society. Although some people on the political right and left use concern about the state of the family primarily to further their respective partisan causes, the debate is real, and it is over genuine issues. The discussion, however, is not well informed and is riddled with historical, theological, and social-scientific ignorance.

This is not unusual as political debates go. The American family debate, however, is especially uninformed and dogmatic. This is understandable, for all people have experienced a family in some way, feel themselves to be experts, and believe that they are entitled to their strong opinions.

The books in this series, The Family, Religion, and Culture, discuss these issues in ways that will place the American debate about the family on more solid ground. The series is the result of the Religion, Culture, and Family Project, which was funded by a generous grant from the Division of Religion of the Lilly Endowment, Inc. and took place in the Institute for Advanced Study in The University of Chicago Divinity School. Part of the project proceeded while Don Browning, the project director, was in residence at the Center of Theological Inquiry in Princeton, New Jersey.

The series advances no single point of view on the American family debate and gives no one solution to the problems concerning families today. The authors and editors contributing to the volumes represent both genders as well as a variety of religious and ethnic perspectives and denominational backgrounds—liberal and conservative; Protestant, Catholic, and Jewish; evangelical and mainline; and black, white, and Asian. A number of the authors and editors met annually for a seminar and discussed—often with considerable intensity—their outlines, papers, and chapters pertaining to the various books. The careful reader will notice that many of the seminar members did influence one another; but it is safe to say that each of them in the end took his or her own counsel and spoke out of his or her own convictions.

The series is comprehensive, with studies on the family in ancient Israel and early Christianity; economics and the family; law, feminism, and reproductive technology and the family; the family and American faith traditions; and congregations and families; as well as two summary books—one a handbook and one a critical overview of the American family debate.

In *Covenant and Commitments,* Max Stackhouse shows how families are profoundly influenced by the economic systems and the ideologies of economic life that surround them. The structural changes in our society—from hunting and gathering to agriculture to trade and early industrialization—and in our economy—from early capitalism to socialism, postindustrialism, and now the global economy—have had a profound impact on the structure, purpose, and well-being of families.

Stackhouse explores not only how families have been shaped by economies but also how the faith or religious vision that families live by can shape economies. Families are not passive reactors to the onslaughts of economic forces; they can guide these forces through their beliefs and commitments. It is widely taught, for instance, that the Protestant Reformation influenced modern economic life. But often its impact on families is not mentioned.

Max Stackhouse demonstrates how "covenant theology" has functioned to guide families, market, and government. He shows not only how this occurred in Geneva, England, and early America but also how it can happen today and possibly in the future. For this age of corporations, global economies, dynamic markets, weakened families, deteriorating civil societies, and beleaguered governments, Stackhouse develops a powerful "public theology" based on fresh interpretations of what it means to have covenant relationships.

We are deeply indebted to Max Stackhouse for showing how Christian theology is relevant to the most complex problems facing families and economies in today's rapidly changing world. We hope that you, by reading this book, will discover that families and economics should not be thought of in isolation from religious faith.

Don S. Browning
Ian S. Evison

Introduction

Everyone who reads or hears of this book and the series of which it is a part will have been supported by and nurtured in a family that allowed him or her not only to survive but also, in substantial measure, to flourish and to be concerned about the well-being of other persons and of civil society. It turns out, however, that understanding the social, psychological, economic, moral, and spiritual dimensions of all that makes this possible is difficult, even humbling. The central question of this book is whether we can develop a viable ethic for family life in our times, in view of the challenges posed by our changing social and economic context. The challenges and changes are registered in the shifting modes of thought about human relationships; in households and work patterns; in home life and religious attitudes; in corporations and the new cosmopolitan interactions of a globalizing, technological society; in debates about welfare programs; and in cynical attitudes about commitment and love. These forces all put pressure on the family.

When we use the word *family*, of course, we are introducing a highly disputed term, in part because it carries moral and religious overtones. Some are convinced that the family is merely an invention of western hegemonic culture and of male patriarchy, reinforced by dualistic religion, and that it therefore ought to be radically reconstructed. Ironically, this conviction recognizes that discussing the family involves speaking of both normative and descriptive matters and that in the long run, protest as we might, convictional, philosophical, ethical, and moral issues will be joined to the material, biological, sensual, emotional, and voluntary aspects of the relationships between sexual partners and between parents and children.

The formation of a family, however, is not only relational. It is inevitably also institutional and societal. The channels by which people find and establish their relationships are often highly, if subtly, formed by longstanding and widespread social practice and governed by legal mandates and constraints that have become second nature to our view of family life. The result is a sexual, social, economic, and political unit in the context of a civil society. The relationships within and between these institutions may be variously arranged, as we can see by cross-cultural study or in families of mixed background. A Japanese man and a Swedish woman may meet at a business conference in Copenhagen, or a Nigerian man and an Eskimo woman may become acquainted at a Canadian university, and each couple may decide to form a family. When they marry, everyone from their cultures will be able to recognize that they have formed a family. But it is likely that each person will have distinctive expectations of what that institution ought to be. These institutionalized expectations may differ from time to time and place to place, but they are never absent from human life.

At one level, all animals find shelter, territory, food, and opportunities for reproduction through patterns of dual sexuality and sometimes in the nurture of the young; otherwise they become extinct. Biologists can tell us in great and fascinating detail how this process works with various species and why humans also must do all these things. Humans, no less than insects, fish, reptiles, birds, and other mammals, are much preoccupied with just these activities, and some impulses seem to be quite common. High percentages of males and females are driven to seek each other for predictable purposes.

What distinguishes humanity from the beasts in all this is that humans develop laws governing household life, negotiate divisions of labor and role definitions that are not determined by instincts, cook the food they share, make love face to face, and know that all these activities are shaped by culture—one that they attempt either to perpetuate or to revise by socializing and acculturating the next generation in quite intentional ways. In the process of deciding what is important to pass on to the next generation, basic value questions come to the fore, and we have to decide what the most important things of life are.

Moreover, in passing our laws, dividing our labor, developing our tastes, expressing our love, and educating the young, we do not simply follow our instincts or cultures as we inherit them, even if we cannot entirely or arbitrarily abandon them. We freely chose some aspects of how we do these things, and we seek a standard higher than the basic requirements of biophysical and conventional social life to guide the way we do them. We develop networks of loyalty, trust, sacrifice, and care; we try to find out what the most important things of life are, why they are as they are, and if they should be introduced into the mix of life, whether to alter its fabric or to support the valid parts of that fabric when they begin to fall apart. It is for this reason that the list of distinctive human activities can and must be extended. Unlike animals, we bury our loved ones when they die and bless the homes we build, the food we eat, the loves we fall into and celebrate. In fact, humans everywhere believe that each one of these acts has to do, positively or negatively, with what is holy. Religion and critical reflection on it by means of theology are the most distinctive activities that distinguish humanity from the other creatures of the earth, however much we share with them.

Recently, James Q. Wilson, the noted social scientist, asked, "What is there in nature that produces not simply sex but partnership?"[1] The answer, as we shall see, is this: Human nature is social as well as biological, moral as well as cultural, and spiritual as well as material. The kind and quality of religion turn out to be critical for the kind of social, ethical, and material systems developed in civilizations—the roles, the relationships, the institutions, and thus the rules and expectations that guide us. And these become decisive for how the attractions of nature are expressed, channeled, rewarded, or constrained. Only some types of religious sensibilities preserve and enhance society and allow the basic structures of human being to become manifest more fully. Further, because theology and ethics are the most adequate disciplines with which to study the relative adequacy of religion, theological ethics turns out to be indispensable to the task of studying the family.

The family, I argue, is at every point an ethical and a spiritual association as well as a material and a biological institution. Humans are social animals able to love and worship, free to do or not to do things in specific ways, and aware that better and worse ways exist for doing things. Since such matters are central to religious ethics, it is not at all strange that among the several studies undertaken in this series, at least one would focus on the relation of theological ethics to the very material side of life.

However, the relationship of theology and ethics to the social and material shape of things changes over time. It changes not only because social and economic and political transformations take place but also because people develop new understandings of the first principles and ultimate ends of life as these are rooted in religion and theology. Such variations have decisive implications for ethics—specifically, for the reshaping of social, economic, and political life in ways that impact on the family. Sometimes, also, changing a theological insight, interpretation, or application as it relates to the ethics of family life or of sexual relationships will have a long-term effect on social, economic, and political forces, and this will rebound to alter religious life in unanticipated ways.[2]

The fact that theology changes has inclined some to argue that theology is unstable and unreliable. But this is an odd argument, for few suggest that because politics, economics, science, law, and medicine change, we should never rely on them. Indeed, I claim here that certain dimensions of theology more clearly grasp how we humans are, at the very depth of our being—especially in regard to the right ordering and ultimate ends of human sexuality—than do most of the alternatives. This is because to grasp our real, existential, sociohistorical existence requires acknowledgment that we do not entirely create the normative principles under which we must live. Real life, real societies, real history is ever touched by a "heteronormative" reality. The question is how best to contain its imperialism when it is falsely extended by racial, sexual, cultural, or religious groups that profess to have it within their grasp, so that they are no longer under it, and how to reclaim it when it is falsely obscured by those who allege that all norms are autonomously generated.

I argue that one main stream of the theological heritage is correct: Sexuality, the formation of households and homes, the nurture of children, and the development of ways to aid those in need ought to take place in covenanted relationships, and we can know, with some degree of reliability, what some marks of such relationships are. At the same time, these normative marks have to be related to other factors in society, such as new conditions in the political economy and new findings in science, law, and medicine. Indeed, as we shall see, a covenantal view at its best is one that includes both elements of voluntary consent and careful analysis of the actual conditions under which we offer the consent.

In previous studies, I sought to identify the ways in which theological ethics may relate to material and social life in several areas—in the necropolis of modern military might, in the ever-widening spread of metropolitan patterns of existence around the world, in the cosmopolitan encounters of cultures and the recognition of human rights as a potentially universal creed, and in the peculiar shape of modern political economies. Also, with the help of several gifted colleagues, I have attempted to trace the implications of some of these developments for theological education, for the moral dimensions of business, and for the formation of a global civil society. But I have not adequately focused (nor has the field of ethics) on the neglected matter of family life, where, much evidence now suggests, many of the critical issues of spirituality and materiality, of morality and actuality, have to be faced.[3]

Indeed, not only we in ethics have neglected this area of institutional life as an enduring and indispensable dimension of life. For at least a second generation, social commentators often have followed instead the conventional wisdom of C. Wright Mills and his generation that "families and churches and schools adapt to modern life; governments and armies and corporations shape it"[4] and have failed to note his inversion of this view when he coined the widely adopted slogan "The personal is political," which shook the world of social theory from the 1960s to the 1990s. In a fresh, new study, Charles Lemert has shown how these themes (the ambiguous causal relation of private and public forces), deeply rooted in John Stuart Mill and Karl Marx and manifesting an antireligious radicalism, fed the sociological imagination of Mills, supported an attack on any thinkers who worked with notions of enduring structures and normative orders (from Alvin Gouldner to Franz Fanon and Michel Foucault), and fueled the social hostility present in many of the militant movements that followed.[5] To be sure, these factions often had differing agendas, but they shared a disdain for "democratic capitalism," a negative analysis of modern technology, and a contempt for the "bourgeois family."

What relates the present study to earlier ones is a set of methodological convictions. I think that we can find the best guides for moral analysis, evaluation, and judgment on controversial issues in the common life by linking the methods of historical social analysis with those of theological ethics. The interactive tools of historical awareness and structural analysis, on the one hand, and of ethical passion that is rooted in a reasoned understanding of what the ultimate warrants for our principles (how, finally, as far as we can discern it, we think God wants us to live), on the other hand, help us identify the several dimensions of decisive institutions and generate operational values for the future. Institutions such as the family are neither merely one thing nor fixed and solid. Because humans ordinarily come in male or female form and rather regularly get together with some intimate intensity, children are not unusual. No civilization can survive without a way of dealing with the result as well as the character of this intimate intensity. We call the variety of regularized means for coping with these realities "family," recognizing that it is constitutive of, contributory to, and influenced by the "ethos."

Many years ago, John Stuart Mill coined the term *ethology* to designate the science of interpreting the value systems that are built into the fabric of social life. He abandoned the effort to establish this science, for it could not be developed on his presuppositions. Karl Marx took up the effort again, and many think that he came very close to realizing the science. But it seems to me that he not only failed but has been proven to have made major errors that led to great human disasters. In contrast, the nineteenth- and twentieth-century post-Marxist social theorists— from Fustel de Coulanges, Max Weber, Ernst Troeltsch, and Émile Durkheim through Talcott Parsons, Benjamin Nelson, and James Luther Adams to such contemporary thinkers as Robert Bellah, Peter Berger, Roland Robertson, and Francis Fukuyama—have provided many of the tools that enable us to discern more accurately the nature and character of the values that dominate our ethos. For one thing, they recognized a certain wisdom in some of the classical philosophers and religious traditions that Mill and Marx, Gouldner and Mills, Fanon and Foucault too quickly dismissed. For another, an amazing array of information has become available about the patterns of life in many civilizations that simply was not previously accessible. What is remarkable about the work of these scholars is that they allowed the longitudinal study of the changes in history to interact with the perennial, structural requirements of political science, psychology, anthropology, and economics as they relate to various possible combinations and coherent arrangements. Still further, these thinkers are deeply interested in how the matters that these sciences investigate interact bit by bit to form complex systems that they can study comparatively, and how religion shapes the organization and direction of the whole.

In this regard, these scholars are all aware that religion plays a decisive role in holding the parts together and in selectively sustaining the values by which the various sectors of the common life find their distinctive principles and purposes and interact, when they do, in viable systems. People's lives, societies, and cultures are everywhere guided by the "ideal interests" people have as much as, if not more than, by their "material interests." For these reasons, a study such as this one depends on the rather specialized historical and social-scientific investigations undertaken by others. Yet it attempts to offer to them a way of perceiving and interpreting the whole from the standpoint of a special focus on the kinds of normative patterns, and their logic, that stand at the moral core of an ethos.

Ethology is, however, finally descriptive and not normative, even if it discloses widely shared operating values, constant structures, or "necessary" moral preconditions. No one, for example, can debate values or engage in scholarly research in ethology unless it is presumed that people will attempt to tell the truth about such information and will alter a perspective if it proves impossible to account for obvious information with a preferred view. Honestly done, ethology should be able to tell us, with a high degree of accuracy, what a society or a subculture in a given period of history thinks ought to be the case and how that view is related to the empirical realities; but it cannot tell us whether that view ought to be embraced or altered or abandoned or condemned. That requires another level of analysis—one that turns to philosophical and religious dimensions of ethics, especially as these are joined in theology.

If historical sociology helps us understand the ethological dimensions of the moral life, then philosophical and ethical theology helps us inquire into the areas of normative thought that are often called "deontology"—whether there are normative obligations and duties that are binding on all humans, irrespective of particular historical conditions—and "teleology"— whether there is a knowable purpose or end to life, its various parts, and the cosmos as a whole. When we combine these questions and come to a persuasive answer to them, we are on the brink of forming informed moral judgments in particular cases or, when considering the larger picture, a viable social ethic, what some prefer to call a "public theology."

I am well aware that various thinkers from time to time have attempted to identify the single one of these dimensions of normative thought that should dominate and guide the others; but while analytical clarity about each one is necessary, ethics is, finally, more a synthetic than an analytical field. We more or less triangulate toward the best judgments we can make, recognizing that each reference point in this effort may need continued clarification, and that when two or more factors are taken into account, some element of freedom of conscience is possible. Just as we allow dissenting opinions in legal traditions and have councils in many areas of life where people come to split votes, so in ethics an element of judgment is unavoidable. Yet ethics is not simply a matter of opinions, for some judgments are either quickly ruled out of bounds as so mistaken as not to be taken seriously or deemed serious enough to refute. And in engaging the debates, we rely on a degree of confidence that arguments, and not only opinions, make a difference. We may discuss the issues in ways that can speak to and with people who are not already persuaded that "our" religion is convincing. This is one reason we inevitably need what I and others call a public theology, a warranted discourse about these judgments that is able both to persuade those who may not agree on social, philosophical, or religious grounds and to offer plausible, defensible guidelines for personal and social decisions.

In regard to the family, we do not have an agreed-upon ethology or a consensus about either deontology or teleology. Although nine out of ten Americans get married, most adult Americans are married now, most are happy with their union, and more than four out of five unmarried adults say they want to get married, we are faced with a sense of crisis in the American family.[6] Lawrence Stone, the noted journalist, was not alone when he recently wrote of the widespread sense of the crumbling family, "The scale of marital breakdown in the West since 1960 has no historical precedent and seems unique. There has been nothing like it for the past 2000 years, and probably much longer."[7]

This view may be valid. It is frequently connected with the view that modern "industrialization, fragmenting people's lives as it did, dissolved [the] . . . sense of obligation and encouraged individuals to look after their own interests."[8] But another interpretation may be equally plausible: The Industrial Revolution was prompted in part by an organizational revolution, one that shifted the means of production from the farm to the factory, from the family to the corporation. Further, the Industrial Revolution was rooted in a deeper theological and ethical perception that we could, and indeed ought to, intervene in nature and transform it to serve human well-being. Economic well-being was henceforth identified with extrafamilial institutions and with matters about which we could make decisions (such as birth control). If this interpretation is accepted, then the perceived crisis in the family is the result of a shift in the status of the household from the primary unit of production and consumption to the primary unit of consumption only.

It cannot be said that in traditional, household-based economies there was no looking after individual interests. Many Victorian novels and surviving diaries speak of the desperate need to marry well, to blot out the heart of love for the calculation of economic advantage—for the well-being of the family or to build political alliances that would allow the preservation or enhancement of its power and position.

It could be, however, that industrialization has brought about a situation in which the family is increasingly purified of its extrinsic dependencies on political power or economic survival, and that the only thing that can possibly hold it together is love. But the problem then is deeper. It is not at all clear that we yet know how to love, develop the appropriate support systems for love, and guide it as it is reformed in new social conditions. What can and should be the shape of male-female, parent-child, traditional and alternative relationships, when they are not propped up by political and economic necessity?

Many commentators are unsure where we are in this matter. The "family values" debate is intense partly because in many areas of the United States, and increasingly in parts of Europe, Africa, and Asia, traditional views of family life are collapsing. Some are convinced that we are in the midst of a great social degeneration; others speak hopefully of a time of transition. As we will see, it is clear that children are often the victims of the collapse of family life and social degeneration, and some efforts to establish government-led "family policies" seem to exacerbate the problems.

In a major study on which this book will rely heavily, Alan Tapper asks the key question "What causes family breakdown?" and surveys the rich trove of social-scientific research on this issue.[9] However, it may be that families were ever prone to breakdown, that it is nothing new, and that the increased rate of divorce is closely related to the decline of constraints on the tendency toward breakdown, as Roderick Phillips's massive study of the history of divorce suggests.[10] We shall have to investigate what the particular pressures in our times might be, as the family and household undergo enormous stress, change, and in many cases breakdown. In the face of these pressures, the question might better be framed: What can and should hold families together, if some of the older props to the family are being altered by choices people make, are repudiated because they are held to be intrusions into love, or are viewed as corruptions of the freedoms people want in love?[11]

Traditionally, the phrases "for richer, for poorer" and "for better, for worse" have been part of what the bride and groom promise before God and the people. They pledge that each will take the other

> to have and to hold, from this day forward, for better, for worse, for richer, for poorer, in sickness and in health, to love and to cherish, till death do us part, according to God's holy ordinance.[12]

These liturgical phrases recognize that marriage involves an interweaving of material and spiritual conditions, historic traditions and new situations, and biological realities and moral commitment. It was made in the context of both a public signing of a legal agreement and public worship. This vow early became a part of a nuptial mass and until today has stood at the center of marriage rites. These phrases from the pledge draw attention to the fact that the formation of and the intent to sustain a marriage are celebrated according to a pattern that faithful Christians believe is intended by God. The law also acknowledges that the new social and economic relationship is intended to endure even if things go badly. The bride and groom form not only a pair, possibly to produce children, but a household, a home, and a new institution in civil society.

Each chapter of this book addresses disputed aspects of family life today. In many Protestant churches, intense debates continue about the nature and character of homosexuality and whether the traditional norm of enduring, heterosexual, monogamous relationship must be honored or altered. Hence chapter 1 explores the various understandings of sex and marriage now under debate and the interpretations of the relation of physical and spiritual factors that stand behind these understandings.

As we will see, many current views of this matter have been shaped by philosophical frames of reference that are rooted in modern social theories. A libertarian view, closely linked with capitalism, and a liberationist view, much influenced by socialism, have offered competing accounts of the history, nature, and economic function of family life, particularly as these can be seen in patterns of work in the household and in modern industry. This topic is addressed in chapter 2.

When we speak of the household, we must immediately consider that the vision of the ideal home has a long and complex history, with many features from the distant past echoing in our common consciousness. Certainly, renting, buying, or building a residence is the largest expense of most families, and how that is done and what its relationship is to political, economic, and religious life are among the least investigated parts of the contemporary discussion of the family. Chapter 3 explores key influences from the past that are with us still and some of the alternative models, religious, pagan, and secular, that are shaping the future. It offers an overview of this enormously influential legacy.

Chapter 4 inquires into the economic and moral consequences of family breakdown, some of which are a product of change, some of which are a cause of change, some of which are confused with beneficial change, and some of which signal changes yet to come. Many of the issues in this area are presently being debated in terms of welfare reform; and in these debates, a vast range of questions appears about the place of children in family life, in the society, and as a responsibility of the state. Key issues of common responsibility, as well as the difficult questions of dependency, the "feminization of poverty," and the demoralization of the next generation, are all considered.

Finally, in view of all the issues of sex and marriage, household and work, home and religion, children and society, we return to the guiding question of this book: Can we construct a viable ethic for family life in a globalizing civil society, given all the intellectual, economic, and historical problems we have surveyed? Chapter 5 suggests that we can and draws attention to neglected dimensions of our theological heritage that suggest universally valid, pluralistic, and dynamic possibilities.

One, unintended result of this book is that it stands as a challenge to the modern churches and clergy. Again and again, these various explorations revealed how central religious life is in the fabric of people's lives and in the formation of the institutions of the common life. It is not clear that contemporary religious leaders realize what an impact, and thus what an opportunity and responsibility, they have in influencing both souls and societies. Key to the last chapter is a "prophetic" recovery and recasting of the classical covenantal traditions, linked to a fresh vision of how the family may best reconstitute the household and find its place in a society where dual careers, a corporate economy, and a limited state are likely to predominate for as far as we can see into the future.

Throughout the entire process of writing this book, and particularly in regard to the statistical and demographic information presented in chapters 2 and 4, I have been helped immensely by my research assistant, a very promising young scholar in her own right, Deirdre Hainsworth. I am also grateful to the "pro-seminar" on "Family Life, Faith and Society" taught at Princeton Theological Seminary in the fall of 1994. The twenty-two students there, representing at least seven distinct cultures and religious traditions ranging from American Unitarian Universalist to fundamentalist Baptist, from European Roman Catholic to East Asian Evangelical, were a delight to teach. And several of the visiting lecturers who joined the class and gave of their insight—Don Browning, Mary Stewart Van Leeuwen, Edmund Leites, William Lazareth, Sara McLanahan—contributed much to them and to me. I am grateful for the many helpful suggestions I have gained from the several doctoral students at Princeton Theological Seminary who offered critical comments on early drafts and from my colleagues both at the seminary and at the Center for Theological Inquiry, where I spent a portion of 1995 working on this material. Special words of appreciation must also go to the Lilly Endowment for funding this project; to Don Browning and Ian Evison, the editors of the series, for their patience and guidance; to David Heim, who took my often turgid prose and sometimes confused thinking and applied his generous editorial skills (and penetrating critique) to an unfinished draft of this book. I draw freely on the ideas of these gifted students, scholars, and friends, although they are not responsible for how I used the material that I learned from them or for any errors or awkwardnesses that may remain.

Above all I am indebted to my wife, Jean, with whom I have spent nearly forty years seeking to contribute to the covenants of civilization and discovering the existential dimensions of the meaning of love. In both this shared pilgrimage and in these more academic explorations, I find myself like Abraham and Sarah, our heroes of faith described in the book of Hebrews. Like them, we are also called to seek a city that has foundations and to connect love with a wider sense of responsibility in society, and under a deeper theological sensibility than was frequently the case in the surrounding world.

> Lift up your drooping hands and strengthen your weak knees, and make straight paths for your feet. . . . Strive for peace with all, and for holiness. . . . Do not neglect to show hospitality to strangers . . . , remember those in prison . . . and those who are ill-treated, since you also are in the body. Let marriage be held in honor by all and let the marriage bed be kept undefiled. . . . Keep your lives free from the love of money . . . ; for he has said "I will never leave you or forsake you." (Heb. 12:12–13:5)

1

Sex and Marriage: An Intense Debate

Most people in the United States go to church to get married. After that, they are expected to found a home, to share their material and personal resources, and eventually to have and raise children. Not only Christians but believers of various other faiths invite the clergy to bless the marriage relationship and expect them to offer guidance about how marital life ought to be lived. The husband and wife do not always live entirely by this advice, but in all traditions it is understood that a couple are joined in a set of sacred obligations and roles. The precise definition of these obligations and roles differs, sometimes dramatically, from culture to culture and religion to religion, but they always and everywhere involve a holy bond of social, emotional, and sexual commitment rooted in the very condition of being human, in the sense of love as a gift, and in the potential to participate in the creation of new life.

During the last quarter century, a debate has raged among Christians in America over matters of sexual morality. It has been most focused in the ecumenical Protestant churches—those that belong to the National and World Councils of Churches. This debate is about sexuality, particularly homosexuality, and it involves a redefinition of normative sexual behavior, the family, and the role of religion in material culture. Roman Catholic, Evangelical, and Eastern Orthodox churches and the African-American denominations that belong to these councils have also been touched by the debate, but they have tended to resist a sustained focus on these matters.

The ecumenical Protestants (sometimes called the "mainline," "old-line," or "liberal" denominations) have produced more church statements, background papers, study documents, books, and proposals on sexuality in this period than in any comparable period of church history. A recent set of books has collected more than 150 of the most important documents, including some key statements from Evangelical and Roman Catholic authorities, and a series of articles have begun to study basic tendencies.[1] Disagreements will, of course, continue; but it is possible to survey the basic patterns. I would summarize the main developments under five points:

1. The churches affirm that genital sexual activity is best confined to a heterosexual marriage; and they agree that even if it is not, relationships should be companionate, exclusive, enduring, and in principle open to the possibility of procreation. All who are called to engage in active sexual lives should seek to approximate the ideals set forth in marriage rites.

2. Most churches that embrace infant baptism[2] (and thus the reality of both sin and gracious affirmation of personhood irrespective of individual moral intent or behavior) have given support to the human and civil rights of homosexual persons but resist giving religious approval to homosexual behavior or to the marriage of same-sex partners.

3. All but two ecumenical Christian churches (the United Church of Christ and the Episcopal Church, both with some ambiguity)[3] officially deny ordination to open advocates of or participants in homosexual relationships, usually because these alliances are not viewed as normatively coequal to heterosexual marriage. Such relationships are, however, often quietly tolerated pastorally or accepted as morally superior to promiscuity.

4. Most churches have approved feminist theories that press for justice, when justice is defined as equality of dignity, status, and pay. They have resisted feminism when it turns all theological questions into gender issues and allies with homosexual advocacy in the name of liberation. In short, "justice feminism" has been generally accepted in the churches while "gender feminism" is generally doubted.[4]

5. Pastoral care for those who are unmarried, homosexually or bisexually attracted, living in enduring same-sex relations, unable to procreate for whatever reason,[5] divorced, or separated is seen as morally and spiritually required, even if these situations are

not celebrated. In this area pastoral wisdom is required, for human situations are so complex and varied that no single strategy can be employed beyond the call to approximate, as far as possible, the normative vision of marriage.

In brief, the overall results of a quarter century of debate reflect a rejection of a radical effort to overturn classical teachings. For all the variations among the denominations, the official statements are remarkably consistent with one another and with the legacy of the Protestant Reformation. The inclusion of justice feminism is novel and is modifying both the uses of traditional symbols and attitudes toward acceptance of women in ministry; but as an extension of concepts of justice to new groups, this change is not revolutionary, and this feminism does not challenge the normative character of the heterosexual family.

The debates, however, have been so multifaceted, so laden with crosscutting arguments and feelings, and so fractured by ideological agendas that both the deeper consensus and the reasons for it have been obscured. Besides, the debates take place while the media portray and sometimes idealize homosexual clergy and same-sex weddings presided over by clergy and while concerted political efforts are moving some states, such as Hawaii, toward the legalization of gay and lesbian partnerships. In these efforts, specifically economic arguments are frequently cited: It is very difficult for a partner to collect insurance or death benefits or to gain control of an estate if same-sex relationships are not legally recognized. Surely that is not just. Further, many churches have not made clear the theological-ethical underpinnings that ground their stances, beyond an appeal to authority or tradition. Yet the ecumenical churches may well have a case that is better than what they have stated, and the burden of proof may well be on those who challenge it. It is the task of this chapter to set forth the key issues in that case and to suggest where the opponents of it may be ethically mistaken about homosexuality but still pose a range of questions that are of profound importance.

The Background of the Controversy

Most Christians believe that it is an enduring, reasonable, and coherent conviction of those religions born out of the biblical traditions to hold that the authors of the Adam and Eve stories of Genesis (with parallels to the Qur'an; see 2:28–37) were, by the grace of God, inspired to see the human situation with a high degree of revealing ethical accuracy. God created the human and gave to this earthly creature a dignity that was nearly godlike, enabling a communion with God as well as a capacity to exercise freedom and to recognize the laws and purposes of God—and thus also to flout them. This most precious of creatures was also distinguished into male and female, a differentiation that made possible an interaction that, in some ways, echoes a relationship with the Creator and makes humans potential partners in the processes of creation.

This pattern is reaffirmed throughout scriptural history. It is against the distortions of this pattern that the prophets later protest. They take the breaking of the basic arrangements of the moral stage of life as an indicator that the judgment and renewal of salvation history is necessary, as we see in Ezekiel and Hosea. Paul appeals to this pattern repeatedly, and it is to this story that Jesus turned (Mark 10:2–12; Matt. 19:3–6) when the issue of responsible relationship was debated in his day. Something of the right order of life, the good end of existence, and the engaged participation in sustaining contexts of life and their relation are implicit in this early story. It is thick with meaning.[6]

Commentators over the centuries have explored each nuance and accent through glasses that have been ground by many cultural biases and ideological dispositions; but on the whole, the heirs of these biblical traditions have held that the ancient authors were not in error.[7] Just as the wall drawings of thirty thousand years ago are recognized as unsurpassed by modern artists, as the pre-Socratic philosophers discovered the still-valid fact that the square of the hypotenuse of a right triangle is equal to the sum of the square of its two sides, and as the deep structure of the grammars of many languages identified by pundits of old signals the capacity of humans everywhere to communicate, the biblical authors saw something of the basic design, purpose, and context of life that transcends every sociohistorical epoch.

As to the basic normative structure for human sexuality stated in the biblical texts, three elements are primary. First, the fundamental relationship that humans are to have with God and with one another is to be one of fidelity in communion (Gen. 1:27–28). One is not to live only by or for oneself.[8] Persons are to be respected and honored. Each is made "in the image of God" (Gen. 1:26). Here is the deepest root of what later became spoken of as the "soul," the seat of human "dignity," the source of "conscience," and thus the center of all rights and duties and the core of the freedom and knowledge that allow for personal responsibility.

Individualism, however, is not the chief implication of this insight. Persons are real and to be honored, but they are rooted in a relationship to God and intended for human relationship.[9] "It is not good that one should be alone" (Gen. 2:18). Indeed, the contemporary biblical scholar Walter Brueggemann only partially overstates the case when he argues that the "image of God" given to humanity is never in an individual alone but only in the community of male and female: "Humanity is community male and female. And none is the full image of God alone."[10] But if we are to exist as associated persons, the question is whether there is a normative character to the relationship. In the biblical view, there is. We are given the freedom and power to name the realities we discover under God's care and to till the garden and keep it, but we are not to decide matters opportunistically, use the creation only to satisfy felt needs, or deny the integrity of the primal relationship that brought all that is into being (Gen. 2:15–17). It is right to be faithful; it is wrong to violate God-given limits: "Of this tree you shall not eat." Personal and relational existence, morally and spiritually considered, is rooted from the start in a divinely ordained moral order that, in some measure, everyone knows.

That order has a purpose, the second element in the structure of human sexuality: generativity. We are to use the resources of creation—the world, the mind, and the body—to see that life flourishes. "Be fruitful and multiply" is one of the earliest and most repeated of the commands. That which defies or stultifies life is contrary to that purpose. The capacity to reproduce is a gift; it is a mark of how God invites creatures to participate in the blessing of ongoing creativity. Humans are to see their sex as a part of the ongoing flow of life, as a blessed link in the generations, becoming fathers and mothers to the generations of tomorrow in a way that can be honored and, as the later commandment says, honoring the fathers and the mothers who went before.

To be sure, the mere proliferation of progeny is not a sufficient mark of vision of or responsibility to the future. Serving God and fellow humanity may call some to renounce biological generativity, as the example of saints and sages in many traditions testifies. Further, the formation of bonds that knit together lives in mutual affirmation may be even more important than those between parents and children, as we see in the life of Jesus. This motif is present throughout the Bible, not only in the stories of Abraham and Sarah and of Jacob and Leah but also in those of David and Jonathan and of Ruth and Naomi, as well as among the first disciples of Jesus (Mark 10:28–30). It may even be that God will recognize greater moral integrity in some same-sex affections than in many opposite-sex relationships. Thus the tradition teaches that we dare not prematurely attempt to separate the "wheat from the tares" in this life. Nevertheless, these alternative affections are not something that can or should displace the common expectation that we should seek to approximate the primary patterns and purposes of human sexuality that were given in creation and have been affirmed in all the long genealogies that appear in the Bible to represent that kind of love which reaches from generation to generation.

Not only are fidelity within a framework of moral order and fruitful generativity within affectionate relationships among the deepest structures of human life, but humans also are called by the biblical tradition to form and sustain social institutions where both fidelity and fruitful generativity become part of the general pattern of the common life. When a man and a woman, in their differentiation and their complementarity, see each other as truly other yet also as the same as the self ("flesh of my flesh," Gen. 2:20–23), they are no longer bound to their genealogical roots. They depart the gene pool and the loyalties from which they come. They form new intimate bonds: "Therefore a man leaves his father and his mother and cleaves to his wife, and they become one flesh. And the man and his wife were both naked and were not ashamed" (Gen. 2:24–25).[11]

Thus to the theological-biological norms of fidelity and fecundity is added the sociotheological norm of family. As an institution, the family is always influenced by the surrounding historical, ideological, economic, political, and legal structures, which give it a specific stamp (as we shall see in subsequent chapters).[12] Real families do not develop in an idyllic setting of plentiful goodness, although falling in love offers echoes of that Edenic state. Real families almost always experience situations of temptation and distortion. The ancient text is well aware of this, and of the fact that when they succumb to these temptations and begin to lie to God and each other about doing so, they compound the fault by trying to hide themselves in "natural" coverings. Love, as it is known to most of humanity, takes place in a context where people try to hide their deficiencies and where the cost of betrayal, scarcity, and pain is well known. At times the family shape has been patriarchal, at times matriarchal; always at least a little tribal or clannish; historically, often feudal or manorial, while more recently bourgeois or suburban and increasingly "dual-career." Each pattern suggests that the actual shape of family life and hence the operating definitions of fidelity and of fecundity are worked out in the context of the political economy of the society at large.

Thus, even if the command to embody "one flesh" remains, precisely how it is to be related to a fidelity to the moral order or to generative fecundity becomes also partly an issue of the whole fabric of society. Conflicts over such matters surfaced in the biblical account—in the hostilities of Cain and Abel and in the establishment of the arts and crafts by which the larger structures of civilization are created and sustained (Genesis 4).

This three-part view of marriage is viewed by most believers as true not because some ancient mythmakers say so but because the stories reveal the way sexuality is at its deepest level and thus how it ought to be when life is not distorted. All who live by these norms, from whatever culture or religion, are recognized as married by those who belong to every other tradition. Most Christians hold that the biblical account of these norms is the most accurate one available, for it tells us that life from the start is rooted in love, and many believe that love has right order, divinely sanctioned purposes, and a need for a socially framed support system. All other options are properly seen as adjustments, exceptions, compromises, or relative approximations.

Although parts of the Christian tradition would accent different aspects of this heritage, this is the triadic standard by which sexuality is classically perceived in Protestant history, and in most Catholic and Orthodox traditions. Sometimes in history, one of these three aspects of a full moral vision has been under attack and has had to be defended by prophetic outcries; but all are necessary to the whole. It would be an error—one that elements in these traditions have made from time to time—to take one of these and make it the whole in the assessment of human sexuality. Thus a view that accents only the right order of things can become legalistic; one that accents only fecundity can ignore affection or vocational responsibility; and one that accents only "traditional family values" can fail to see the changing place of family life in the fabric of social history. The parts belong to a moral structure that repeatedly has to be reaffirmed by being reformed in a changing context.[13]

All attempts to approximate this structure stand within a larger vision, one that suggests that sex and marriage are not the ultimate matters. God, in this tradition, has no consort and is neither sexed or gendered, even though human images of or terms for God are. Further, Jesus argued against those who held that such matters were ultimate—"There is no giving or taking in marriage in heaven"—and the end-time vision of the New Jerusalem has no mention of marriage (Matt. 22:30; Mark 12:25; Luke 20:35).[14] Thus, when we speak of sexuality and the moral forms it is to take, we are speaking within the confines of creation and history as they bear on ethical life, not of the most ultimate aspects of theology.

Still, creational and historical matters are not to be decided by appeals to idiosyncratic historical experience alone. It would also be an error, in this view, to begin with an understanding of this or that person's sexual inclinations or desires and then to construct a morality or spirituality that would support those dispositions. Such a nihilist strategy would subordinate all normative ethical visions to individual constructions and deny that history itself is experienced as being under norms that it neither contains nor exhausts. It is more accurate to recognize that everyone knows something of these normative standards and qualities, for what is revealed in scripture and in Christ accords with how God formed all humans at their deepest levels.[15] The religious themes thus are not something imposed on people or distinctive to one cultural-linguistic group but are revealing of how life is really constituted. That is why many believe that all morally honest people know that something is wrong with relationships that are driven only by instinct or emotion or that do not sustain fidelity or hope. That is why people feel violated by the infidelity of those they love, lament infertility, resent social policies that weaken families, and seek to legitimate alternative lifestyles by trying to show how much they approximate normative patterns.

Because such truths are rooted in one of the deeper tissues of human existence, reason, the Christian tradition has held it proper for the church to guide the formation of public thought and of the institutions in which sexuality is most directly expressed—especially the family but also education, law, homemaking, and economics as these influence or inhibit the development of the social channels in which sexuality can find expression. The earliest Christians began to advise believers how to live their sexual lives, as we can see in the Pauline and pastoral letters and in early books of moral instruction. Furthermore, whenever Christians have had a chance to shape civilization, they have sought forms that sustain fidelity, fecundity, and family and developed critical stances toward attitudes and policies that would distort these, even when the distortions came from sources within the faith.[16]

Reformation Perspectives

The biblical view represents the deepest perspective on sexuality now debated in Christian circles; but the current debates in Protestantism make little sense unless they are seen in the context of discussion and certain disagreements with both Jewish and Roman Catholic views. Some of the disagreements focus on the relationship of biological membership in ethnic communities to religious membership in religious communities. On this point, Christians tend to differ from Jews in that the former believe no one is or can be "born" into church membership, the way Jews are born into a people. On the one hand, the "natural" community of origin for Christians is humanity, for all are made in the image of God, all have a propensity to use the potential freedom to distort life and to rebel against the frameworks given by God to guide life, and all need a manifest savior. On the other hand, membership in the community of salvation, old and new Israel, is seen as marked by baptism (a "circumcision" available to both male and female) and confirmation and not by the natural process of birth. Thus, while Jews and Christians share the view that God created humans good, Christians have a more pronounced sense of the human "fall" from that goodness and a greater sense of the necessity of grace to participate in the community of redemption.

Protestants also tend to disagree with Catholics about the role of women in leadership, about birth control, and about abortion. These matters are central to Roman Catholic ethics, and when the issue of homosexuality is debated, it is in a context of decided reservations about each of these questions. However many Protestants share these reservations, homosexuality poses greater difficulty than these other issues where theology and sexuality touch. This is due in large measure to the influence of natural law theory in the Catholic tradition and to the suspicion of it among Protestants. The disagreements involve a view of the relationship of grace and nature. Protestants are doubtful that unambiguous moral logic can be read from the teleology of biophysical functions and are thus much less attached to naturalistic arguments in ethics.[17]

Protestants focus more on grace than on nature and are doubtful of the Catholic view that grace completes or perfects nature. Grace is held to be constitutive of creation in most Protestant views, and they often hold that what we call nature is "fallen"—the purposes intended by God are contorted, garbled, or made ambiguous in the actual operation of things. What we examine when we study what is "natural" is what is distorted, incomplete, or contingent, even if it bears traces of God's grace in its capacity to be reformed toward order, purpose, and reliable relationship.[18] Thus, in most Protestant traditions, humans may—or even have a duty to—alter natural patterns of life to limit its defects and to use technology to alter what is out of accord with God's intent so that it may more nearly approximate grace-filled, right principles;

good ends; and a viable civil society. Because of this, Protestants, for example, have come to advocate (sometimes reluctantly, but actually in concert with these accents) social reform, a right to divorce or abortion under certain conditions, the equality of women (including in church offices), technological innovation, and birth control as a moral obligation.

Ecumenical Protestants also tend to believe that religious and ethical insights can be shared outside the believing community. While they may draw from a number of "sectarian" movements, which apply their religious and ethical principles only to their own particular communities, ecumenical Protestants, as well as most Catholics, hold that what can be comprehended through theology by the careful use of its convergent sources for knowing grace—scripture, tradition, reason, and experience—is pertinent to the whole of society and to all people. Of course, the Jewish tradition and many members of sectarian groups also feel themselves called to be a "light to the nations" and thus witness to the fact that what they have to offer ethically is of significance to all. But the ecumenical Protestant (like the Catholic) tradition ceaselessly, if not always effectively or wisely, seeks to join public discourse in a more intentional way.[19] They feel a compelling responsibility both to interpret and to shape the common life—not just the life of those who adhere to their confession—on theological grounds.[20]

The debates about homosexuality in the ecumenical churches thus are neither new nor only about the inner life of churches. They are truth claims about what the fundamental order and purpose of created nature is all about. The Protestant traditions hold that there is an onto-theological order that everyone almost knows, although a few deny it. Some doubt it because they have not had it clarified in ways that are persuasive—hence, preaching and teaching are of vital importance. Others deny it because they want it to be otherwise—thus they obscure and resist with ideological flourish what they dislike. The churches' truth claims echo convictions that touch the nerves of the civilization's heritage far beyond the issue of tolerance of people who are "different." It is unlikely that we can grasp the profound reservations about homosexuality in our society if we do not understand that these are rooted in a fundamental philosophical-theological conception about the nature of human identity under God and of how human life therefore ought to be lived in society. On the whole, this public theological tradition has held that what is found in symbolic and mythic form in the Genesis stories and reinforced by the New Testament is the most public and universal truth that humanity knows about the basic normative structure for sexuality. It is how God wants us to live.

Of Sacrament, Covenant, and Contract

We can clarify this vision of how God wants humanity to live by inquiring whether sexual love has a shape, a normative order. The answer to which most ecumenical Christians have come to is that it does and that this form is "covenant," an idea that is similar to but not the same as either "sacrament" or "contract." Thus, to clarify the nature of covenant in marriage, we first have to contrast it with the Roman theology of sacrament and the secular theory of contract. We take up rather subtle questions on these matters for the remainder of this chapter. (Since the family is a decisive part of civil society, a range of related issues is addressed in the next three chapters, and we return to the more general implications of a concept of covenant in the concluding chapter.)

In a long, slow process, Christian theology came to articulate the biblical heritage in terms that also drew from nonbiblical and postbiblical ways of thinking. Sexuality is one of those areas, like political power, economic wealth, legal authority, or higher learning, that can either bless life or tempt humans to the distortion of their own constitution and lead them to relationships or behaviors that harm persons and the fabric of the common life.

When Christianity broke with Judaism, it denied the incorporation of religious and ethnic identity. Later, as the Roman Empire began to collapse, society tended to devolve from cosmopolitan city to feudal household—a process we trace in greater detail later. Parts of the church pressed toward a theology in which celibacy was seen as the ideal and marriage a lesser possibility. This prevented Christianity from becoming another ethnic religion, for celibacy obviously breaks the link between gene-pool identity and religious identity. The interpretation of certain ascetic passages in scripture was joined to antimaterialistic philosophies, however, and these interpretations sometimes became so deeply laden with antimaterial, antisocial modes of thought that the larger ethical vision was threatened. It was not until the medieval period that the emerging Roman Catholic theory of marriage became explicit and woven into a full theory of sacramentality.[21] This view fostered many authentic gains in seeing love, with increased consent and relative equality, and marriage, with its inevitable physicality and demand to attend to the material well-being of the family, as central to responsible relationships between men and women and between parents and children. Marriage was still viewed, however, as an imperfect if natural institution, a concession to human lust made spiritual and acceptable only by the sacramental infusion of grace.[22]

Against this view, some liberal Catholics, typified by Erasmus, who elegantly restated what was already in a number of the scholastic and canonical authors, challenged the sacramental heritage. They recognized accents that have become a part of much Protestant thinking. The Erasmian strain saw a certain theological legitimacy in the ecstatic joy of sexuality—one that bonded the couple together in mutual pleasure and drew each out of self-control and into a committed vulnerability to the other. This delight was itself a proper end of marriage, "a foretaste of the joys of heaven" as it was said, often with reference to the Song of Solomon.

Erasmus and others refined the idea of friendship, already well developed in monastic thought and rooted in the ancient Greek and Roman philosophers, and applied it to the relationship between male and female. Margo Todd has investigated the debates over these matters and corrected the more ideological postures about them. She has shown the deeper affinities of Catholic humanist thought to Protestant understandings of the biblical concept of "covenant" in marriage, as found in, for example, the Reformers Heinrich Bullinger and Theodore Beza. These views embark on a quest for that kind of friendship in which there is "an especial sweetness to have one with whom ye may communicate the secret affections of your mind." This relationship is not only endorsed by scripture but also is taken to have a self-confirming quality in experience.[23]

As is well known, Martin Luther became convinced that the Roman Church had misinterpreted the scriptures by presuming a sharp contrast between spiritual and material reality and thus had falsely given a privileged place both to celibacy and to the priesthood's capacity to confer grace on nature through sacramental performance.[24] He saw marriage not as a part of imperfect nature needing grace to complete it but as an order of creation graciously given by God to sustain life and to constrain lustful tendencies in society, even if marriage continued to be celebrated in and registered with the church as a part of the church's proper, public role. Implicit in this challenge is a repudiation of the synthesis of "lower" nature and "higher" grace that had been worked out in medieval theology. Grace and nature are woven together in a different mix, with some things under the law and some things under the gospel. Thus many of the features of marriage were relegated to the civil order and became matters for princes, the state, to decide and guide—still widely the case in Lutheran lands.

For Henry VIII, the reinterpretation of the sacrament of marriage was a matter of obligation to the larger fabric of society, represented by his duties of the crown, which required an heir in a system in which primogeniture was the least violent means of succession in a predemocratic era still tied to gene-pool identity. He needed a divorce to marry a wife who might give him a son, and the Roman authorities would not allow the divorce because of their theory of sacrament. To fulfill his vocation in society, he felt he had to break with Rome. These challenges to the authority of the church brought with them a search for a new normative definition of marriage. New doctrinal developments, drawn more intentionally from biblical sources, gave rise to new liturgies that gradually became standard in many Protestant traditions. They shaped, expressed, and routinized in both culture and law the common expectations about the proper context of sexuality.[25]

Erasmus, Luther, and Henry did not break fully with the medieval patterns of marriage (which, for example, supported feudal patterns of inheritance and succession as well as the legal authority of males [potestas patria]). Nevertheless, they stimulated a quest for an alternative understanding of marriage that preserved the theory of mutual consent.[26] Over time, a new view became installed, in some measure, in the legal traditions of the West[27] and has increasingly been exported to and accepted by those areas touched by western influence around the world. This view was based in covenantal theories derived from Reformed ways of reading the biblical tradition, which gradually became distinct from contractual theories, although the latter became more and more predominant in modern law.[28]

The covenantal heritage shaped not only modern patterns of marriage and church life but also constitutional democracy, the modern corporation, and notions of human rights, based on the conviction that humans are created in the image of God and thus have a dignity that ought not be violated by denying people opportunities to exercise their will and debate issues of right order and common good.[29] In this view, by God's bestowing of "common grace," all people are endowed with a primal sense of freedom and capacity to know something of the laws and purposes of God (justitia originalis). Thus they are able to recognize, in some measure, authentic religion and genuine morality when these

appear, and to learn how to order the several spheres of society ethically, so that humanity may flourish.[30]

On this basis, all are to form covenants of binding commitment that
give shape to life in ways that approximate, under conditions of sin, the
patterns and purposes of holy living that God intends.[31] This is true in
regard to power and politics, culture and learning, and wealth and economics: states, universities, and corporations are potential centers of
covenantal responsibility when we recognize their deepest ethical principles and purposes as obligations under God, and the implications of
these developments are traced in subsequent chapters as they bear on
family life more broadly. It is even more true in regard to sexuality and
marriage, for these are the most widespread and most directly personal
of covenantal spheres. Marriage, understood as covenant rather than as
sacrament or only as contract,[32] is the primary theological-social relationship by which the defects of the Fall, known in broken nature and
manifest in lustful desires, find their evils constrained and their residual graces, effaced but not obliterated by the Fall, enabled to approximate holy living.

This covenant is to take place in accord with the laws and purposes
of God, as discerned and made manifest in the mutual pledges of enduring faithfulness under God between a man and a woman and as confirmed by the community of witnesses to be in accord with the first
principles of righteousness and the well-being of society. The wedding
thus is a public declaration before God and the people, and the church's
and the society's public honoring, of a valid covenant, which will actually have been made privately in pledges of love.

Puritan Contributions/Conflicts

The several Protestant traditions enacted many variations on these
covenantal themes, but the eventual adoption of this model in the rites
of marriage stands as a symbol of a shift from sacrament to covenant as
the primary way of understanding not only human sexuality but also
the social and ethical context in which sexuality was to be considered
in much of modern theology and society.[33]

Because of frequent misinterpretations, we must note certain differences between the views of the Puritans, who both modified and mediated this Reformed view of covenant to the Anglo-American world, and
of the Victorians, who not only were indebted to the Puritans but re-
asserted the older tradition that spirituality and materiality, grace and

nature, soul and body were contraries. Thus many heirs of both Puritanism and Victorianism became convinced that the more religious or moral one was, the less concerned with the physical side of life that person would be.[34] This view not only fed moralistic protests against the rising influence of the secular sciences but also issued in a prudery with regard to human sexuality, to adherents of which the term *puritan* is sometimes applied. Indeed, entire philosophies have been developed to expose the evasions, hypocrisies, and denials of these developments.[35]

However, most Protestants did not think that sex was evil or bad, an indicator of inferiority, or a brutish necessity that had to be endured. While undoubtedly laden with residues of patriarchy, most of Protestant thought held that God had created not only sex but also covenant and marriage *before* the Fall, for our companionship, increase, and well-being—even if, after the Fall, sex was sufficiently distorted that the covenant became all the more necessary as a decisive way of limiting sin and guiding our desires in constructive ways.[36] Still, many Protestants temporarily lost sight of the classical view that the ecstasies of sex echo the innocence of creation, bond us more firmly to our covenant partner, and allow us to anticipate the bliss of the kingdom yet to come.[37]

Sex in marriage thus was designed to regenerate not only the species, thereby connecting us ethically, biologically, and socially to the nurture of the future, but also the spirit, reminding us of the divine life and empowering the spirit to order life rightly, so that the paired complementarity of God's design for humankind could be concretely manifest in ways that would also overcome the terrors of loneliness and the egocentrism to which humans are prone. Sinful humans would be drawn into structured bonds of interdependence that would link the interpersonal unit of the family to the institutional composition of civil society and tie the affections of the soul to godly living.[38] Fidelity to and in this covenantal relationship was an emblem of our fidelity to God's covenantal design for life as it was to be actualized in all areas, even if it sometimes led to the sufferings of the cross. The attention given to familial covenants thus became a manifestation of a very high estimate of sexuality, not of its low estate. In this context, humans had a "duty to desire."[39]

This tradition never advocated celibacy (or disengagement from politics or vows of poverty) as a mark of faith. Puritan divine John Cotton was quite typical when he argued that "God was of another mind" than those who held to the "Excellency of Virginity," for God had created man and woman for each other.[40] Nor did this tradition speak of the "rights of privacy" as an individual right—although it often sought the independence of the church, the press, the school, and business, as well as the home, from state control. Covenanted "societies" had a sacred inviolability and were the primary units in which persons worked out their gifts and callings.[41] It cannot be said that all moral difficulties were overcome by these developments or that those who lived according to this view were fully righteous, any more than it can be said that every Hebrew after Sinai refrained from idolatry, adultery, and covetousness or that every Catholic after receiving the sacraments lived a holy, pure, and sanctified life in accord with the highest possibilities of human nature. But these developments offered a prophetic interpretation of the previous biblical and theological traditions that is both faithful to their deepest structures of reason and revelation and conducive to modern, complex civilizations in a way that brought greater possibilities of a just social order.

Freedom and Ideals

The covenantal emphasis brought with it both an accent on freedom before God and from state control and a new resolve to live in disciplined interpersonal and social relationships, even in the face of the inevitable failure to live up to the highest ideals. Decisive in this development for our concerns was the growing sense of distinction between sin and crime, and thus between moral shame and legal guilt.[42] The Protestant churches generally have come to argue that not everything that has been treated as sinful, such as some abortions, should be criminalized, and not all that is criminal, such as some civil disobedience, should be treated as sinful. Indeed, each of these could be, like just revolutions, the least evil option, which one may be called to undertake with a humble courage while holding with confidence to the promise of forgiveness offered to those who seek to discern how God wants us to live in this world. We should be tolerant, especially legally, but we should not engage in or approve of behavior that increases the likelihood of abortion or war, even if some people genuinely feel desires that could lead to those results. Similarly with homosexuality, we should not criminalize people who feel profound inclinations in this direction and may even be legally tolerant of homosexual acts between consenting adults in private; but we have no obligation to approve, in communities of faith or in the privacy of the voting booth when trying to vote in a way that accords with our deepest ethical convictions, those religious or political leaders or those doctrines or policies that would demand moral legitimation or common support of homosexual behaviors.

The distinction between sin and crime augmented the tendency to see marriage as a purely voluntary act and neither as a covenant involving fidelity, fecundity, and family in society under God nor as a sacramental institution involving an imperfect nature made perfect and complete by an infusion of grace. The distinction thus aided the growth of contractual views of marriage in the culture. Yet these perspectives did not seek to exempt sexual feelings and behaviors from moral and theological guidance, for in the covenantal view, all areas of human life are subject to theological discernment, ethical evaluation, and social judgment under standards of the ideal of an enduring, faithful, equitable, monogamous, heterosexual model that is also potentially fecund.

Those who live in other kinds of relationships are to be accepted as members of churches and recognized as persons under God's care; but their inclinations and their behaviors, whether intended or not, are among those that are not affirmed as ideal. It is indeed likely that, in this view, few or even no marriages fulfill all aspects of the kind of covenant God established with Israel or Christ with the church, and thus every human approximation to the marriage covenant has elements that are deficient or problematic. That is what most ecumenical Protestants affirm when they are alert to the tradition's deepest roots, and that is why the Old and New Testaments, which witness to these covenants, are deemed revelation and taken as the standards for our relative covenants.

This is also the basis for the Protestant view that "all are sinners in need of the grace of God." Sin, in this view, is less the intentional betrayal of some principle or norm than a basic condition that makes saving grace necessary whatever our intentions, and even in spite of our best intentions. In addition to this "state of sin" that we call "original" there are particular "sins," specific acts that we do, duties we neglect, attitudes that we take, feelings that we savor, egoisms that we indulge—either willfully or without moral or spiritual protest—that are contrary to what we know to be right and good and fitting. Even more distorting are the rationalized forms of denial of our sin or of justifications for our sins, which compound the fault. The resistance to the ordination of gay clergy is, at its deepest levels, rooted as much in this issue as it is in certain behaviors. Protestant pastors are not inclined to argue that separated, divorced, unfaithful, or abusive relationships are fully compatible with the ideal, and in most of theological history, homosexual pastors did not claim that their situation was normative either. Under contemporary ideological conditions, however, pastors in these sorts of relationships and churches that would ordain and support them in those relationships would communicate a distortion of the normative message, thereby morally and spiritually legitimating sin or sins with the authority of their office.

Temptations to rationalize a particular bias attend us all, not only gay clergy and their supporters. Yet, in spite of the general condition of sin and our particular list of sins of omission or commission, ecumenical Protestants hold that we can make some relative discernment as to the marks of a properly covenantal relation, just as we can, with a relative degree of confidence, tell the difference between better and worse political regimes, corporate behaviors, and academic institutions. And in this area, ecumenical Protestants throughout their history and still today are doubtful that homosexual relationships are or can be as nearly approximate to the ideal as heterosexual ones. Congregations thus are suspicious of unmarried clergy, even if the distinction between sin and crime and their own awareness of their own defects leads Protestants to believe that "it takes all kinds to make a world" and that Christians ought to "live and let live" in terms of legal policy.[43] In accord with this emphasis, a number of the ecumenical churches have increasingly advocated the decriminalization of homosexuality, even if they have not moved toward approving it.[44]

True or False Prophets?

Some religious bodies that grew out of the same root as the ecumenical Protestant tradition have broken with it. This can be seen if one looks at the heirs of the Puritan movement in America. Many have remained close to the center of the tradition, but others have turned in directions that appear to undercut more widely shared theological and ethical principles. In the nineteenth century the Unitarians denied the doctrine of the Trinity, with its attendant, covenantal understanding of God as a living reality who both is internally differentiated and relates to humanity in dynamic, historical, and interpersonal ways. The denial partly reflected and partly augmented the affirmation of deism or, as frequently, an immanental pantheism that frequently celebrates "the spirit of man." The Universalists broke with the tradition because its adherents believed that Christ had fully overcome sin and the threat of condemnation. They did not believe that a good God would condemn anyone ultimately. Hell, if there was one, had no population; punishment was excluded from religious destiny. The old joke on this matter is that the Unitarians think humans are so good that God would never condemn anyone, and the Universalists think that God is so good that no one would ever be condemned. Judgment and exclusion were ruled out of religious truth in these "new doctrines" that claimed to be prophetic of the religion of the future, no longer tied to the dogmas of the past. Such developments prompted H. Richard Niebuhr to speak with contempt of those traditions that preached of "a God without wrath [who] brought men without sin into a kingdom without judgment through the ministrations of a Christ without a cross."[45]

These two traditions have now merged in an intentionally post-Christian denomination that has not joined the ecumenical councils of churches and has taken the most accepting or affirming attitude toward homosexuality of any organized religious group in the world. Central to their common perspective is the appreciation for themes that, in fact, were already partly embedded in the humanism of Erasmus and some liberal Puritans—the finding of "sweet friendship," of one with whom one can communicate "the secret affections of the mind"—which they consider a self-confirming evidence of moral legitimacy.[46] Many see no reason that this quality cannot be found in same- as well as opposite-sex relations.

Comparable tendencies are also widely present in the United Church of Christ (UCC), which has remained in the ecumenical fold.[47] These accents appear in constant UCC references to the empirical fact that many church members and clergy live in arrangements that do not fit the classical norm and do live in committed relationships. In this view, people ought to be free to establish the most meaningful agreements with partners of their choice, and diversity in this area is something to celebrate. Sometimes these affirmations are made to counteract the violent effects of homophobia, but more frequently the motivation is to prevent people from feeling judged, from seeing their lives as failures, from thinking their loves are not worthy, from believing that God is not interested in their spiritual well-being, or from fearing that the community of faith has rejected them utterly. Often this position also arises from a sense that no one and no body can set relational norms for others; it is a private, individual matter. Most profoundly, this emphasis comes from a recognition of the pluralism of the kinds of grace that can come to people in all sorts of conditions in their lives, which sometimes reaches the point where leading spokespersons for the tradition are tempted to an antinomian "angelism," as James Luther Adams called the poetic and sentimental celebration of every deeply felt variety of spiritual possibility, without clear analysis of the incarnational long-term and normative implications.[48]

In such views, the tradition of covenant is being set aside in favor of a fully "dispositionalist," contractual understanding of sexual relationship for both heterosexual and homosexual couples, as is frequently the case in the culture generally—"if it feels like love, it must be of God." This is a motif that the churches have included but never acknowledged as morally adequate, for it implicitly denies that love has a normative and discernible form.

The concept of contract is relatively easy to recognize in this view. It is a perspective in which the satisfaction of the felt needs of individuals is sovereign, with doubt as to whether any normative order exists for such relationships. What is required is that all parties consent to an arrangement that the parties construct and agree upon. It may imitate a covenantal order, but it resists the idea that one structure of sexual life is normative, above any other. Love becomes less a manifestation of a binding architecture of mutuality, established by God for the well-being of humanity, than a routinized partnership. Herbert Davis treats it as

> the response of any person who knows that loving actions always end in good and positive and happy results. Love (and often love-making) is a utilitarian act. We love because love produces positive results. . . . Our happiness is supreme and God's task is to see that our happiness is fulfilled.[49]

Robert Bachelder, in commenting on the triumph of these views in post-Christian circles, says that all this finally "is to assert the supremacy of personal relationship. . . . Human experience, then, becomes the rule of faith and practice (and neither revelation or the wisdom of ages or logic of morality that is higher than our experience)."[50] Both Davis and Bachelder wonder if this does not reflect the commercialization of our culture. Although we are dealing with feelings more than with money, decisions depend on weighing gains and losses in pleasure or pain, with refined calculations of costs and benefits. That this has always played a role in family life and sexual decisions can hardly be doubted, but here the background framework that constrained and guided such decisions seems much weakened, if not lost. Love, in other words, has no transcendent form and is ordered essentially by human feeling and will.

But another factor has influenced the UCC. For many, a key issue is the question of the mission of the church. The UCC was formed in 1957 out of the old Puritan tradition in conjunction with independent movements from immigrant and Southern dissident groups. In some ways, disproportionate to its numbers, it led the ecumenical churches into the historic struggles for the freedom of oppressed groups. All of this has given the tradition an anti-institutional bias. Many claim that the key to church history is found in the "prophetic struggles" against those structures of society that are the source of oppression—earlier, the tyrannies of Europe; then slavery; and more recently, the discriminations that have denied full dignity and liberty to workers and to women. All of these conflicts involved social change and the recognition that freedom demands, above all, the liberty of the individual conscience. Many in the UCC believe that the church must now carry forth the struggle for another oppressed group and allow each person to find the form of sexual fulfillment that is best for him or her.

In recent years, advocates of comparable changes in all the major Protestant ecumenical denominations and organizations have taken up these issues in parallel ways.[51] On the issue of homosexuality, however, the ecumenical churches have rejected the doctrinal denials of the Unitarian Universalist Association (UUA) and the tendency toward contract in the UCC. While they recognize the decisive role of the church in the common struggle for justice, as is advocated by the national leadership of both the Unitarian Universalist Association and the United Church of Christ as well as by leaders of the World and National Councils of Churches, some suspect that this particular advocacy undercuts the larger theological tradition that sustains persons in viable relations and in just societies. In the final analysis, the wider community of the ecumenical Protestant heritage does not think that these positions are truly prophetic; they may even be false prophecy. They do not preserve covenant or guide freedom to holiness.[52]

Positions voted in the UCC by a two-thirds majority in the last decade, for example, were voted down by the United Presbyterian Church General Assembly ten to one; and a recent Evangelical Lutheran Church in America draft of a potential church position, which has wording quite similar to that of the UCC, created such a stir in early discussion that it was removed from the agenda and will not be voted on.[53] The Disciples of Christ, Reformed, and United Methodist Churches have had parallel disputes and have thus far resolved the questions in a way essentially compatible with the decisions of the Presbyterians and the Lutherans, to the consternation of the advocates affirming homosexual ordination and partnerships.[54] In most Protestant denominations, vocal minorities champion positions that are indistinguishable from those of the UUA and the UCC statements.[55] When we examine these debates, we stand at a line that divides the wider ecumenical heritage from more radical current positions. Who are the true and who the false prophets on this question?

Marking the Divide

In "Misogyny and Homophobia," an essay often reproduced and quoted by the advocates of the UUA and UCC positions, Beverly Wildung Harrison of Union Theological Seminary argues that the majority statements of the churches are "antisensual," and this is because the authors of these statements do not understand the body "as mediating spirituality directly." Instead, "the males who rule over and represent the masculinist norms" of society tend to accent a "false dualism," in which the rational and the spiritual are distinguished from the emotional and the physical. This makes it impossible to affirm physical love unequivocally. Religion thus "involves living and acting as though a split between lower 'nature' and consciousness were part of fundamental reality." Christian culture, influenced by these ideas, has come to accept the priority of mind over body, "as if mind is not a function of body experienced in a certain way, or the 'transcendence' of spirit over nature, is often held to be the essence of religious conviction. 'To believe' comes to mean believing such nonsense."[56]

Harrison is surely correct that forms of dualism adopted by some Christians have been antisensual. But the protest against that distortion does not justify the opposite error, which she seems to make. Those same forms of dualism have demanded that Christians deny all contact with political power, with economic wealth, and even with cultural philosophies. Mars, Mammon, and the Muses can seduce the soul no less than Eros, but that does not mean they are to be utterly avoided. The overwhelmingly dominant Christian view is that they are to be engaged, converted, and then embraced on a qualified, cautious, ethically guided basis. None of these areas is, in the Christian view, to be endorsed "unequivocally." They are, as sex is, a potential gift of grace to preserve and enhance life, if—and only if—they are engaged on "equivocal," theological-ethical terms that transcend and transform what they are actually in a fallen world.

In Harrison's view, Christianity's qualified and only selective embrace of the powers of erotic sensuality—and indeed, of economic and political and cultural materiality—and its treatment of them on principles other than their own substance are what help generate, even if they do not fully explain, both the misogyny and the homophobia of society and the irrational resistance to a materialist view of economics, politics, and culture. Our "society's revulsion from sexuality itself is an important element in homophobia. Homosexuality in our social and cultural context, represents a break with the strongest and most familiar control on sexuality—compulsory heterosexuality."[57]

Harrison goes on to offer an analysis of the reasons for the "hysterical" reaction of church leaders to gays, to women, and especially to lesbians and indicates that this response arises because people have not properly understood their own sexuality. No doubt a good bit of autobiographical bias does enter the discussion of this issue, as it does on other matters; but acknowledgment of this fact can easily entail an exaggeration of the amount of "projection" involved in serious discussions. Harrison, however, suggests that all transcendent standards or principles in theology and ethics are projections of unresolved psychosocial dynamics.

The problem with this stance is that it is self-defeating: if all morality is a projection of psychosocial dynamics, resolved or unresolved, then the same can be said for Harrison's own stance. This approach denies the possibility of speaking of any realm of mind or soul or spirit that is other than body and its material operations. We are hard pressed to know, on her view, why the church and theology and normative ethical views and marriage ceremonies and laws should exist, for they all point to realities that are never fully manifest in the world. Thus her analysis turns out to be antitheological, anti-ethical, and anti-intellectual. And in her thought, the suspicions of the Christian tradition that the deepest impulses of the gay and lesbian advocates are methodologically opposed to spiritual, theological, ethical, and intellectual life as a guide to the material, economic, political, and social life find confirmation. For these reasons, some hold that her views, not those she opposes, are dehumanizing.

Perhaps the most frequently cited theologian on the topic of homosexuality is James Nelson.[58] He has served as a consultant to several church statements and is quoted in all the major ecumenical ones. He does not intend to exclude theology, but he does believe that we are in the midst of a major paradigm shift, away from an old view of human sexuality in which forms of Christian theology taught that sexuality was either incidental or potentially harmful to the divine-human relationship. Further, the old perspective focused on problems of sin that are manifest in wrong sexual acts or violations of norms.

In a new paradigm emerging from feminist, black, and third-world perspectives, Nelson says, human experience provides the source and norm of the most important insights. God's presence is viewed as incarnational—that is, as God became flesh in Jesus Christ, so the Divine can be experienced in the pleasures of the flesh. In this view, sin is alienation not only from God—and from the neighbor—but also from the flesh. Sanctification means, indeed, growth in the capacity for sensuousness.[59]

Nelson makes self-conscious use of theological terms here, but he employs them in a way that undercuts the very notion that love has a normative form and a purpose beyond our own pleasure or self-fulfillment. This view provides us no reason for the church, the gospel, the faith, or the theological tradition. All that is needed to learn of God and to experience God's presence can be found in the romantic naturalism of a nudist colony.

A much more careful view of the divide over homosexuality, however, can be found in a recent book by Patricia Jung and Ralph Smith.[60] They discuss many of these views and challenge the ecumenical conception of covenantal marriage on another ground. Jung and Smith are convinced that the real problem is the normative "heterosexism" on the part of the Christian tradition. They define heterosexism as "a reasoned system of bias regarding sexual orientation." By "reasoned system" they do not concede that it is justifiable, only that it is "not grounded primarily in emotional fears, hatreds or other visceral responses. . . . Instead, it is rooted in a largely cognitive constellation of beliefs about human sexuality."[61] In offering this definition, they do not load the argument, as many other current studies do, by making all who disagree with current advocates presumptively guilty of moral bigotry or pathological irrationality.

Jung and Smith's study is useful on a number of other counts as well, not least because it provides a handy compendium of the arguments most often used in Protestant debates today about the "real" meanings of scriptural passages (as interpreted through "liberating" and "antipatriarchal" schools of analysis). In this connection, an almost evangelistic emphasis on the self-authenticating character of personal testimony comes to the fore, and many vignettes appear as evidence. In these terms, Jung and Smith pose the decisive issue: Is it true that the Christian tradition is and has been heterosexist, and if so, is a bias toward heterosexism wrong? Their answers are yes and yes. They see the liberation of society from that sin as the basic goal. They seek an unleashing of "the erotic" so that it may be a path to the holy, although there is no clear definition of what holiness might be.

The authors locate an ambiguity in the Protestant heritage. It rejected the sacramental view of marriage and did not see the wedding ceremony as a means of grace; yet it located sexuality in the context of a covenanted relationship of joyful love that required both voluntary commitment and equality between partners, and it found the grace of God present in this relationship. Why could covenant, love, blessing, joy, voluntary commitment, and equality not apply also to homosexual relationships?

The answer, from the standpoint of the deeper assumptions of covenantal theology, is that they may. Indeed, homosexual relationships, when they exist, should seek to approximate these patterns, and relationships that manifest these qualities in greater degree are morally better than those that do not actualize them at all. But the normative view is not only about qualitative relationships between persons or about the freedom to make individual contracts; it is about these in a wider context that includes the right order of God's creation, as manifest by the structure of male and female, by the capacity for generativity, and by institutional arrangements that most fittingly sustain civilization until history is no more. The truly prophetic view thus is one that not only respects the particularity of each individual, nurtures good relationships, and liberates people from oppression but also guides and evaluates each of these in terms of the higher principles, the longer purposes, and wider patterns that God intended. Otherwise sexuality becomes entirely a matter of civil contract, to be permitted or restricted as the whims of social sentiment dictate. "Sins" quickly become defined as "crimes"; norms are decided by charismatic leaders on one side or by prudish leaders on the other; neither relationships nor families have a shield from manipulative control; and the deeper founts of moral vision to guide public discourse dry up.

Can We Know What God Intended?

For more than a century it has been doubted that we can know what God intended with regard to human sexuality. Indeed, since 1869, when Karola Maria Benkert invented the term *homosexuality* to offer a biological description of a "third sex" not subject to moral or religious evaluation, efforts have been made to remove the question from theology and to turn it into a medical issue.[62] It was held by Lamarckian, Darwinian, Freudian, and other schools of thought, which do not agree with one another, that homosexuality is a matter of "nature," produced by natural causes and to be properly understood not by theology but by "science." Over the same time span, the arts of "higher criticism" were developed to show that the biblical sources were, in fact, highly redacted versions of ancient materials and thus neither direct dictations of God nor the recorded observations of eyewitnesses to miraculous events. And simultaneously, a number of the social sciences were being founded, which argued that social institutions were not eternal and constant but products of historical and cultural development. One might even say that Greenberg's monumental *The Construction of Homosexuality* is the epitome of the attempt to show how much of sexual orientation and of our assessment of it is socially constructed. In the context of such insights, not only medical and biological understandings of nature but also theology seemed a feeble basis for ethics, for it became viewed as a product, an epiphenomenon, of these "deeper" roots.[63]

Contemporary perspectives born out of such reflections present a great ambiguity. On the one hand, they are cited to suggest that we should have a tolerant attitude on these matters, since responses to and practices of sexual conduct change from time to time. Yet insofar as they undercut all "essentialist" arguments that some people are unalterably destined to be same-sex oriented, the door is left open for multiple experiments in biomedical and psychiatric engineering to alter attitudes or behavior. This exposes the fact that every attempt to guide or control the behavior is someone's agenda. So who shall set the agendas? If it is not to be the churches and the theologians, should it be the doctors and the psychiatrists? And since these professionals are licensed by the state, should the lawyers and the politicians guide them?

In a new study, Pim Pronk explores these issues in depth.[64] Not only does he review the basic arguments that have developed over the last century, but he also shows that nearly all, if not all, of the posttheological positions taken today depend on the naturalist fallacy. Indeed, he shows that those who have tried to develop ethics on purely dogmatic bases, such as Karl Barth, are naturalistic in this area. So are most of the gay advocates (with whom Pronk largely identifies) and those pleading for "tolerance" (some of whom he sharply criticizes). Both the advocates and those who plead for tolerance tend to demoralize and often thereby dehumanize homosexual persons by claiming that it is their nature to be the way they are, thus there is nothing they can do about it. Both become deterministic in their view of what drives homosexual behavior, whether their assessment is positive—"This is *my* nature, I must fulfill it"—or exonerating—"I know you can't help yourself." In the matter of moral logic they presume a naturalism, and in this they do not differ in approach from those who are negative ("That contradicts all that is natural").

Pronk forces us to recognize key ambiguities in Protestant ethical thought, specifically in two areas: "nature" and "will." That we are conflicted about the notion of "nature" can be seen in the fact that we are not clear what its opposite is. What could "unnatural" mean? Is it diseased, distorted, imperfect, unusual, artificial, superficial, cultural, unnecessary, or what? And how does the appeal to what is natural relate to what ought to be accepted in society? Many things exist in states of nature that we deplore and spend enormous amounts of political rhetoric and tax money to alter. Pronk knows that it is a distinct—and a mistaken—move to jump from a descriptive statement of the way things "naturally are" to a prescriptive statement about the way things "ought to be," because it is "natural" (positive) or "ought not to be," because it is only natural and not spiritual (negative), without an intervening ethical or theological step.

The Protestant tradition generally has broken with the theory of natural law, but it does not know what to do with nature, with the naturalistic references in scripture, or with the changing concepts of nature in medicine and the sciences, physical and social. How are these to be woven into the moral wisdom of Christian teaching in the area of sexuality? Many past hypotheses have proved inadequate. Will current findings and models also soon be replaced? What on earth is natural? Nor does it help to appeal to scripture on this point.

Pronk knows that the religious traditions have not satisfactorily settled the question of which parts of scripture should prevail over others. Specifically in regard to the references to homosexuality in the Bible, which ones are pertinent to the whole of humanity, which to the church only; which to ancient contexts, which to now, and which to all times? The ethics of human sexuality therefore cannot be settled by an appeal either to nature or to scripture. In Pronk's view, it must be dealt with on the grounds of the modes of moral discourse that are worked out in the context of the formation and maintenance of human relationships, quite within the confines of practical reason.

His methodological move here has important consequences for the future, and it accords with a number of pastoral responses to homosexual persons.[65] However, it is not at all clear that we can draw such sharp lines between the research of the sciences, the systematic reflection of the theologians, and the exercise of the will in practical reason. On most important questions they overlap. In fact, it is inevitable that they will intersect when we come to the issue of the evaluation or discernment of basic norms governing how we ought to live. The strategy of flattening the moral world, so that the findings of the scientists and the systematic insights of theologians are left out of these debates or appealed to only when they aid the practical reason we choose in a given culture or time period, makes all ethics a matter of voluntary construction. In certain ways, Pronk represents the current consensus in academia.

At this point, Pronk forces us to face the question of the will in this matter, and thus he allows us also to separate the issue of homosexuality from issues of race and sex. There is no possibility that personal will plays a role in being black or white, female or male, and any suggestion of moral responsibility for these conditions or any suspicion that the will of persons of particular races or sex is disordered in its very constitution is moral nonsense.[66] Further, no specific set of sexual behaviors or preoccupations can be presumed of anyone who is female or black (or male or white), and it would be sexist or racist to suggest this.[67] And in neither respect can it be said that identity independent of morality is dependent on innate drives, affections, or behaviors independent of the will. It turns out that it is simply not clear that some people are gay or lesbian in the same way that people are black or white, female or male.[68] For these reasons, many properly doubt the reports in the ecumenical churches when they make the issues identical.

Yet the church's reason for being is one that does not hold that practical reasoning is everything. The will is taken seriously, for it is seen as both rooted in the gift of the "image of God," which is present in each person, and capable of being directed toward God and the right ordering of creation that God intended. Thus the church rejects what is, finally, a nihilistic element in Pronk's argument, one that has brought moral disaster with it in every known experiment: it makes all that passes for religion, science, and ethics purely a matter of the power to mobilize group will. More radically than the reductionism of Harrison, the romanticism of Nelson, and the permissiveness of Jung and Smith, Pronk presents us with a flat pragmatism that has no place for either ontological or theological insight.

It is doubtful that the church can or will accept such arguments. The classical theological heritage has long recognized that nothing will suffice except an onto-theological view, and it now sees itself challenged by this issue to abandon its claim to have such a view to offer to the world. The church is likely to continue to claim that the deepest ontic structure, given in creation; the purposive presence of a loving Creator and Redeemer in history; and the gift of the graced human consciousness to grasp the relation between these in the midst of time are, together, necessary for life. Science at its most profound levels can and does point toward this deep ontic structure of things, even as it recognizes a non-ontic element in what it studies whenever it aids the technological alteration of things as they are. Science thus implies a distinction between the ontological, if not always the theological, which humans cannot alter and the phenomenological, which can be constructed or deconstructed at will.

The Problem of Technology

To raise the question of will or choice in relation to issues of the ontological or theological structure of sexual orientation points us toward a set of very complex and controversial ethical matters that is seldom discussed. Can the will be transformed by technical means? And if it could, ought it be? In Protestantism, as has been mentioned, nature is not seen as the same as creation.[69] God "created" the world good, but in the Fall, the way things are became distorted, and nature has subsequently become flawed and inadequate. Hence to argue that some moral aspect of life is "natural" on the grounds of its frequency or "innateness" or because people feel it is intrinsic to their way of thinking, feeling, or being may not be to state that it is the way God intended it to be in creation. It may be, in fact, to state that what is experienced as natural may be in need of alteration, remediation, and redemption. Protestants are prepared to believe that the world, including our sexuality and the cultural roles we establish for males and females, stands under a higher order than our natural being and for a divine purpose greater than our personal sense of the presence of God, for even identity and spirituality may be fallen and in need of repair by bringing them under theological, ethical, and biosocial norms not of our own desire.

Such a perspective is often lost or forgotten in contemporary life. The chilling implications of such a loss, however, need to be contemplated. It is frequently thought that if we understand ethical and social matters as constructions, people will become more tolerant. On the contrary, if all is a social construction, then we can and should raise the substantive question posed by genetic and social engineering: Why should we not construct people the way we want them to be? If there is no "right order" or "given purpose," then we shall have to face the question of why we cannot reconstruct the genetic makeup of the fetus to our liking. If we come to identify "gay genes," endocrinologic predispositions, or how a propensity to homosexuality is induced by certain early experiences, why should we not attempt, by the control of nature or nurture or both, to reduce the number of homosexual persons? Further, if we become able to manipulate the genetic makeup to our liking, we can expect that gay and lesbian parents will want to affirm their lifestyle and subculture by using the same techniques in precisely the opposite direction. We should have no illusions about this: people will seek to control these matters. Not only the legal and political but the moral and ethical questions will have to be faced.

Indeed, the issue ducked by the last couple of centuries floods back into the picture: Can we reliably know anything about how God wants us to live? Perhaps it is not surprising in this regard that we are now facing an upsurge of Christian Evangelicalism and Roman Catholicism and their increased influence in ecumenical circles. This is not simply because people are fearful of change and are seeking old-fashioned certitudes in the face of new insecurities, any more than resurgent Hinduism, fundamentalist Islam, the new Buddhist missions, or the Confucian revival are emerging for only these reasons. These traditions are vibrant because of a profound doubt that we can treat moral issues, including homosexuality, without reference to a normative, onto-theological notion of a right order of things and a vision of divine purpose to the gifts of creation.

Changes in theories of nature and technology have deep connections with the peculiar structures of modern society, which are currently dominated by economic understandings of reality: all can be changed by technological manipulation, if it is to our benefit and if we can afford the costs. This has had great influence on the theory of the family as well as on that of sexuality. We shall shortly turn to various schools of thought—some liberationist and others libertarian—that have put increased pressure on theological reflection. The issue of how to understand this economic shift is decisive, since it is certain that these fundamental changes have taken place also in the organization of the household. Just as the debates regarding homosexuality have helped define the inner economy of human relations, so a series of other issues force wider explorations of the economy of the family. These views, too, have their own reductionist advocates, whose positions cannot be explored here; but we can note that they have become intertwined with the debates about homosexuality since the 1960s, when the critique of capitalism in ecumenical circles, and then its celebration in evangelical ones, promoted distinctive agendas regarding family life.[70]

The ecumenical churches have not ignored these matters. In long and sometimes rancorous debates, the ecclesiastical bodies have modulated harsh and judgmental attitudes toward homosexuality, acknowledged the sexually and economically exploitative role of many historical familial arrangements, sought to overcome the legacy of Victorian prudishness, and recognized the changing place of the family in society. Most particularly, they have recognized the changing roles of women. These modifications, embraced with quite overwhelming votes, however, are quite in accord with the classical, covenantal view.

2

Household and Work: On Sex, Economics, and Power

In the face of intense and sometimes rancorous challenges, the ecumenical Protestant churches have reaffirmed the classical theological ethic on sexuality, marriage, and family. Some of the church disputes have been less about specific sexual issues such as homosexuality, however, than about the organization of the family, the division of labor within the family, and the roles people play relative to economic and political life. These questions have arisen with particular urgency in our time because the realm of the family and the realms of politics and economics have grown increasingly distinct.

In most societies, sexuality and economics and power—what can be referred to as the forces of Eros, Mammon, and Mars—have all been combined in a family-based "household." The household has been the primary locus of production as well as of reproduction, of childrearing as well as of consumption, and the center of social power as well of authority.[1]

For most of the world, the fortunes of individuals are fatefully tied to the material and social resources of the household. It is in the household that one learns how to love, how to work, and how to order the common life. The relative effectiveness of the household and its capacity to integrate spiritual and material units into moral communities opens or closes options for people. The next generation is more or less able to productively enter the various areas of life according to the viability of the household—as every schoolteacher, police officer, sports coach, business employer, or medical professional knows. The social location of one's household and its patterns of love, work, and authority may not be entirely determinative of the individual, but it inevitably shapes the individual's capacity to participate in society and to reproduce a next generation able to contribute creatively to the common life—as every pastor and social worker also knows.

Over the last century, anthropologists have documented with great subtlety the variety of household forms that humans have devised. Despite the variety, however, it is a rare society in which the household is not the central institution for both sexual and economic life. Indeed, some scholars hold that the nuclear family has been a core organizing unit of all societies:

> Only within our own generation has the emphasis on the special importance of certain types of solidarity of kinship units . . . been identified. . . . In this context, the nuclear family has gradually been perceived to be a very special case because, though there are certain secondary variations, it comes nearer than any other unit of kinship structure to having universal structural significance.[2]

During the 1960s and 1970s, however, the central role of the household came under attack. Social critics and researchers were intrigued by apparent evidence of alternative modes of social life, including the possibility that earlier societies had been matriarchal and only later, with increases of military capabilities, became patriarchal.[3] Others denied the notion of the primacy of family altogether and returned to some nineteenth-century theorists whose work had been "surpassed"—it was suspected, for ideological reasons. One nonfamilial theory was advanced by Lewis H. Morgan, one of the few Americans quoted extensively by Karl Marx, and later supported by Baldwin Spencer and F. J. Gillen's studies of aboriginal societies. These theorists argued for the early existence of groups who held all things in common, including sexual partners in a kind of "group marriage."[4] Morgan identified several types of partnering that took place under various conditions and attributed them to a combination of factors, including the attempt to develop social solidarity and the prevailing economic means of subsistence.[5]

A key concept deriving from Morgan's contemporary John McLennan and perpetuated and modified by Sigmund Freud in one way and by Margaret Mead in another was the theory of "primitive promiscuity," the notion that spontaneous sexual expression, with multiple partners, was the primal mode of human interaction, preceding the imposition of socially constructed norms at the hands of those in control of economic and political life. Sexual expression sadly became manipulated, through the invention of taboos and repressive controls, by elites who gained power, wealth, and sexual advantage thereby. Mammon and Mars, in other words, sought to control Eros; but Eros, in this view, is the natural enemy of or even the cure for Mammon and Mars.[6] In other words, an idyllic condition of both harmonious communal economic cooperation and radical individual sexual freedom was posited as the primal reality, destroyed by the artifices of (especially modern, western, religiously influenced) civilization.

These views are now largely dismissed by specialists, although it is difficult to underestimate their influence at the margins of the social sciences. Among those alienated from the Jewish and Christian traditions, from American cultural values, and from western modes of social analysis that took these matters quite seriously, they had a striking resurgence in the 1960s. Numerous studies of the industrialization process and of the formation of modern democratic capitalism have been produced using precisely the presuppositions and methods of this view. Perhaps the most thorough summary and restatement of what this view means for our questions can be found in *The Social Origins of Private Life* by Stephanie Coontz. Her energetic style weaves into a single web of artful interpretation most of the studies written from this perspective during the last generation.[7]

In this view, both the nature and character of the person and the shape of an individual's intimate relationships (with the opposite sex, with parents or children) are products of the changing means of production—animal, human, and mechanical—and of the struggle by elites to gain domination over them, destroying in the process both the equitable autonomy of the individual and a spontaneous, primal communitarianism that are presumed to have been the natural condition prior to the introduction of bourgeois, conquering, hierarchical, and transcendentally oriented (male) white authority. However, some tendencies toward modernity are celebrated, for they are seen as opportunities to reestablish a solidarity with others in the formation of class consciousness and a new autonomy in which a man or a woman may have free choice about material relations, including sexual ones, with any and all potential partners who are willing, without financial or social penalty of any kind.

After her introduction, for example, Coontz sets the contours of her study by establishing a contrast between the western Euro-American and the Native American cultures, in the latter of which:

> the role of the family . . . was to circulate people and resources, ensuring that all individuals would have a call upon the labor or products of specific others. This militated against the development of economic inequalities. It also reinforced an ideology that made sharing or generosity rather than accumulation the main source of prestige.[8]

Further, in this society, as she reads the data, the nuclear family "had no functions that were not shared by other social groupings"; "was not a property-holding unit since resources and land were available to all"; freed "girls as well as boys for sexual exploration"; and was an institution in which "full rights of separation or divorce were common for both men and women," "sexual division of labor varied from group to group," "women had a high degree of autonomy and played a respected role within their societies," and so forth.[9]

Coontz then offers the sharply contrasting view of the settlers who encountered and disrupted these practices, bringing with them "private property, which was inherited through families, state institutions, . . . conscription, and social control. . . . They were also agents for the reproduction of class differences." Further, they "were connected, albeit at different points, to an international mercantile system whose conceptions of wealth, trade, state authority, and national rivalries stood in sharp contrast to the collective subsistence and individual autonomy of Indian life."[10] This led rather directly to hierarchy, patriarchy, slavery, and witch trials, the substance of the remainder of her chapter. In brief, Coontz offers a dialectical materialist interpretation of the American family, based on the schematized historical logic derived explicitly from Karl Marx and Friedrich Engels as well as from a stream of romantic anthropological theory on which they, too, depended, to trace these themes throughout the nineteenth century.

Meanwhile, since the landmark work of C. N. Starcke and Edward Westermark,[11] the evidence has been accumulating that the household is pervasive in every known society and that it is critical for the shape of both economic and political life. Most political units in most cultures and most institutions of production and consumption have been household based, not as late developments but as a part of the human society as far back as they can be traced. The larger hut of the village headman may have become the castle of the nobility, defending, governing, and taxing the peasant; but both ordered their lives and society in households.

A number of cultures have a maxim to the effect that "a man's home is his castle." It suggests a widespread moral claim that even the most humble household has a dignity that the powerful ought not violate economically or sexually. Something sacred, something inviolable, is at stake; and for that reason, no culture has been able to treat the household, large or small, without reference to social forces that are greater than the potencies of Eros, Mammon, or Mars—without reference, namely, to religion. Certainly, as we pointed out in the previous chapter, every civilization has religious rites or rituals to sanctify the household, bless the marriage, and invoke divine help to assure both fertility and the abundant life. But because nearly all of these reinforce the structure of the household in one or another direction, they are sometimes interpreted as a naturalized, ideological expression of other, more fundamental forces.

Cross-cultural studies show the relative stability of the religiously normative ideas of the household. The great religious traditions—those that have demonstrated an ability to guide the organization of complex civilizations and many peoples over long periods of time—give a central place to the household, although they have treated the relationships between household, economy, and political order differently, as I have elsewhere argued.[12] Some have given priority to the familial side of the household, seeing gene-pool, and thus sexual, identity as basic, and others have accented the political or economic place of the household and seen familial relationship as subordinate to the wider interests of the political economy.

We may consider a few examples. The ancient Hindu tradition produced one of the great options for humanity.[13] It placed the nuclear family in an expanded household, called the "joint family," and the joint family within the subcaste, called the *jat,* which was often defined in terms of the kind of work the members of that highly extended household did in and for the whole society. But the *jati* were parts of "ethnic classes" (called *varna*), arranged hierarchically, and near the top of the hierarchy was the "warrior-ruler" caste. It was superseded only by the priestly caste, the Brahmans, who guided the organization of the whole society by ritual and instruction. They provided the intellectual guidance for the distinctive "social spirituality" of India. Their identity, and that which they demanded of others, was defined by closed gene-pool marriage and heredity. The most heated issue in India even today is whether the secular democracy established in 1947 can survive or whether *Hindutva*, a religiously guided national solidarity, will reassert itself.[14]

The Muslim tradition presents a contrasting major option, for it saw combined in the person of its founder, Muhammad, a trader in a family business, a political-military leader, and the prophet of a radically monotheistic view of God, in which differentiation and pluralism are not accepted (as, for example, they are in the Christian doctrine of Trinity and, in another way, in Hinduism). This integrated focus allowed the raging feuds between the Arab clans to subside under a singular brotherly mutuality, a moral simplicity, and a legal unity. During Muhammad's lifetime, family life, economic prosperity, military expansion, and religious intensity were combined in a way that consolidated sexual, political, economic, and religious power.

Not long after Muhammad's death, however, Islam split over the issue of whether succession should be by familial descent or by political authority.[15] The Shiite wing holds that the true biological heir of the prophet (now hidden from view, since the visible heirs were wiped out in a massacre) will be revealed in the future and a restoration of the primary grandeur of Islam will result. In the meantime, the clergy must guide ruling families or even assume rule if the ruling families distort the tradition—as the world has seen recently in the Iranian revolution led by Ayatollah Khomeini.

The larger wing of Islam early turned to the rule of the caliph or sultan and subordinated both family life and religious leadership to political authority. Since the collapse of the Ottoman Empire, royalty has often been responsible for the appointment of religious leaders and for preserving the purity of Islam. We can see this not only in Saudi Arabia, Jordan, and the smaller states of the Persian Gulf, but in tendencies of "strong man" rulers to enforce Islamic family patterns, from Egypt to Malaysia.[16] Both wings of Islam continue to see the household, whether that of the bazaar merchant or that of the palace soldier, as the center of economic life and distrust other kinds of economic institutions, such as banks, corporations, or religiously bonded (often Sufi) groups of artisans or traders.[17]

One could trace other traditions similarly. Buddhism, for example, tended to accent the role of the warrior-king and to make the brotherhood of clergy (the *sangha*) the jewel in the emperor's crown.[18] Further, the characteristic vows of celibacy and poverty on the part of the monks reduce the moral and spiritual focus on family and wealth in certain ways. This could seem to make Buddhist cultures less influenced by sexuality and materialism; but these in fact play a substantive role in the life of the vast majority of the population, who are neither monks nor royalty. Indeed, it could be that the lack of positive normative engagement with these elements, since salvation comes from forsaking them, means that both sexuality and economic interest have a license that may become libertine, as long as they do not disrupt the regime by forming other centers of loyalty in society.[19]

The Confucian heritage, which integrated family into a total imperial system, offered one of the most detailed, nuanced, and stable forms of society in the world. But its former totalistic character was destroyed through selective adoption into other systems, as in Korea and Japan; by the exodus of "overseas Chinese" into much of the Pacific world, especially Singapore and Taiwan; and by the nationalist and then the Communist revolution at home. Each change has led to new relationships between political, economic, and familial organizations.[20]

Western Views

In chapter 1, we introduced the covenantal view of marriage that emerged out of biblical and Reformation history; we shall return to those motifs in the final chapter. But western civilization contains at least two major competing traditions. Both streams grew out of the philosophies in ancient Greece and Rome and persist in various permutations in the contemporary era. One stream regards the household as secondary to the requirements of the political regime; the other regards the household, and the political regime itself, as secondary to the personal needs and desires of the individual.

Many Greek and Roman philosophers regarded the *polis,* the city-state, as the defining and comprehending institution of the common life. The *oikos,* the family-based household, was subordinate to the life of the political regime. Plato in the *Republic* (especially in book 2) locates the roots of the city in economic interests and in passionate desire. These unruly forces need control, which can be attained by education and religion when they are rightly organized by a wisely guided political authority. Aristotle, in his *Politics* (book 1), sees the household as the basic unit of society, defined by the relationship of a man to his property, his wife and children, and their servants. Beyond that, the clan and state stand as increasingly comprehensive units, each one subduing the turbulent character of the lesser unit. And Cicero, representing the Roman tradition as an advocate of the traditional Roman family, comments in the *Republic* as well as in the *Laws* on the priority of regime over the family, pointing to the nonfamilial myth of Romulus and Remus being raised by a she-wolf and founding the state to control the wolfishness and animal sexuality that, paradoxically, also nurture civilization.[21] Thus much of the concentration on the polis by the most famous Greek and Roman philosophers was inspired by the need to control or guide the individual, the repository of unruly passions, who was able to acquire virtue when rightly guided by philosophy and political authority.

Throughout this long history of Greco-Roman philosophy, another tradition, with roots in a contrary ancient pattern of thought, can also be seen. As the ancient polis and the later Alexandrian Empire began to fall apart and the Roman rulers began to become more cynical, Epicurus and then Lucretius (among others) repudiated the traditions of Plato, Aristotle, and the Stoics and resisted the constraints of any political order. They set forth an atomistic view of human nature and offered positive assessments of material interests and of the reliability of sense-based, individual intuition.

Epicurus claimed that the primary insight that should govern human life is the incontestability of personal experience. Sense data alone are the source of reliable knowledge. All scientific generalizations and all forms of ethics are probabilities constructed out of particular sensations. They depend for their reliability on whether they evoke feelings of pleasure or reduce feelings of pain. Hence the most important thing to do is to attend to one's own feelings or felt needs. Everything else is "abstract." To be sure, the immediate experience of these does not guarantee the gaining of good and the avoidance of evil over time, so intelligence must develop practical wisdom—the calculation of the probabilities of pleasure and pain by the exercise of memory and anticipation.[22]

In this view, both sexuality and the structure of household life, with its inevitably economic and political and religious overtones, were subordinated to personal cultivation. Indeed,

> Epicurus warned against the assumption of heavy responsibilities and serious involvements, whether public or private . . . , [and recommended instead] the cultivation of friendship, the enjoyment of carefree pleasures, and even attendance at religious festivals in order to remind [us] . . . of that complete tranquillity of which the gods are the perfect exemplars.[23]

Lucretius early became entranced by Epicurus's thought and developed parts of it further, particularly its materialist implications and the relation of these to a notion of free will. For instance, in book 2 of *On the Nature of the Universe* he argued that it is not necessary to have determinism if one holds an atomistic theory, for the inner disposition or sentiments of each person can incline him or her to willfully "swerve" toward cooperation with another and bring the novelty of convergent creativity, when it is in the natural interest of all parties to do so. Thus what was "natural" can begin to construct something "novel." That is what leads from the possibilities of "natural justice" to various compacts between persons and, indeed, to human communities.[24]

In commenting on Epicurus's view that natural justice is a bargain for mutual profit that "does neither hurt nor do hurt," Lucretius points out that not everyone keeps the bargain. However, he has a very optimistic understanding of human nature, and he argues that a large majority do so because they are naturally inclined to find agreement with one another. For the most part, they do not need the elaborate structures of politics, religion, law, and family. As R. E. Latham points out:

> Thus the fact that mankind has survived at all is adduced [by Lucretius] as a proof that there must have been such a compact. But it also serves to explain the occurrence of such a compact along Darwinian lines, as an example of survival of the fittest. . . . By this evolutionary approach to the problem, Lucretius escapes the absurdities of some later theories of "social contract." He finds the basis of social cooperation not [only] in calculated self-interest, but in a natural instinct that impelled the strong to take pity on the weak.[25]

In these brief summaries, we can see that the West is heir to a stream of thought besides that of the theological heritage and distinct from that which reaches from Plato and Aristotle to Hegel and Marx and the communitarian political traditions of today. If the polis-oriented tradition tends to swallow the individual, family life, economics, and religion into political collectivities by making the household a governmentally controlled cell, this other tradition combines an individualist, naturalist, and sense-oriented theory of human nature and will with an evolutionary, biologistic view of history. It reaches from such thinkers as Epicurus and Lucretius through key founders of modern scientific thought, such as Adam Smith and Charles Darwin, to key contemporary theorists of the family, such as Gary S. Becker and Richard A. Posner.[26] As representatives of the "Chicago school of economics," with its radical emphasis on "rational choice theory" supported by a "sociobiological" set of background beliefs, these contemporary thinkers tend to swallow religion, family life, and politics into a theory of naturalistic economic activity.

The two nontheological streams of thought that have come to us from ancient Greece and Rome have interacted with each other and with theological influences at many points, as can be seen in a variety of authors, such as Thomas Hobbes, Baron Montesquieu, David Hume, John Stuart Mill, Jean-Jacques Rousseau, and Michel Foucault.[27] In whatever combination, these streams have come to dominate the thinking of many in our era. They provide the intellectual roots of what today can be identified as the liberationist and the libertarian view of family life and human sexuality. Both views, I argue, tend to destroy the family. They both misunderstand the nature of human sexual identity and the place of the household in the political economy. Thus they undercut the foundations of civil society.

The Liberationist Reduction

Plato, Aristotle, and Cicero share with Hegel and Marx the notion that the political order is the guarantor and the enforcer of those virtues necessary for human well-being. All these thinkers believed that the state should dominate the household and thus guide both sexuality and the economy. But the ancient philosophers differed from the modern ones in their view of time and in the virtues they wanted to have enforced. For the ancients life was flux and chaos, and they sought an order by which to live in time. They saw wisdom as the grasping of the deep order of things. It was able to guide to justice, with politics as the means to establish it.

For the moderns, life seemed trapped in convention and imposed order. They saw liberty as the hidden dynamic and purpose of history. It had its own cunning, if not quite wisdom. The chief means to grasp the logic of history was reason. But reason would not reveal wisdom as constant order; it would discover the logic of change. That is what could generate a process of expanding liberty. The process, treated variously as "progress," "development," and "revolution," was above all one of "liberation"—of consciousness and society.[28]

G. W. F. Hegel saw the movement to liberation in the expanding incarnations of consciousness, whereby rational freedom became exercised in wider and wider units of civilized life. Rational freedom moves from the direct control over property, through the agreements on contracts with others and the basic religious realizations of morality, to the higher ethical levels of marriage, with its expanded possibilities for capital and progeny. From there it moves to civil society with its cooperative divisions of classes, as ordered by law and actualized in the state, the locus of true freedom.[29]

Marx both incorporated and creatively reconceived the Hegelian vision. Drawing on notions of a primal, natural communitarian life, as portrayed in Rousseau's philosophy and Morgan's anthropology, he argued that the structures of property, morality, religion, family life, and civil society were actually inhibiting liberation and obscuring true reason—which, Marx claimed, arose from the material struggle for existence, not from any "spirit" or "consciousness" progressively actualized in them.

The opposition to liberation and its progress, then, were not located merely in personal resistance to reason or to the state; they were based in the resistance of that class—the progeny, women, and servants who constituted the proletariat—who were subject to the laws of property, morality, religion, family life, civil society, and the state that were perpetuated by the founders of the cities, the bourgeoisie. Subjected to the "citizens" and exploited by them, the proletariat were stripped of their idealistic illusions about the rationality of society. After all, they were the ones who did the real work of the society and thereby learned how things really worked. They could know actual rationality and see through the rationalizations offered by the system. When the realities of their lives were brought to consciousness, they could use the actual rationality that was within them to mobilize the political structures of power to liberate themselves and the whole society.

There is little doubt that real exploitation of women, children, and conquered people has taken place in human history. At many moments, a *master-slave relationship* (the term Hegel and Marx borrowed from Aristotle) has been at the root of social arrangements. But it is doubtful that it can historically be identified with the city, ancient or modern; with the crafts and industries connected to it; or with the owner-worker relations and husband-wife, parent-child patterns that developed in it, as Marx thought it could. More frequently, this relationship was located in labor-intensive agricultural economies with low technology and high-command management at the hands of imperial, feudal, or manorial hierarchies, who identified their control of land with their control of the peasantry and of the fertility of the family, the land, and often the gods. The monuments to this view of life can be found in the ruins of ancient Babylonia, Egypt, India, and China; in the castles of medieval Europe; in the temples of pre-Columbian Latin America; and in the plantations of both pre–Civil War North America and conquistador South America. These are the wreckage of civilizations that opposed independent cities with their independent households, schools, businesses, and religions. Hegel and Marx, in others words, misidentified the sources of evil and thus perpetuated the evils they opposed. They decivilized society.

This error is fateful. Wherever this ideology came to domination, whether in the rightist or the leftist state, the inner tissues of civil society, including the religious, educational, trade, and associational life that sustained the independent household and a more equitable family life in the cities, were deconstructed. The impact of these views on the family was, as Gertrude Himmelfarb points out, "especially brutal"; it invited a nihilism that has played itself out both in the apocalyptic militarism of National Socialism and later in the historicist politicism of Soviet socialism.[30]

In both forms, socialism subverted the fabric of moral and spiritual life, which is the core of civil society, and swallowed every institution and sector of civil society into a political struggle—first to gain control of Mars and Mammon, the political-military and the economic establishments, and then to control the people by means of them for the sake of political, military, and economic development. Churches, clubs, businesses, schools, hospitals, unions, and professional associations, as well as family relations, were seen as part of the bourgeois, liberal past, which the radical solidarity of the future either had to abolish by force or had to sweep into the party-state apparatus.

As for the state itself, it was incorporated into a single, organic unit of society, with all resources focused on the accumulation and exercise of power on the one hand and on the production and distribution of material goods on the other, as led by the party—the "executive committee" of "the people." The former turned out to be, inevitably, a new "royalty" of interlocked households, acting to liberate the "folk" (in the case of National Socialism) or the "masses" (in the case of Soviet socialism). In both cases, the state controlled housing, marital eligibility, gender roles, jobs, income, education, medical care, and entertainment and tried to control religion, neighborly interactions, and friendships. The household became either an instrument of the state, deprived of any independent role in society, or an encapsulated enclave—often the only network besides certain religious groups that one could trust.[31]

A civilization may be able to tolerate this for a time, especially if it abolishes even older tyrannies and oppressions; but over time it will degenerate, precisely because it will replace those older pathologies with new ones. This ideology does not liberate, as Hegel and Marx thought; it controls, as Plato and Aristotle believed was necessary. In the long haul, the state is not capable of discovering wisdom or sustaining reason, procreating or forming the next generation, producing wealth or meeting needs. It certainly cannot inspire trust and meaning at an ultimate level. For these it must depend on other dynamics, such as religion, culture, the family, the household, and the market. The life of the spirit and the fabric of civil society are prior to the state, and the state must honor the one and be the servant of the other if life is to flourish. Hegel almost saw this but then subverted his own insight when he identified the Prussian state as the fullest manifestation of reason's consciousness actualized in history.[32]

Marx almost saw this too, at another point. He was doubtful about the dominance of the state. He believed it had arisen in time and would disappear in time. He therefore recognized the priority of society to politics; but he saw society entirely in terms of the dialectic of material interests and human will, which developed ever-new means of production and engendered the class struggle in history, and the struggle itself required the centralized state to accomplish its purposes (as V. I. Lenin in one way and Mao Tse-tung in another rightly saw). Thus Marx interpreted not only the state but also family, culture, religion, and all other aspects of civil society both as by-products of a class struggle and as tools or weapons to use in the fight.[33]

It is not certain how much Marx endorsed all of the ideas set forth in Friedrich Engels's *The Origins of the Family, Private Property, and the State* (1884), which combines elements from Hegel and Rousseau and draws heavily from the theories of Lewis Morgan, mentioned above.[34] What is clear is that they both believed the primal communitarian, possibly matriarchal, form of life was disrupted by a new division of labor that was both brought about by new technologies and manipulated for class advantage by the strong, male heads of households. These developments, they held, established the possessive structure of sexual monogamy and explained the subordinate status of women, children, and servants in the household and in society. They concluded therefore that the monogamous family ought to be abolished along with capitalism. In fact, they and many of their disciples saw the relative absence of these repressive structures among the proletariat as both an echo of the primal condition of humanity and a forecast of the liberation yet to come.[35]

The effort to abolish the family was among the first aspects of the theory to be abandoned after Lenin came to power in the Soviet Union. This failure of the theory is telling—as is the failure of the system to eliminate completely religion and various independent cultural and economic activity. In spite of enormous pressures, aspects of religion, culture, family life, and business survived. They formed the residual civil society that sustained bodies and souls. The communitarian, liberationist political theories were no more able to form or sustain a civilization in the modern world than they were in the imagined ancient one.

But the ideas developed in the liberationist stream are not dead. They live in the minds of us all; they supply much of the repertoire of social and historical analysis of all theorists, whether they know the sources of these ideas or not. And they have become deeply intertwined with no small number of religious perspectives.[36]

The Libertarian Reduction

Epicurean individualism, which subordinates the society, the family, and the household to individual choice, also flourishes in our time. It appears most dramatically in the "rational choice theory" that has been applied by Nobel prize–winning economist Gary S. Becker to the family[37] and adapted by the noted jurist Richard A. Posner to legal decisions about sexual and family matters.[38] Neither Becker nor Posner, any more than Hegel or Marx, offers a detailed analysis of the material aspects of family life, although both frequently refer to supporting information. What counts as reliable information is itself a matter of dispute, for the footnotes of those who follow the traditions of Hegel and Marx and those who follow Becker and Posner almost never overlap.

Rational choice theorists are, in any case, most directly interested in clarifying how people make decisions in regard to sexuality and family life—choosing a partner, deciding to live together, dividing the work of the household, allocating responsibilities between the family and the larger society, deciding when and how many babies to have, planning how much and what kind of time to spend with children, calculating how to invest in children's education through direct payments by the family and through tax policies, bargaining over the prospects or terms of divorce (pre- or postnuptially), and the like.

The underlying presumption is that people approach sex and marriage the way they do commercial transactions: they estimate costs and benefits and seek to maximize gains and to minimize losses. The goods of sex and marriage are, like commodities, scarce, so there is competition for them. Getting married is best understood, then, in terms of entering a marriage market; having kids can best be grasped in terms of children's marginal utility.[39]

While not essentially focused on public policy or on preserving the family for religious or ethical purposes, Becker recognizes that external conditions such as the legal structure of a society or religious values influence what people take into account in making their calculations and why they view one option as more desirable than another one. At the same time, he presumes that such legal and religious, and thus cultural, values are themselves matters generated out of practical experience over time as to what produces the greater benefits. Care for children—"altruism"—for example, is itself a product of this preconscious but rational choice phenomenon:

> If children "inherit" culturally or biologically a tendency to be like their parents, families with greater altruism would become relatively more numerous over time. Such a selection mechanism operating over thousands of years would have made altruism toward children common in modern times.[40]

Yet Becker is convinced that families are weaker today—performing fewer social functions and breaking up at higher rates—because other institutions have assumed what were familial roles. Wider "market and government mechanisms have evolved to train and educate young people, and to protect against the hazards of old age, illness, premature death, prolonged unemployment and other economic disasters."[41] These "market and government mechanisms" are, in brief, the movement of women out of the household into positions of paid employment and the development of the welfare system, both of which are explained by Becker as increasing the rational choice of individuals and thus, although he hides his preferences, to be approved.

The connection between libertarian economic theory, with its focus on the individual who uses rationality to calculate the relative costs and benefits of choices and its (often forgotten) roots in both the ancient Epicurean and atomistic patterns of thought, and the modern utilitarian and biological ways of viewing problems is even more dramatic in Posner. For one thing, he focuses more on sex than on the family, and for another, he is more overtly hostile than Becker to religious and philosophical perspectives that claim to provide moral guidance for civil society. That, in his view, is the task of law, and law ought to be based on modern secular and scientific grounds. In this connection, he is also explicitly suspicious of feminists, such as Salvatore Cucchiari, who resurrect McLennan's theories to propose that the earliest humans were a "bisexual horde" who only divided into two "genders" and of "social constructionist" gay advocates, such as Michel Foucault, who hold that while there may be some "sexual" differences, most of the meaning we attach to them is socially and culturally constructed.[42]

In contrast, Posner holds that existing social patterns are not altogether "fluid, contingent, plastic, or manipulated by a ruling class." Instead, many "institutions, customs, laws, and other features of the social world" are quite rational and "specifically might be durable adaptations to deep, though not necessarily innate or genetic, human capacities, drives, needs, and interests." This is a "functional outlook that economics shares not only with evolutionary biology but with influential schools of political science, sociology, and anthropology."[43]

This functional outlook, which Posner substantially shares with Becker, is, however, used here to guide the revision of the law in the face of a massive sexual revolution. Posner argues that between 1920 and 1980, most of the western world saw dramatic changes in sexual mores as the world increasingly repudiated what he variously calls "the distinctively Christian attitude toward sex . . . fashioned primarily by Paul," "Augustinian asceticism," "Catholic moralism," and "our Puritan heritage." In the place of this religious vision, society has turned belatedly to the wisdom of sociobiology, as anticipated by Charles Darwin and David Hume, and of economic utilitarianism, as found not only in the liberalism of Jeremy Bentham and John Stuart Mill but also largely with the social Darwinist William Graham Sumner and his contemporary advocate E. O. Wilson.[44] Posner outlines the following changes in sexual mores over this transition as among the most remarkable:

> Premarital intercourse has risen steeply.
> Abortion, sex education, and contraceptive use have increased.
> Teen pregnancy and illegitimate births have soared.
> Marriage rates have fallen.
> Divorce rates have skyrocketed; so has the rate of people cohabiting.
> Average age of first intercourse has fallen dramatically.
> Pornography now circulates more widely than ever before.
> Homosexual activity is increasingly tolerated.[45]

In the literature on the modern family and sexuality, this list of changes is not particularly unusual. What is interesting is that Posner sees these developments as a by-product of the expansion of individual choice. All groups, particularly women, youth, and homosexuals, are now more free to make their own decisions about sexual behavior. It might be said that the Jewish, Christian, and even Puritan ideals of the companionate marriage, freed now from all traces of religious and moral obligation, are coming to full fruition. In fact, according to Posner, from the standpoint of what we ought to consider regulating, we have come to the point where sex needs to be treated as a "morally indifferent" matter. Above all, we need "a laissez-faire approach to sex—an approach that . . . would limit sexual freedom only to the extent required by economic or other utilitarian considerations."[46]

The causes he cites for these changes of attitudes during the so-called sexual revolution can also be identified in terms of the market. They are due to

> a handful of factors, such as the sex ratio (more variable than often assumed), the extent of urbanization (and both the anonymity and the multiplication of possible partners that goes with it), and, above all, the changing occupational role of women. That changing role is, in turn, a function of infant mortality, the value of children, the technology of contraception, the existence of labor-saving devices in the household, and the degree to which well-remunerated work not requiring great physical strength or stamina is available in the economy.[47]

In other words, Posner sees sexual behavior as a function of the market economy and thus believes that the behavioral trends need to be evaluated by means of market theory. His aim is to update the law to take into account current conditions, thereby further maximizing individual choice, so that the ongoing evolution of economic life can proceed with the least amount of friction. He writes of a series of decisions in the 1960s and 1970s in which the Supreme Court "created a constitutional right of sexual or reproductive autonomy, which it called privacy." Later, he points out, the Court cut back on the range of this right. Posner does not focus on the jurisprudential theories by which this was done; but he is interested in "the motives or forces that impelled the Court first to become a standard-bearer in the sexual revolution and then to falter in that role."[48]

The problem is that liberalism itself has become confused since at least Mill, and its misinterpretations continue in current culture wars.[49] One side wants the state to control economic life to promote equality, while allowing maximum freedom in areas of sexuality; the other wants the state to control sexual deviation, while allowing maximum economic freedom to promote productivity. Posner suggests that both err. Each forgets its own libertarian roots. Sexual liberalism would best be identified with economic liberalism. All these matters, plus a number of disputed issues around adoption, pornography, gay marriage, artificial insemination, surrogate motherhood, and the like, should be treated as matters of commercial contract.

It is doubtful that this libertarian economic perspective can sustain the common life any better than the liberationist political one of Hegel and Marx was able to do. The former, too, undercuts the structure of civil society and the place of the household in it. In fact, as we see in the next chapter in greater detail, some of the Scandinavian countries have attempted to combine socialist political policies to redistribute wealth with market economic policies for the production of wealth, as well as laissez-faire policies on sexual matters; but the decay of civil society generally and the family particularly is quite pronounced.[50]

This is not to say that these authors have not recognized certain factors that do indeed play a role in the political economy as it bears on family life and on our moral assessment of how things work in society. They are surely correct that people make many of their decisions regarding whom to date and mate with according to who is available in a given "market." And people do calculate, in refined detail, the relative merits of various options about partners, children, colleges, balances of work and family, and the costs of public policies. Becker and Posner are also surely correct in recognizing that the household is no longer the center of production and that not only the fathers but also the mothers have become part of the labor pool and do their work outside the home—no longer being dependent on an income-producing partner.

Yet Becker's and Posner's approach depends on a circular argument: They think that the revolution into free-market sex needs to be enacted into law because of evolution, yet this evolution is based on a free-market logic that enacts in law what has evolved. They also ignore certain political decisions that have played a more decisive role in matters than economistic theory allows. In his new *Beyond Individualism*, Michael J. Piore points out the separation of production from the household was not only a creation of economic forces but was also allowed and promoted by political decisions that both encouraged the formation of corporations and nurtured the idea that each family should have a single wage earner. While this was more an ideal than a reality for most Americans, the ideal drove policy formation and shaped the development of the labor market for the better part of a century. Piore points out the enormous energy put into social reform and legislation that reinforced this ideal, including

> restrictions on female and child labor, compulsory school attendance, secondary education supported by the state, the minimum wage, restrictions on industrial work at home, support of trade unions, . . . [and] the New Deal labor market policy. . . . And in

the 1950's, when the women who had been drawn into the market by the demands of war production were driven out again by returning male veterans and the New Deal social programs combined with the wages of the newly organized manufacturing workers to provide income security for most adult males, that model became the norm of middle-class American life.[51]

It was only after the Civil Rights movement in America, which converged with the invention of the birth control pill, the rapid expansion of both the corporations and government services needing labor resources, and the flood of women into higher education, that this model was seriously challenged. These medical, economic, and social changes, while having obvious economic dimensions, are rooted in value and social-organizational changes that are not simply driven by economic forces. And it is not altogether clear that, as people survey the available market in potentially available partners and the costs and benefits of having children or of trading off time at the job for time with the scout troop or the Sunday school class, they calculate only so opportunistically. Indeed, people do not simply join the "labor market"—they get jobs in stores, firms, agencies, offices, companies, clinics, or schools, and these social institutions have to be built, sustained by surrounding institutions, and held together by cooperative commitments that are very difficult to buy. Where these institutions do not exist, efforts to join the labor market fail. The atomistic, pleasure-pain calculating self, driven by instincts and hormones, may be able to form certain temporary liaisons, but it is not likely to have been able to form or sustain either communities of love or viable societies in the ancient world, at the height of eighteenth-century utilitarian philosophy, or in contemporary "functional" life.

Sex, reason, and institutional formation are not best understood in terms of the motivations and calculations of the crowd in a singles bar, and neither the general public nor the bar patrons want it to become so. The tolerant society will, to be sure, allow such forces to operate; but this form of calculation will be viewed as a safety valve, at the margins rather than the center of the social channels by which people find opportunities to fall in love. Those who meet in settings such as the singles club are nearly always searching for something more and leave the scene as soon as it fails to produce what they want. It is, in other words, false to Eros to define it essentially in terms of Mammon and to deny the power of Mars and, finally, of God in it. Indeed, unless we see the role of political law and order, the poetry of love, and the deepest of human convictions about the laws, purposes, and graces of God as manifest in all of these spheres of personified powers, we will not understand how human sociality works. In the libertarian view, partial truths are valued more than is valid, and laws made on this logic will neither command respect nor long endure.

At times, Becker and Posner seem to recognize as much. Becker exercises extreme caution whenever value questions arise, even as "externalities." And Posner sometimes points out that parts of the biblical and theological tradition are valid (because they fulfill an evolutionary and utilitarian purpose) but more often manifests a barely controlled rage against religiously based moral doctrines and sentiments. The caution and the hostility suggest that these factors have a great power in human lives in this area, and that there is more to society and culture than the logic of evolution and the calculus of economic gain.

It is the proper function of modern academic disciplines to attempt to explain as much as possible from their own singular perspectives. But that systematic reduction, now present in both liberationist and libertarian perspectives that want to guide human destiny, blots out too much of human life too energetically. These approaches deny the truth of truly "liberal" insights, insofar as these recognize that humans have a basic freedom to exercise their wills beyond the logic of social-historical forces and collective, class interests and beyond the evolutionary logic of survival and the blind rationality of gene perpetuation. The question is how to use that will. Of course, to recognize the factors that theorists like Becker and Posner neglect would force alteration of the arguments and views that they hold with dogmatic tenacity; but families, households, civil societies, communities, and civilizations based only on the economic factors they trace will collapse as surely as did the Prussian state and the Soviet Union.

Another Option

The political economy of the household and the civil society at the core of it cannot be understood by either the liberationist or the libertarian model. No civilization could survive on these bases; these theories falsify the way families work, distort the foundations of human cooperation, and prescribe solutions to social difficulties that compound the problems. To follow them leads to moral, intellectual, and social disaster.

This is not to say that the long philosophical traditions and the anthropological data from which they draw have nothing to offer. As we shall see in the next chapter, when certain aspects of this heritage are seen, as they must be, in conjunction with deeper influences of religious, affectional, legal, and ethical loyalties, they take on a thicker, richer texture. We have already hinted in the previous chapter at the more adequate model by reference to a pluralist understanding of social reality, suggested by the references to covenantal theory. In this view, the family as a unit bonded together by inner ties of commitment and exterior ties of mutual obligation is the core of the household, and the household is an integral unit of society, interacting with, supported by, and mutually supporting other covenanted institutions in a federation of associations.[52] In this view, the family is not a subsidiary of a sovereign political order or a contracted alliance of sovereign individuals driven by calculations of pleasure and pain or potential gain or loss. Families are greater than the sum of their parts, and the bonds between husband and wife, parent and child, formed in love and sealed in promise, make a unit of sharing of bodily, emotional, material, political, moral, and spiritual resources that constitutes an internal economy called the household.

We explore other dimensions of this unit in subsequent chapters, but for now, we focus on those aspects that have to do with the specifically economic functions of the household. It is in the household, in every social context—including the rapidly changing context of contemporary social life—that decisions are made about the needs, resources, opportunities, and obligations of each member and about the proper relationship of the household as a whole to the larger political economy. This unit accumulates not only material capital but also social and moral capital—shared values and enduring loyalties, common virtues and habituated commitments—that deeply influences the character of persons, the quality of directly interdependent institutions (churches, schools, political parties, businesses, etc.), and the ethos of civilizations. If people do not grow up within this kind of matrix, it is doubtful that they will be able to make deep contributions to these other institutions, and it will be with only great difficulty that these other institutions can reconstruct a viable organization to perpetuate society.

Something like this is true in every culture, even if it has been obscured by hyperpolitical or economic theories or distorted by bad anthropology or philosophy. The work of individual family members affects the family as a whole; in turn, the work of the family within the home affects the support individuals have behind them in offering their gifts to the wider society. Quite practically, if children or ill or elderly persons are in the household, someone must provide care for them. Meals must be prepared; houses must be cleaned; food, heat, and shelter must be provided; decisions must be made as to whether to support or oppose current political regimes; and, if it is a genuinely human community, songs must be sung, stories told, disputes negotiated, pain soothed, and a degree of order maintained. Women have known this for centuries, and in spite of the attraction of some women to liberationist and libertarian theories, perhaps in order to gain a critical leverage against unjust conditions, the deeper contributions to understanding are likely to come from those who study the richer, more complex functions, relationships, and loyalties that constitute household life. Many practical matters are demanded of the household; they are what families that work do. We cannot imagine a time or a location where these things have not been, are not, and will not have to be done. No classical, no modern, no liberationist, no libertarian theory can survive that does not attend to the work of the household as a matter constitutive of society.

Household Work

The work of the household can be described under three categories: the work that household members do outside the home; the work they do inside the home to keep things operational; and the work of forming the next generation.

We have already noted that, in most cultures, the household has been the center of production, reproduction, childrearing, and consumption. The most remarkable change for the household is that productive work is now largely performed outside the home. Modern industrial economics have removed much of production from the family farm or shop into factories or offices separate from the household, a trend that has accelerated over several centuries, is most pronounced in the United States, and is increasingly the case around the world. Much has been written on the fact that first the father and the son and then, more recently, the mother and the daughter go out of the home to work, selling their time, energy, and skills to support the family. The relocation of production alters the family as a unit that shares in productive labor, and it sets boundaries between "private" and "public" life. The contrast here, between premodernity and modernity, can be exaggerated, for wage work and apprentice systems took people outside the home in many periods of history. Nevertheless, something new in household life did emerge with the social and economic transformations of the modern period.

Later in this book, we shall give a more extensive account of the continuities and discontinuities between premodern and postmodern patterns of family life, and we shall recognize that religious developments played a greater role in these changes than either the liberationist-communitarian or the libertarian-individualist hypothesis suggests. For instance, it is quite likely that the Protestant emphases on "calling" and "covenant" had something to do with this transformation, for these inspired a creative concern for "technology, innovation, organization, and a host of other factors related to the quality . . . of labor, [and thus to] . . . a rational approach to problem solving, and a preoccupation with the here-and-now that inclined individuals to master their environment through innovation and labor."[53] But these Protestant views themselves rest on deeper presuppositions. We shall examine the influence of such religious developments on the household later on, but for now we can note that positive attitudes toward technology, innovation, organization, and labor were morally and spiritually embraced in the United States and were organized by a legal theory of the corporation.[54] The results helped generate the peculiar shape of the Industrial Revolution in America and drew workers in massive numbers into the factories, and into the building of the canals, railroads, and turnpikes that serviced them, as the settling of the frontier was drawing to a close.

It was these developments that drew massive numbers of immigrants to the United States, even more than land drew them to, for example, South America or Africa; for they sought not only land but also structured opportunities for community life, trade, and jobs. By the 1860s one-half of the labor force did some work away from the farming household.[55] The successive waves of immigrants, with nationalities and often religious loyalties changing by the decade, may not have endorsed or even known of the Puritan doctrines of calling and covenant or of the deeper religious foundations of the social developments they sought. Further, they brought with them distinctive family traditions and non-Protestant convictions; but they quickly adapted to the social institutions established by this heritage, and their mixtures of religious, home, and work experience simultaneously sustained and broadened the role of the household, even as production was gradually removed from it.

One of the most remarkable changes was the alteration of the roles of women. Whether most of the production was done in the household or whether a mixed pattern of seasonal work on the farm and episodic work for pay, factory workers often used their income from outside the home to support the faltering household economy. But even if most of the production took place outside the home, "nonmarket" work remained—work that was the necessary support for everyone who worked for wages elsewhere. It is the combination of this work at home with work at the company that has shaped the role of women in the workforce. More than men, women have borne responsibility for maintaining the household *and* for contributing to the income, whether by taking in washing, keeping chickens and marketing the eggs, selling handicraft products, or taking a "job." Nancy Cott has shown that from the late eighteenth century, women were also engaged in schoolteaching, innkeeping, midwifery, and other "crossover" occupations.[56]

In the allocation of tasks, women were expected to be the protectors and managers of the household, tasks formerly assigned to men, as well as the chief laborers in it; men, meanwhile, were expected to provide the income earned outside the home, to be the managers or workers in industry and the experts on public affairs. As Ann Douglas has shown, religion also increasingly became defined as something pertinent to the household only and was thus largely "feminized" for a time, until the rise of abolitionism, the Social Gospel movement, and, for Catholics, the inauguration of the Social Encyclical tradition, all of which demanded religion's pertinence to and engagement with public (and thus "manly") matters.[57]

But this sharp division of private female and public male worlds was unstable. The deeper traditions of calling and covenant, and the social influence of democratic government and the economic corporation shaped by them, drew women into the public world—in spite of the efforts of government and of both labor and management to keep the spheres separate. Union leader Samuel Gompers argued in 1898 for a "living wage" for the male worker, so that he could support an "average-size family."[58] Henry Ford's concept of the "five-dollar day" was another effort to establish a wage able to support an entire family. Ford argued, "The man does the work in the shop, but his wife does the work in the home. The shop must pay them both."[59]

Part of the reason the division between men's and women's spheres did not hold is that not all men had five-dollar-a-day jobs. Poor white women often supplemented their husbands' incomes, and black wives worked outside the home at four times the rate of white women, a fact that is directly related to the insufficiency of pay to minority males.[60] But men's income levels cannot account for middle- and upper-class women beginning to go to college in higher and higher numbers and joining the labor force at a geometric rate of increase. Nor can they wholly account for why these women have remained in the labor force after their early twenties (the median age of first marriage), even when their husbands have good incomes, or have stayed employed longer during pregnancy and returned to the workforce in increasing numbers before their children reached school age.[61]

One could attribute such figures to a kind of personal hedge to protect one's fortunes in the face of increased levels of divorce;[62] but teenage mothers and black women, who have the highest rates of divorce, do not follow these patterns. What seems to be the case is that women increasingly feel themselves to have callings in at least two covenanted communities: They want to be loving wives and mothers in the family and to be responsible producers and earners in the public world of work.

As work outside the home changed, work at home changed as well. While women may have done more of the cooking and men more of the planting and harvesting during the preindustrial eras in the West, the adults living in the household shared a remarkable number of the tasks. While some things were differentiated by gender—women made and mended cloth garments, men made and mended leather ones, for example[63]—many tasks were gender-neutral, such as milking cows, grinding grain, and feeding pigs. Nor can it be said that these allocations of tasks were determined by the kind of political economy or by the level of technology, for what we know of medieval China, India, and Africa, for example, suggests that they divided precisely these tasks differently in spite of the similarities with the West of subsistence agricultural technology and feudal-royal governance systems. What was decisive in all of these societies was the structure of the household systems and the range of persons who were engaged in its interdependencies.

But when, in the West—and now, increasingly, in other cultures— more members of a family take jobs outside the household, someone still has to do the household chores. To be sure, the technology that changed methods of production in factories also changed the methods of doing household work. "Labor-saving" devices such as cooking stoves, sewing machines, vacuum cleaners, washing machines, and the like, all made possible by gas supplies, running water, and available electricity, may have reduced the strain of physical drudgery, but they also made it easier for one person to do more. Technology brought a reorganization of, rather than a reduction of, household work.[64] And women who left the home to work in the mills or factories or offices returned to this domestic work after their extrahousehold jobs. Some argue that the housework hours put in by wives have remained basically constant over the twentieth century—fifty-one hours per week in 1920, compared to forty-nine in 1990—in spite of all the household technology and housekeeping aids now available. The result has been rising standards of cleanliness and health—sometimes with absurd expectations, as television ads for cleaning materials indicate.[65]

One of the key reasons for the social delegation to the woman of household managerial as well as labor responsibilities is the physical fact that women bear children and, especially if they nurse, they must be near the children for an extended period of time. The man does not have this restriction of movement. He can continue to hunt, gather, work in the factory, or go on a business trip during his mate's pregnancy, delivery, and lactation. This fact prompted some to define the "callings" of men and women entirely according to biology.

But callings are only partly related to material factors, and how much this physiological difference between men and women has influenced gender roles and is genetically programmed into their emotional and dispositional lives is a matter of considerable dispute. Certainly, its importance is somewhat reduced, whatever its level, by the fact that men can run the home technology as well as women and women can run the company technology as well as men. Besides, a calling is more properly understood as a spiritual matter in the context of covenanted social arrangements, and one theological reason for treating work in terms of calling is to deny the notion of a fixed, naturally determined status in life for which there is no moral responsibility and no exit. We are responsible first of all to God and to those given to us to love, and not merely to "nature," for how we live our lives. For these reasons, we find many efforts to bring an increase of equality between men and women in the way they allocate tasks of the household, now the locus not of production but of reproduction, consumption, and altered childrearing.

The Work of Nurture

Until quite recently, when both mother and father began to work in institutions of production outside the home, the care of children was entirely in the purview of parents. Children were conceived in the household, born in it, raised in it, and quickly taught to become part of its labor force. To be sure, elite families could delegate much of that care to a governess or tutor or boarding school, but these, too, were seen as a manifestation of both love and the stewardship of children's lives, entrusted to parents for a time by God.[66]

The education of the young, for most of western history (from Plato and Aristotle through Locke to Freud) and for many in Chinese, Indian, and African cultures, was especially the responsibility of fathers, although clearly, women passed on all sorts of skills and lore to their progeny. (Modern historians interested in women's history have recovered aspects of the mother's role in this, especially for the daughters.) The earliest American laws regarding schooling were in seventeenth-century New England, under which the parents, especially the fathers as "heads of households," were required to ensure that their children were prepared for adult life through learning to read, especially the Bible and often a catechism, and to master a trade and the basics of math. Towns began to establish schools under the authority of religiously informed local governments. As the colonies developed in the eighteenth century, a variety of schools were founded, including schools from multiple religious orientations and specializing in a wide range of trades. Only in the nineteenth century were the "public schools" developed by states. This paralleled the development of the factory and the corporation, which took parents increasingly out of the household and even out of local communities. In the twentieth century, school attendance became compulsory.[67]

At the same time, education became more and more the responsibility of women. In both home care and formal education, childcare was marked by increasing professionalization as reformers and settlement-house workers, the forerunners of social workers, instructed immigrant mothers about "proper" modes of home economics, health, and nutrition and provided much needed childcare for working mothers. The marks of "mother love" were increasingly stamped by "professional standards," a development that had the unanticipated results of further removing fathers from responsibility in these areas, reinforcing and extending the period over which mothers had primary responsibility for nurture, and inculcating professional skills and standards of performance, and thus a desire for more formal education, in women. Not only the early education of the young and schoolteaching but also departments of education, social work in the colleges, and divisions of religious education in the seminaries became "women's work."

With the influx of women into wartime factory production during World War II, mothers demanded, and got, corporate provision of childcare facilities. Thus the profession of nursery-school teacher was born. When the fathers marched home from the war, took over the jobs at the time of the great postwar boom, and built suburban homes on GI loans in areas that had no schools, no churches, no community traditions, and no centers of recreation, the mothers temporarily left the professional world and constructed semblances of a new "civil society" on volunteer time. But the longer-term patterns were already established. From the 1950s on, women entered the workforce in record numbers and also became the advocates of childcare, nursery schools, extended hours for school, better schools, and more responsibilities for educators and social workers—and, over time, the possibility of participation by all professions in the childrearing tasks. They did not particularly advocate but they also soon had to recognize the influence of the entertainment industries, which intentionally cultivated the loyalties and tastes of the young. All these developments, of course, meant the greater distance of fathers from the work of nurture.[68]

Current Trends

In the course of outlining the work of the household, we noted several recent developments that have put new pressures on the household and threatened its ability to accomplish its critical tasks. First, industrialization has relocated production outside the household. Husbands, wives, and children do very little work together. Second, this relocation of production has reallocated (and technologized) the division of labor between men and women in the household, and in the society at large—which gives ambiguous signals regarding the expected roles of men and women. And third, these developments have both professionalized childcare and removed parents, especially fathers, from the work of nurture, although the management of childrearing remains a stereotypical duty of mothers.

These changes have induced a great ambiguity about the relationship of household obligations and employment obligations. People feel caught between their commitment to spouse and children and that to job and earning. Yet enormous numbers of people want to keep both and would feel deprived if forced to choose between one and the other.[69] We do know that the working hours of Americans have been rising steadily since the 1970s, after declines over most of the twentieth century,[70] but we also know that productivity has been rising and that increasingly the gains have gone into household spending.

Some workers, of course, struggle to find full-time work or work that will offer them benefits and security, and many face the problems of holding more than one job, having to work more hours to maintain the family, having fewer periods of time off, and facing reduction of benefits and job security in view of global competition in the labor market. But this partly reflects the fact that more and more people around the world are joining the middle class (by Asian, African, or Latin standards), adopting an ethic in productive areas not unlike that developed in the West, leaving the farms, working in factories that compete with American ones, adopting household patterns closer to those known in the West, and making the less-skilled workers in the United States more vulnerable.[71]

But for most Americans, the main issue for both sexes seems to be the conflict between commitment to paid work and commitment to home life. They find it difficult simultaneously to meet the demands of their jobs, to keep everything working at home, and to raise their children. A 1987 study showed that 41 percent of women and 32 percent of men in dual-career families reported that paid work interfered with family life.[72] What seems to be important in determining the effect of employment on family life is the type of employment and the level of control, over both work and schedule, that it affords, with routine or uninteresting jobs that offer little control creating negative effects.[73]

For example, marital satisfaction decreases and the probability of divorce increases when a spouse engages in shift work.[74] Earlier studies showed that part-time work by wives correlated with greater marital satisfaction for both spouses than did either full-time employment or full-time homemaking; however, later studies point to the negative effects of part-time work's lower benefits and autonomy. One study showed that dual-career couples who have commuter marriages, due to different job locations, experience less work-family conflict than dual-career couples with a single residence; however, they also experienced generally lower levels of marital satisfaction.[75]

Overall, the impact of married women's employment, specifically, on marital stability and divorce is mixed. However, a 1992 study found that the attitudes toward the division of labor according to "traditional" gender roles had a greater impact on perceived quality of marriage than did the particulars of the wife's work, and that there was less conflict when both spouses' attitudes were open, even if the wife's job was higher in income or status than the husband's job.[76] A 1990 review of research into the effect of these attitudinal factors concurs, citing study findings which show that men's attitudes about working wives had a stronger effect here than the views of women, as measured by marriage stability.[77]

Both housework and childcare by fathers has increased among families with employed mothers as well, from 14 percent of all arrangements made for children under age five in 1977 to 20 percent in 1991. This is related to increases in shift-work arrangements by parents[78] and to care by unemployed fathers.[79] Finally, cultural factors and gender-role socialization play a significant but unmeasured role in determining the housework and childcare involvement of married fathers. Scandinavian studies on paternity leave and other social programs, for example, show that despite the lack of economic penalties incurred by fathers' increased involvement with their children, the programs have not shifted the childrearing duties significantly from mothers.

Dual-career couples studied, as well as those in marriages with wives in the home, agree that wives take more responsibility for the work of the household across all areas: cooking, cleaning, shopping, and bill paying.[80] The division of childcare responsibilities follows similar lines, despite very different perceptions by men and women of the allocation of the tasks involved. Forty-three percent of men in dual-career families perceived that they shared childcare equally with their wives, while only 19 percent of women agreed with this assessment. Wives in dual-career families with children actually spent 3.75 hours on an average workday caring for children, compared with about 2.6 hours for men; these women also spent about half an hour more per workday on chores than did men in similar families. Time away from work was similarly allocated: On the average day off, women spent more than 14.5 hours on children and chores combined, while men spent fewer than 12 hours on these.

How do work-family conflicts play out? The heaviest effects are on the families themselves, rather than on the work site. Forty percent of workers studied report that household chores were not done, 35 percent report their personal time affected, and nearly 25 percent report their family time affected due to job responsibilities. Yet workers apparently were willing to make significant trade-offs for benefits that were family-supportive: Of those workers not offered health insurance, slightly more than half would change their employer or give up salary increases and other benefits to obtain it. Thirty-five percent of parents with children under age 13 would change jobs to obtain flextime arrangements, and almost 30 percent would change jobs in order to be able to work at home. Over 35 percent of parents studied in Ellen

Galinsky, James T. Bond, and Dana E. Friedman's *The Changing Work-force* would trade salary and benefits for childcare at work.[81] Women overall valued flextime more highly than men did, while men and women were equally willing to make trade-offs in salary and benefits to obtain dependent-care assistance (at-work childcare, flexible spending accounts, childcare vouchers).

The movement of married women and mothers into the workplace has, in some ways, made clearer the value of the work done in the home. Household tasks that began to be professionalized early in the twenti-eth century have become businesses themselves. Phyllis Palmer has ar-gued that "servants" have not disappeared; they have simply become professionals, moved out, and formed their own companies.[82] Others claim that, for the poorer sectors of the population, the servants have become the bureaucratic welfare workers.

Yet there are parts of the "work of the family" that cannot be pur-chased through market transactions or engineered by political pro-grams. Care, trust, mutuality, acceptance, and parental involvement and the affective bond underlying it are beyond price or governmental authority. Nurturing and being known are not services; they cannot be readily commodified, any more than they can be generated by political programs. Children spend their lives in a variety of institutions that shape how they feel about themselves and look at the world, but the stewardship and guidance of the parent-child relationship and the modeling and intimacy it involves are not subject to the ordinary laws of political economy. They assume a level of involvement and motiva-tion that is not measured in hours or easily quantifiable. We know them more by their absence and its affects on a child's later life, and thus on society, as we see in the next chapters. And if what people are presently seeking in family and economic life is hard to find, it may well be that they are unclear about the multiple dimensions that influence those spheres or about the theological and ethical foundations on which their integration rests. It is to further explorations of these dimensions, in quest of the deeper foundations, that we now turn.

3

Home and Religion: Sharing and Home Life

Some of the complex and multiple meanings of "family" as it relates to religious and economic life are becoming clear. Family is rooted in issues of sex and marriage and thus tied to the question of the morally and spiritually valid forms of physical intimacy, as we saw in chapter 1. It also is integrally related to the way labor is divided for production, consumption, reproduction, and nurture, as we saw in chapter 2. Although both contemporary interpretations of sexuality and newer patterns of economic life complicate many aspects of family life today, it appears that a sense of sacredness persists in attaching itself to home life. At the same time, the family is not, and under present conditions cannot be, the sovereign center of loyalty. It can flourish only in a setting in which family is one (crucial) part of the network of civil society.

In tracing the key dynamics of changes in the context of an increasingly complex civil society thus far, we saw that the structure of marriage and the household, and indeed of the corporation, the school, and reproductive technology, depends on factors more deeply rooted in the religious dynamics of life than is recognized either by the current theories of sexuality or by evolutionary and economic theories. These sweeping views cannot account for the sanctity of marriage that is present in every historical culture or for the actual economic dynamics of how people live. Nor can they answer the question of how we ought to live and why we ought to live one way rather than another. But if these theories cannot do so, what might? Surely, they are correct that how we live is in continuity with social constructions of our deeper past. What might these be?

We more accurately see how we live in families and how they are related to social history if we note certain family-based activities that are so obvious as to be overlooked. Some apparently simple activities, such as the giving of gifts, the making of a home, and sacrificing for the next generation, turn out to be profoundly significant. For instance, the media routinely report that one of the most important indicators of how the political economy of the United States is doing is the rate at which people do Christmas shopping. Every year, from Thanksgiving until New Year's Day, the stores are flooded with goods, shoppers, and special decorations. It is estimated that well over 10 percent of the nation's retail economy depends on that season.[1] Some authors suggest that holiday shopping's contribution is significantly greater. Leigh Eric Schmidt, in a fresh treatment of American holidays, states:

> Indeed, many department stores as well as smaller retailers count on Christmas for a quarter of their annual sales and because of higher margins in pricing, half of their annual profits. And sometimes the percentage for Yuletide earnings run even higher—up to 70 percent of the year's profits. In all, according to one recent estimate, Christmas gift giving is worth some $37 billion to the nation's economy. . . . If an anthropologist were to draw up a "temporal map" of American culture, Christmas would have to be inscribed in giant red letters.[2]

One might dismiss all this as nothing more than an invention of the store owners for their own gain. There may be something to this argument, but most efforts to manufacture holidays for commercial purposes fail. If that were all there we had to say about this matter, we would also have to admit that it is a brilliant strategy, for these commercial interests are evidently able to recognize that people have become so conditioned by deep cultural values that they are delighted to spend more than one-tenth of their annual income just at this time of year and just in this way. More profoundly, the deeper roots of cultural values and symbols find expression in these rites.

Of course, no one thinks that everyone who buys toys or jewelry, scarves or books, neckties or TVs, turkeys or eggnog, is a believer or deeply motivated by Christian charity, or that every manufacturer, advertiser, or department-store manager is driven by festive motives—as every preacher who holds forth on the perils of materialism in this sacred season knows very well. But the significance of holidays to the economy does mean that at least part of our culture is shaped also by an ethic of gift giving, of sharing, and of caring.

Further, if one examines who buys what for whom, it turns out that members of the family, various relatives (extended family), and family friends, along with selected workmates or business associates, are the purchasers and recipients by a high percentage in this elaborate ritual of material sharing. Even more, remembering, more or less, what everyone in the family circle likes or wants or needs and trying to match that, and at the same time keeping a mental catalog of what each did for everyone else over the last several years, to make things relatively appropriate and proportional, constitutes a massive religious-familial-social-economic phenomenon, seldom, if ever, named in any theological or ethical text.[3]

A related practice is that people, especially the ill or the elderly, take great pains to distribute their assets and heirlooms, to be sure insurance arrangements and wills are in order, and to plan legacies for children and for churches, schools, hospitals or other charitable institutions. While some of this may be a matter of "golden handcuffs" that bind the younger generation to the older, to make sure the latter is cared for and to satisfy their emotional needs, much of it is experienced as caring and sharing. Economically, generational generosity and philanthropy are enormous sources of capital; and America is about to enter the largest transfer of wealth from the older generation to the younger that has ever taken place in history.

Yet another significant but taken-for-granted element of everyday life is that couples almost always seek a place of their own. Most couples dream of, save for, and plan on a house that can become their home, knowing that it is likely to be the largest single material investment of their lives, consuming 30 percent or more of family income.[4] And in seeking a place for their family, couples refine, often with disagreements, their shared commitments and sense of propriety, even if they are dream-rich and money-poor. Matters of location, design, decor, and proximity to institutions—religious, educational, cultural—that they want to enjoy, enhance, and encourage to the next generation become critical. A house reflects the distinctive values of the culture at large; the fashions of the times; the couple's particular subculture, modulated by what they can afford; and what the architects, engineers, builders, bankers, interest rates, designers, and furniture makers can supply, as guided by building codes and liability laws.

That the finding of a place for a family to share is greatly shaped by what is financially possible is, of course, rooted in the larger, society-wide economic realities and in the family's place in them—including a family's ethnicity, class, education, and age. Some couples want to be close to parents; others want a degree of distance. Some desire a retreat from the world; others want a locus for hospitality. Some simply want a place to sleep, with easy access to external centers of activity; others look for a self-contained center for work, hobbies, exercise, and entertainment. Some accent private space for each family member; others emphasize common space. Some love antiques; others delight in contemporary. Some feel at home with rich complexities of hues and design; others seek simplicity of color and line. Both what people desire and what is possible are shaped by economic factors. Yet what is most striking is the fact that what people do with what they have to establish a home is shaped by value factors, and specific clusters of value factors make specific forms of family life more or less possible to establish and to sustain.

In the United States, in the last quarter of the twentieth century, some 65 percent of households consist of detached, single-family houses, not counting the additional 5 percent or so who live in mobile homes in established locations.[5] In addition, most condominiums, cooperatives, and rental apartments occupied by families compare in size and value with detached homes, although 65 percent of apartments are occupied by unmarried, widowed, separated, or divorced women or single men.[6] These dwellings are sizable compared to the housing of most of the world over most of human history. Seventy-five percent of family dwellings have two rooms per person, and about 10 percent are plagued by overcrowding (officially defined as 1.5 persons per room).

The fact that most of the houses people live in, and the homes married people seek, are located in suburbs, exurbs, or small towns is also significant. Living in these homes is intimately connected with the cost of going to work; for every three persons who go to work by train, bus, or subway, more than one thousand go by car, and more than 75 percent of the cars have only one rider. These commuters generally drive less than one-half hour. In other words, the hopes for a place to live are intimately tied to issues of how to get to get to work and back in an affordable manner.[7] If Americans have a mass transportation system, it consists of cars.

Moreover, the dream of a house—plus a job to pay for it and a reliable, stylish (where possible) vehicle to get to and from it—is intimately tied to the hope of having children. Indeed, the next largest investment that a family makes, after the house, is the education of their children. It may be that the best some families can do is to make sure their children are properly washed and clothed for public school; but most families go through all sorts of sacrifices of time, energy, and money, to the limits of their abilities, to seek out the best options available for their children, to motivate them to do their best, to prepare them to become responsible members of families and society in the future. In this process, parents want the children to live up to their God-given gifts, actualize their callings, do some good in the world, find some happiness in what they do with their lives, and establish homes of their own. Of course, what people define as "responsible," "gift," "calling," "good," and "happiness" may vary from subculture to subculture. But it is not unreasonable to suspect that there is also a sense of sacrificial dedication to the future of homemaking.

Such behaviors confirm our suspicions that efforts to discuss the family simply in terms of sexuality and social construction, as we saw in chapter 1, or simply in terms of economic and evolutionary forces, as we saw in chapter 2, are extremely shallow. Commitments and loyalties are present in parents' actions; they cannot be understood without reference to the ways in which religious values shape family life. The specific forms of sharing mentioned here—gift giving, homemaking, and sacrificing for the next generation—are embodied in the social practices of civil society and have very deep, and increasingly forgotten, roots. The contention of this chapter is that if we do not understand these roots and offer a better overview of social history than has been heretofore presented, then we are unlikely to understand the relationship of faith, economics, and family life. Indeed, we may be tempted on the one hand to a kind of familism, an idolatry of the family, or on the other hand to a neglect of the family's sacred elements and its proper place in society.

From Hearth to Hearth

In 1864 a classical historian in Strasbourg, Fustel de Coulanges, who was later to become the director of the École Normale in Paris, wrote a major study of the family in ancient Indo-Aryan, Greek, Roman, and Semitic culture. Although contemporary scholars have gathered more data since that study, de Coulanges saw deeply into the implications of what he had at hand, and his major hypotheses have turned out to be remarkably accurate. He recognized that family life, including its sexual, economic, and legal dimensions, was fundamentally shaped by religious influences, and that specific kinds of religion shaped distinctive economic and social systems.

In his masterwork, *The Ancient City*,[8] Fustel argues that ancient religious beliefs and rituals surrounding "hearth" accurately reveal the

forces that shape life. When people marry and bury and say their
prayers, they try to do what is right before the ultimate authority they
can imagine. Thus we can look at ritual patterns and classic forms of
creed to which people turn when they make judgments about how to
order life. These convictions and routines may be mostly preconscious
and unexamined, but they inform the daily rounds of life and the ordinary fabric of community, even if they are not recognized as "special"
because they have become, over time, "second nature."

Ancient beliefs and practices centered on the sacred fire of the hearth.
The hearth not only was the means for cooking food and of providing
warmth for those who lived and loved in its presence but also was the
center of a profound "domestic religion." People prayed together daily
at the hearth, the altar of the family gods. They prayed to the spirits of
dead members of the family, who had descended to the underworld
when buried in the earth of the family property, and to Hestia, goddess
of the hearth and of fertility. These spirits were a living presence at the
hearth and near the tomb. The pouring of libations and the leaving food
from the hearth for those who were deceased and the tending of the
hearth and the earth where living and dead resided together became
the most holy and binding duties of all, the source of loyalty and
law. Here is the root of the claim that those who pray together, stay
together, and of the recognition, known to every pastor, that people's
religious convictions, economic behaviors, and political loyalties are
profoundly intertwined with their enduring bonds to relatives, even in
dysfunctional families.[9]

The implications of the family, the land, and the household being
bound together by the presence of holy spirits in their midst are many.
For one thing, marriage was absolutely sacred. When marriage took
place, the woman (sometimes, several women; polygamy was not un-
known) left not only the home in which she was born but the religion
in which she had been raised. Marriage was a conversion. She was ini-
tiated into a new cult by her husband or the senior patriarch, and she
thereby adopted new ancestral spirits with whom, to whom, and for
whom she was expected to make ritual and material sacrifices. This
bond also made divorce most unholy and unthinkable; all her goods,
activities, and loyalties were henceforth to be dedicated to this, and no
other, sovereign and sacred tradition. (When a groom today carries a
bride over the threshold, he not only is entering a new and holy estate
but is doing so in a way that reenacts a bit of the ancient ritual of the
hearth cult.)

This view of sacred reality also made private property absolute—although what was private was less personal than familial. The family was bound by sacred ties to the land it occupied, since land was not only the primary means of production but also the permanent residence of the family spirits. Thus ownership was deeply tied to the sacred obligation to carry on the line, so that the sacred fire and the offering of sacrifices to the spirits of the dead present in the land would bless life. Each person found his or her fate linked to the social unit of the family. Those fathered by the same seed or suckled by the same breasts belonged to the same patriarchal cult and held the land as a common and perpetual legacy. It could be expanded by cultivation or conquest; but these would not make it home. Homemaking took place in the establishment of grave sites and the dedication of a sacred hearth; friendly departure by a younger brother would properly entail taking some of the bones and coals from the hearth with him. The end of the line of a family meant the extinguishing of the fires of life and the death of the gods—a haunting source of ghosts and evil spirits, for which no one wanted to be responsible.[10]

Fustel recognized that other peoples in other places had many practices that were similar and yet had distinct ways of organizing their families around other pieties. He makes specific reference to the "mobile peoples" who lived by cattle or horse breeding and whose views of the divine were less related to constant space than to changing times. Although there may well be similar bonds to kith and kin, such concepts are of a somewhat different order and have distinctive social implications. "The tent covers the Arab, the wagon the Tartar; but a family that has a domestic hearth has need of a permanent dwelling. . . . [Such a] family did not build for the life of a single man, but for generations that were to succeed each other in the same dwelling."[11]

The "mobile peoples," we should add, were likely to focus on tribes or clans as well as families and to develop greater loyalty to the gods of the sky than to the deities of the earth. Among the mobile Germanic tribes, the mode of organization sometimes took the form of a warrior brotherhood—the *comitatus,* as it was named by Tacitus—whereas in India it took the form of the hereditary caste. Yet another tradition, decisive for the West and distinct from these Indo-Aryan forms, is that of the Hebrews. According to Fustel, God is understood as the "primitive proprietor, by right of creation," of land in the Bible—a quite distinct difference. But when this God delegates to specific human groups a stewardship over various portions of the earth, something analogous to the religion of the ancient hearth is occuring. The extended family becomes the decisive center of responsibility regarding its property and its members. Thus both similarities and differences appear again when we read in the Hebraic tradition of Genesis that the husband is to leave his father and his mother to join in marriage—contrary to the hearth tradition. And we read that the Lord told Abraham, Sarah, and his household to go out from the land of Ur and later told Moses and the Israelites, "Go up hence . . . into the land. . . . Unto thee will I give it." In the calling of Abraham to go out of the land, we see an understanding of God that is not tied to family and land in the same way as the hearth tradition held. Fustel thinks that Christianity developed this idea of being called out of the household and tribe of origin, taking a more radical direction that has subsequently been fateful for our cultural history.

Fustel recognizes that domestic religion was not the only form of religion in the Greek and Roman traditions. Some religions centered in the principle figures of "Zeus, Hera, Athena, Juno, . . . of the Hellenic Olympus, and of the Roman Capital." These multiple deities were understood to be "the Gods of Physical Nature" and were closely tied to the heroic and warrior traditions. These powers were not, however, fully integrated into a conception of a single god ruling the universe, for no notion of a universe had yet developed. Instead, the world was conceived as a series of "rival forces," each one having its own will, living together in "a sort of confused republic."[12]

De Coulanges traces the rising influence of those religions established by warrior-heroes as they settled in clusters, lived off the labor of the slaves they conquered, and drew into their family compounds. Their settlements, however, were dedicated to these nature gods, who were honored by the establishment of communal temples with sacred hearths. This, he argues, was what led to the founding of the great city-state traditions of ancient Greece and Italy, but it led to a great tension between the private sacred space of the family deities and the public sacred space of the city deities.[13] The question was posed: Which is most "natural" membership for humanity, the spiritual relation to earth and family or the spiritual relation to city and fellow cult member? The spirits of the *oikos* and the spirits of the *polis*, each holy in their own way and each tended by a specific group, evoked tensions of duty and conflicts of solidarity. These tensions were a contest of the gods, that is, a struggle as to what the sovereign powers of the universe actually were and thus which were to reign in society and in the deepest loyalties of the people.[14]

For a time, city religions came to dominate: The father-priest of the hearth became subordinate to the priest-king before the sacred fires of the temples of the polis. The elders who worshiped the gods of the cities established republics of families able to claim the loyalties of, and set the laws for, the relationships of the families. But their basis was fragile, and they were threatened by any who challenged their pieties. These are they who forced Socrates to drink the hemlock, for with his relentless inquiries he challenged not only the deities of the families but those of the city as well.

But all these deities were not able to command the loyalties of all, and both the conflicts among the families within the cities and between the cities demanded, or at least invited, an empire. It is significant that Alexander was tutored by Aristotle, who was quite suspicious of the household except as an economic unit and of the city cult except as an instrument of control for the unphilosophical masses. Called *soter* (savior) by the time of his death at the age of thirty-three, Alexander sought unification of rule and took into his entourage all the father-priests and priest-kings and philosophers who would serve his purposes, and defeated the rest.

In the empire, the old familial spirits and the deities of the city-states became ghosts of the past, and constraining duties to them were easily ignored. Instead, the powers of Eros and the heroic virtues were presumed to be located in the individual citizens and especially the empire's leaders, in mixed degrees. Clearly, some of the stories of the sexual behavior of the gods suggest that the powers of Eros resisted any constraint. Yet, without the old religions to guide them, the best philosophers of the day argued that these powers needed state control, as we see in Plato, or at least carefully habituated political guidance, as we see in Aristotle, even if a few, such as the Epicurians and some dramatists, argued that they should be lauded and cultivated.[15]

De Coulanges traces the several developments that led eventually to the rise of Rome—the decline of the gods of the city-states at the hands of both populist democracy and increased military authority, which led, in turn, to the celebration of Mars and the deification of Caesar, much as domestic religion had been relativized by increased loyalties to the city cults, with no small amount of the uninhibited worship of Eros at all levels of society.[16] Yet he notes that the Romans, to keep their rule, not only had to develop a civil religion but had to expand both the empire's armies and its capacity to feed the urban populations. This involved including new peoples in the armies and developing new, massive tracts of land to produce wheat, wine, and oil, the staples of the imperial city.[17] Soldiers and sharecroppers were needed to operate these plantations and to fight wars. A number of northern Europeans, at the margins of the empire, were organized in bands of fighting men, the *comitati* (as has been documented more fully by contemporary scholars, who have traced down materials Fustel could not have known).[18] They took sacred oaths to support one another under their chief or lord, who, in turn, looked after his men. They did not live in independent households around sacred hearths or in cities dedicated to the natural gods but as bands in clusters of huts built in sacred groves. Some fought the Romans, others fought with the Romans; many are remembered from later history as Celts, Slavs, Vikings, or Norsemen. The Romans drew some into the Roman army and many on whom they preyed into protected sharecropper villages, and they drove others to the margins of civilization.[19]

However, in attempts to tame the frontiers, the Romans had established laws that dealt with issues of household, property, village, and piety. These laws were based on the older traditions of family and civic order, and that legal heritage allowed practices that, in very subtle ways, sustained the forms of family life, sometimes with the legal obligations of the old "sacred hearth" tradition, but without overtly stating the ancient religious meanings. Ownership was perpetual and hereditary, for example, and the father was to protect the purity of the family. Although these obligations had been surpassed by both the Greek city cults and later imperial religion, they were reinstituted by Roman law and further reinforced by the Roman doctrine of the *potestas patria,* the nearly absolute authority of the father as citizen of the empire to become arbiter of law at the local level.

Later, during the political and economic disintegration of the empire, farmers found themselves in need of protection and bound themselves and their villages to the leaders of the *comitatis* with their retinue of "knights." They gave over their lands to the emerging petty nobility and received in turn the right to farm them, under the protection of their lord and with the understanding that the lord of the manor would receive a share of the produce of the land. By analogy, the relationship of each man and his wife and children was viewed in ways similar to his relationship to the lord of the manor, thus establishing superior and inferior forms of relationship in terms of loyalty, ownership, and rights to use. Deprived of their mutual sacred obligations, property and power increasingly dominated house and home.

In brief, the medieval history of the West, in a new location and with many new features, blended, preserved, extended, and revitalized certain ancient traditions, sometimes well blessed by interpretations of the patriarchs and Davidic rule in the Bible. Feudalism, with its combination of familial *and* economic authority, tied to warrior power and echoes of imperial order, partly redefined but essentially reinforced traditional lines between the personal and the political, the private and the public, familial membership and property, with habitual and legal residues of the old sacredness of the hearth.[20]

From Altar to Sacrament

Fustel concludes his study by pointing to the distinctive social contributions Christianity made. For Christians, the Divine is not identified with the hearth or the city or the regime, not with Eros, Polis, or Mars. God is not to be confused with spirits of the ancestors or the powers of Eros, with the gods of the polis or the imperial rulers, with Mammon or the laws of property. God stands in a realm above them all and yet is present in and among the people, in Christ and the Holy Spirit as they live in and among all of these.[21]

Such a perspective is evident in scripture and in the liturgies that are still said. When Jesus taught his followers to say "Our Father, who art in heaven, . . ." and instructed them to "call no man father," the absolute and divine power of the male head of the household was relativized. (The practice of calling priests "father" and taking them out of the household has some comparable sociological implications.) Biblical references to God as King of kings and Lord of lords portray God as above the political power of all kings and the economic power of all lords. Thus, when the imperium fell, it was this religion that picked up the fragments and established a new, more universal understanding of the Divine and the human.[22]

A generation ago, C. N. Cochrane argued that Rome fell because it had a metaphysical disease: It could not sustain the bases of society on the grounds of the religions it cultivated.[23] It soon became clear that the church, if it was to provide a cure for the metaphysical disease, had to work out a positive and constructive relationship to the fact that, for people to live, family life, economic life, and political life had to continue, even if some members of the church took vows that removed them from these activities in order to signal their loyalty to the God who was above them all. Gradually, the sacramental forms of marriage were worked out (as suggested in chapter 1), drawing on certain Greek ritual elements as well as the Roman legal concept of voluntary contract and the rights of property for new family but (as mentioned in chapter 2) demanding both voluntary consent and a mutual exchange of vows.[24]

What is most remarkable about these developments is that the sacred character of the office of husband or wife, and of the duties of intimacy that led to procreation as well as of the rights of the family unit to perpetuate property, was treated as not intrinsic to sexuality, household traditions, or procreative fecundity by themselves. Sacred rights and duties were conferred by God at the altar through sacrament to form the family. The activities of marriage were not understood to be, in themselves, sacred. They required grace from beyond themselves to be holy.[25]

The power of the altar and the sacrament in the medieval period further dampened the hearth fires, and the spirits of the fathers, Eros, Mars, and Mammon had no role in guiding house and home. Believers were not supposed to offer oblations to ancestral spirits any more than they were to offer incense to Caesar or to covet the wealth of the lord or the power of the princes. Their altars were to be in churches, where people from all families and nations, of all classes and ranks, might worship; where the keepers of the altars took vows of poverty, chastity, and obedience; and where spiritual loyalties were to be directed to the One who stands over these earthly powers and converts them to other ends.

The development of the sacramental altar in contrast to the hearths, in tension with the feudal integration of powers, bore within it implications for the common life. At the foot of the cathedrals, markets developed; around the crossroads, settlements based on an economy other than that of agriculture began to be nurtured. Decisive here was the formation of a postfeudal civil society, on new foundations. The new cities that arose around the cathedrals brought a fresh form of integration of the ancient motifs. The new synthesis was based on a new religious sense of fellowship and trust brought about by a fascinating and intricate weave that included participation in the mass; in the new economic patterns of trade, craft, guild, and urban property; and in a new definition of law based in oath-sworn agreements by all "citizens" of the city, as Max Weber demonstrated in one way and Harold Berman in another.[26] Implications for house and home were immediate. The home became a workshop, a locus of economic production and the training of apprentices, as well as the center of consumption, the locus of intimacy, and place for the rearing of children.

But in contrast to the hearth that was the center of the land wherein the spirits of the ancestors lived and to the village surrounding the lord's property, with their shared understanding that the land was critical for production, the skill and diligence of the craftsman, trader, shopkeeper, and merchant became the mark of productivity and the definer of rights and duties, and even membership, in the guild and in the citizenry of the city. The modern, urbanizing world where people try to find their place was born in the shadows of the cathedral, with the home now recognized as the graced hub of both production and reproduction, of both consumption and nurture. The locus of the home in much of western civilization is, first of all, at the altar.

The great story of European history is one that sought to address old paganisms, medieval feudalisms, and newer, bourgeois ways of living, perpetually trying to understand and shape these realities, constantly recognizing that they were formed by both previous pieties and persistent material interests, simultaneously blessing them on a selective basis and challenging them to transcend their own temptations.

Home in America

The Christian understanding of home life was mediated to America chiefly by the Puritans. They wanted to purify all of life, and they were convinced that the European churches had succumbed too much to the residual power of pagan forces. These forces had obscured not only family, economic, and political life but the life of the church itself, and hence the truth of the God for which the church was supposed to stand. Above all, the Puritans wanted to purify the faith, the church, the raucous, paganized practices during holy days, including Christmas, and thus set family, political, and economic life on a new basis. In short, they wanted to do, in northern Europe and America, what the early Christians did to Greco-Roman life: depaganize it and reorder it on the basis of a theological vision.

How much the Puritans influenced America, how long that influence lasted, and how deeply it shaped the world in which we live are much debated.[27] We cannot fully enter that debate here, but we can trace certain key influences from that stream of continuity as they shaped the definitions of house and home in American history. It is now clear that the experience of homemaking in the United States is rooted, above all, in the Puritan foundations of the society. It stands in contrast to the notion of the hearth, the family, as the center and the foundation of civilization.

In the Puritan view, the church was the center of life. The family was thus the "little church" and, secondarily, the "little commonwealth."[28] That is, the family was to be modeled above all on the kind of covenantal bonding and dedication to spiritual nurture that governed faithful communities and just governments. Already the theory of the covenant had shaped the Independent and Congregational Churches and on that basis had been extended to the constitution of the common life, as we see in the Mayflower Compact and in the founding speech by Governor John Winthrop to the new settlement in Boston, "Modell of Christian Charity."[29] For the Puritans, the congregation was the core of civil society, and the general court required the church, on this model, be the basis for "the ordering of towns."[30] The entire society was ordered around the church; no town could be founded without one. "Once land allocated for a township had been sold, newcomers had to find a minister and begin another community."[31]

At the same time, the town had to have a political economy, a commonwealth—a method of governance able to set the conditions for the economic flourishing of the people. Hence government, both at the state level and at the local level, was to be a covenanted commonwealth, a constitutionally organized polity founded on what later generations called the "self-evident truths" assumed by people choosing to be bonded together for human well-being. It was responsible, among other things, for the securing of property and for the founding of schools so that the young could read, write, and cipher.

This was a context in which the family played a critical role.[32] The family as "little church" meant that parents served as elders of the congregation in the home. They were to so channel the emotions by common prayer and mutual responsiveness that they would not only lead each other to the love of God but also would nurture the young in the faith, on behalf of the larger community. That nurture included teaching children how to be productive participants in society. It was families who represented the church, just as it was families who were both the units of political citizenship and centers of economic life.[33] Gwendolyn Wright puts it this way:

> The meeting house was always the first important building to be erected. . . . The church was the congregation, not the structure where they worshiped. In many ways the meeting house looked like a large dwelling. Since Religion extended to every aspect of life and the building was not considered sacred, it was the site for many other public assemblies, and often for schools, in addition to religious services.[34]

Thus the town was laid out around a village square that contained the meetinghouse, which served as the center for worship, the schoolhouse, the locus of political meetings, and the place where disputes concerning property rights and other matters were settled; and in the square around the meetinghouse, as in the shadow of cathedrals in the late Middle Ages, trade was carried out and harvest festivals were held. Over time, a town hall or courthouse was built, distinct from the church, just as a schoolhouse, inns, shops, smithies, and other centers of the crafts and, later, banks were founded around the church green. Surrounding all of these was the town, a cluster of households, each of which remained the local concretion of church, school, commonwealth, and craft, preparing the next generation for responsible participation in the arts and disciplines of all.

This pattern did not long endure in its pristine forms. Some think that it was at an end by the time of the American Revolution. Others date its demise to when the last New England state disestablished religion in the 1830s and the populist Jacksonian tide signaled the power of the western frontier. But the legacy remained deeply ingrained in America, defining patterns of leadership in social, economic, legal, and professional life. In his study of Puritan Boston and Quaker Philadelphia, E. Digby Baltzell points out that not only the Adams's, the Lodges, the Lowells, the Gardners, the Cabots, and others in Boston, and not only the Biddles, the Ingersolls, the Cadwaladers, the Morrises, the Whortons, the Peppers, and others in Philadelphia, but the Roosevelts and Rockefellers of New York, the Mellons of Pittsburgh, the Du Ponts of Delaware, the Tafts of Cincinnati, the Mathers of Cleveland, and others elsewhere have perpetuated values roughly comparable to these early Puritan ones, although translated into an industrial era.[35] Those who established the social tone, formed the opinions, led the schools and colleges, and guided the fiscal and cultural institutions of the society held to the values of the early traditions. Baltzell is surely correct that up until World War II, these values formed the basis of what people meant by the word *society*. They perpetuated the ongoing legacy of "Puritan-Yankee culture," which

> spread westward, first into Ohio and then throughout the Northwest Territory. They set the matrix for a church—and later what might be called generally a "voluntary associational"—theory of social life that is rooted in a pluralism of social institutions of which the family is one key part, preparing generation after generation for participation in the common life, and serving as a center itself of culture, learning, political responsibility, moral formation, and, above all, piety rooted in commitment and accountable authority.[36]

To be sure, the Puritans were not the only cultural group where certain of these characteristics were developed. Other groups developed out of biblical traditions, with only indirect influences from this elite culture and under quite different conditions. Particularly striking was the culture that developed among the slaves. Many of the white political leaders of America who came from the South had been influenced by Protestantism in another way. They agreed with the Puritans on many items, including the overcoming of royalty in the political sense. Thus they opposed the idea of private castles and all these had meant in European cultures as *castello, tour, Schloss,* and other fortified centers of nobility and chivalry. But when Southerners turned to economic life, the plantations they established perpetuated the feudal structures of the landlord in a quite different way than that of the citizens of the New England and Middle Atlantic towns. The South's economic vision was rooted in the *latifundia* and the Roman legacy as it became institutionalized in the feudal heritage of the villa, the *Hof,* the château, and the hacienda, surrounded by peasants who occupied the *casa,* the *maison,* the *haus,* the cottage, or the cabin. But since serfs did not exist in America and Native Americans made poor ones (although some efforts were made in that direction, more in Latin America than in North America), the heirs of the feudal tradition developed the peculiarly American institution of chattel slavery. In turn, the slaves, when they turned to Christianity and interpreted it through their experiences of suffering as well as their repressed memories of African communal traditions, developed another set of American values about the common life that had similarities to parts of Puritanism.

Slaves had semipublic spaces in the slave quarters. The worship services, weddings, and funerals were held in the common land between their cabins and sometimes in the clearings or the shacks at the stills hidden in the woods, and these became centers of cultural independence, mutual exhortation, economic swapping, and underground politics, as well as courtship. To be sure, family life was fragile at best under slave conditions, but it was treasured and precious, even if subordinate to the moral and spiritual formation of a larger community vision of justice and righteousness.[37] However, since slaves had no access to the formation of the institutions of civil society, their religion and ethics frequently took highly moralistic and intensely personal, not structural, forms, with a wide tolerance for the adjustments people made in order to survive the brutal system under which they lived and on which they were dependent. With some notable exceptions, this brought a relative disjunction between religious ethics and responsibility for the general social order. On the whole, it understandably fomented a private moralism linked to a very slender sense of public responsibility and a pronounced countercultural sectarianism, at least until the movement led by Martin Luther King, Jr., and the rise of "black theology."[38] Nevertheless, black religion in America has, for the most part, distinctive affinities to this wider Protestant tradition, and the elite leadership from the Puritan-Yankee background has often supported black movements in calling for principles of justice, equality, and social transformation that parallel certain Puritan themes.

Catholic (Irish and Italian, especially; subsequently, Polish, Latino, Hispanic, and others) and Jewish communities of European immigrants (eastern Europeans fleeing the pogroms and, later, central and western Europeans fleeing the Nazis) entered the social environment formed out of this American crucible and took advantage of the relative religious, political, and legal freedom formed by Puritan-Yankee values, as well as of economic opportunities. From the middle of the nineteenth century to the present, they formed distinctive subcultures rooted in churches or synagogues. At first these were quite self-enclosed and self-protective and often quite hostile to America's nontraditional society and its religious and social arrogance, but they later developed their own traditions toward those institutional arrangements that echoed the designs of the settlers of Plymouth, Boston, and Philadelphia, who had drawn their insights substantially from the same religious sources that had shaped these immigrants but had developed them in distinctive directions.[39] For many of the heirs and allies of the Puritans, for much of black religion in America, for the Catholics, and for the Jews, the family is seen increasingly as a bonded context for love, education, economics, and cultural identity, guided above all by the biblical tradition and having the duty to shape people to take responsibility in church, civil society, and political economy under fair laws. The deeper structures of society have been less changed than adopted and adapted.

The prominence of these structures was not something that the founders of the nation had envisioned by other forms of leadership in America. Thomas Jefferson, although he lived much in the manner of a feudal lord, saw the yeoman family as the center of society, periodically joining with others to renegotiate a social contract that would allow their lives to flourish. James Madison, too, lived in such an environment but accented the individual and his rights, while John Adams saw the family as the moral school for citizenship: "The foundations of national

Morality must be laid in the family."[40] For these leaders, the church was not central to the constitution of the whole or to the fabric of civil society. Neither churches nor families, nor any other of the organizations that constitute civil society, are mentioned in the Constitution that America's founders wrote and defended before the people. The only collectivities mentioned therein are nations and states.[41] All other agents are individuals, and all other relationships—conjugal, commercial, social, or political—are treated as contractual. The family, the church, and the civil society generally were held to be the beneficiaries of individual liberty and political sovereignty.

The covenantal view—centered on church, civil society, and family—and the contractual view—focused on individual liberty and governmental rule—have been sometimes complementary, sometimes at odds. (We mentioned this in chapters 1 and 2 and treat key issues of theological conflict and convergence in chapter 5.) The decline of covenantal practices, in spite of their residual influence, and the gradual increase of contractual ones left the nation open to the resurgence, in new places and ways, of all the ancient themes—new hearths, new cities, new feudalisms, and new imperialisms.

New Hearths, New Cities

As Puritanism was disestablished, as non-Protestants flooded to America's shores, and as Alexis de Tocqueville wrote *Democracy in America*, major changes were already underway on the farms, in the cities, in the newly industrial towns, and in the federal government. The United States was a beneficiary of the conflicts between France, Spain, and England, all of whom contended for the control of the American continent. When the hostilities among these nations intensified, the United States was able to purchase the Louisiana Territory in a series of treaties between 1803 and 1819. The question remained, however, of how best to settle the new territory. After the Revolutionary War, attempts had been made to form chartered companies to purchase parts of the Ohio Territory and establish colonies, but the companies ran into financial difficulties. The Texas Republic, however, had found another technique for settlement: It attracted people with the Homestead Exemption Laws in 1839, which prevented creditors from seizing plottage, house, or chattel—within given limits—from an active farmer who, with his family, worked his land, even for debts he had incurred before he took possession of the land. New York adopted similar provisions in 1850, and the rapid growth of Texas and western New York was remarkable. But the explosion of growth came after the Civil War, when veterans and settlers from abroad realized the potential of the Homestead Act, passed in 1862. Not only was a homestead exemption enacted but free land was given to a settler who would reside on and cultivate the land for five years, with no cost except the minimal taxes and registration fee. Most prominent among all who headed west were families, who established their homesteads from the Mississippi River to the California coast. They settled the land, sanctifying it with their toil and the bones of their beloved. The family farm became the new center of society.

Churches were, to be sure, formed by the thousands rather quickly. Every town, trading or military post, and crossroads became a potential locus for a church. Those communities of commitment preserved a profound vision of a higher law and wider purpose and deeper context of life than merely the conquest of the Wild West, even as they brought an interpretation of "family values" to trapper, hunter, cowboy, Indian fighter, mountain man, bar girl, whore, and schoolmarm, and to all the many fugitives and misfits of eastern U. S. civilization. This was true of a great number of the frontier evangelical traditions. They "settled" the West.

But ancient religious loyalties were also reborn. Quite possibly, no religious movement in America represents this quite so clearly as the Mormons do.[42] In this tradition, we can see certain tendencies of the deep traditions reemerging in a radicalized form, claiming an ancient teaching now recovered with miraculous, relevatory authority. Among the key doctrines of this tradition, which echoes much of Puritan and frontier piety in so many other respects, are the conviction of the usefulness and validity of a revelation outside the Bible, the practice of the baptism of the dead, and the doctrine of "sealing" in eternal or celestial marriage—views not far removed from ancient traditions of the sacred hearth.

The notion that the scriptures are best able to guide the common life when the understanding of them is joined to philosophy, science, and the interpretation of social practice had long been maintained by the theological tradition; but these other disciplines were always secondary aids. The Church of Jesus Christ of Latter-day Saints (Mormons) held that the Bible was best interpreted through another revelation, one that paralleled, mostly confirmed, and partly refined the Bible, putting it in another context of interpretation. This view is not unique. More dramatic examples can be found in Islam and in the Unification Church ("Moonies"), and slightly less dramatic ones among the Quakers and the Christian Scientists, each of which brings with it a distinctive modification of the classical teachings about family life and its relationship to economics.

In the Mormon faith, the baptism, by surrogate means, of those who have died before they have come to faith points to a sense of deep continuity of the family. This is so deeply felt by this tradition that the most extensive genealogical records in the world have been developed, as an act of conviction and devotion. People can trace their ancestors, and honor them, by offering them this opportunity for repentance and salvation.

The doctrine of "sealing" refers to the belief that only those who are able to establish an eternal covenant with their partner will find salvation and that this form of marriage may be "sealed" at a higher level than that of those who decide to live together, however enriching, satisfying, or loving such relationships may be. That this doctrine is especially focused on women and at certain stages of the tradition, and in various branches until today, both provided permanent security for the women and permitted polygamy[43] is an indicator of the residue of the ancient father-priest tradition, one that, it is held, was practiced by the Hebrew patriarchs as well as in the Greek *oikos*. On the basis of these powerful views of the family, an elaborate system of hereditary land and water rights (in the arid territory where the Mormons settled) was established and has since been taken as the model for the western Plains states.

It is not insignificant that in 1850 the Mormons requested "home rule" for the territory of Utah. The attempt at the time to establish a patriarchal and polygamous theocracy, on the model of ancient Israel, from Idaho in the north to Arizona in the south failed. But the Mormons applied the concept of home rule to Salt Lake City in 1852 and built a city that became a "New Jerusalem," with a centralized temple and place of pilgrimage for their scattered, family-based believers. This matter of home rule touches both ancient traditions and new developments that extended beyond the Mormons. As forts, trading posts, ports along rivers, and terminals for the railways thickened from the Alleghenies to the Rockies, many became aware that charters granted by state legislatures were precarious things, for legislators could always revise the terms of the charter or revoke it completely. A legal instrument was needed for common action, one closer to the autonomy granted towns under the Puritans but without the required formation of a church.

In 1875, Missouri established a home rule charter that allowed cities and towns to govern themselves, without any overt religious patterns, without interference by the state authorities, and without being subject to county governments—many of which were dominated by rural representatives.[44] Similar action was soon taken by other states, and the stage was set for cities to control zoning, property-tax assessment, building codes, sanitation, health and safety, and police powers on the basis of practical economic interests—matters that deeply influenced homemaking throughout America. In some ways, the city-state was reborn, in a new form, and the foundations for the great cities of the country were laid. Political power was allocated to state, county, or city government according to particular function, and households were specifically linked to the city level. Homes became intimately related to the commerce, trade, and industry around city hall. Here, too, however, churches were built, and issues of moral and spiritual leadership to guide city life were complemented by simultaneous concern for home, nation, and the world's peoples. As we shall see shortly, however, the cities quickly became divided into a series of classes—each with its own churches—as defined by the kinds of work people did outside the home.[43] The idea of "local control" has religious roots as well as economic interests and familial loyalties.

The secularized form of this quasi-religious character of city identification is present in many common loyalties that develop beyond the class and racial divisions. We can see it during the sports seasons, when the city's teams become the emblems of social loyalty, enormous financial commitment, family scheduling, and church planning. We do not understand the religious life, social psychology, economics, or family life of the town or city unless we recognize the influence of these matters. Responsible fathers take their children to the games and become involved in leagues to train their youngsters how to play various sports; responsible mothers take their kids to practice or cheerleading or band rehearsal to get ready for a school or league game. Pastors go to the games, where the people are, and offer a blessing on the team. People develop specific identities around teams, "becoming" Yankees or Cubs or Cowboys fans. The same motifs are also found in towns and colleges around the country, and in high culture—the Boston Symphony Orchestra, for example, is compared to the orchestras of Cleveland, Philadelphia, or St. Louis, and jazz is compared to country, folk, rock, rap, salsa, or polka. The teams, totems, cultural treasures, and artistic expressions of a city make up a part of the values and loyalties that people pass on to the next generation as part of the civil society that is "home," and having the family attend a game or a concert or bringing sports teams and musical groups into the home via TV as a part of the celebration of Thanksgiving, Advent, New Year's, or Easter is a practice thick with family, religious, and economic meaning.

The density of interaction and the new combinations of religious, ethnic, and national traditions, in the dynamic mix of cultural and economic creativity and in an environment entirely constructed by human hands, brings a heady sense of the marvels of the human spirit. The city gives that spirit full rein to build a new civilization, no longer tied to powers of the earth or the gods of the sky.[46]

Resurgent Feudalism

For each family that established a home on the prairie, another moved to the city; and within only a couple of generations, the children of the homesteaders also began to go to the city. The Industrial Revolution, spurred on by wartime production demands during the Civil War and by the importation of technology from England, meant that a couple could farm more land with fewer hands and send more products to a growing city than their parents could. Cash crops displaced subsistence farming. Spinning, weaving, and food preparation were increasingly removed to the factories. Children were less necessary to production in the fields or food preparation in the kitchen. Young people went to the city, to be followed within generation by fathers with small farms who could not keep up with technological innovations, and later by the mothers who, like their husbands, took jobs in factories. We treated some of the implications of this development for household economies and the division of labor between the sexes in chapter 2. But we have not noted the development of a new kind of town, an industrial town dedicated to manufacturing. Landless workers from abroad and ex-farmers from villages and homesteads came to these towns by the hundreds of thousands. Where were they to find a place to live, a home to call their own?

Two early plans signaled later developments. One, suggested as early as 1791 by Alexander Hamilton and backed later by Andrew Jackson, involved an attempt to centralize, at government expense, industrial parks in rural areas, outside crowded cities, in a planned system of "national manufactury." Although Congress debated this idea in 1791 and accepted the idea of a centralized bank, it rejected the plan to centralize this aspect of the economy. Instead of a government branch or project, a corporation, rather than an individual or a city, was given a charter to develop an industrial-residential center. A joint-stock corporation hired Major Pierre L'Enfant, a friend of the Marquis de Lafayette who was also the engineer-architect who had laid out the national capital, to design a new kind of town. The result was Patterson in New Jersey and Manchester in New Hampshire. When, during and after the War of 1812, consumption of manufactured goods began to expand, Patterson was the fastest-growing town in America, and row after row of cottages were constructed for the workers. Modest and cramped as they were, and dreary, dangerous, and oppressive though the labor was, workers flooded to the area to get a company job and a company house.[47]

Most experiments of this sort, however, remained small and local until Samuel Slater, called by Andrew Jackson "the father of the American factory system,"[48] brought to America the Arkwright mill system from Great Britian, which integrated the carding, spinning, and weaving processes. He also brought a plan for nearby villages of worker housing for families (preferably large) and their boarders, with the understanding that all members of the household would work in the mill. In southern New England and Pennsylvania, where this plan (first tried in Rhode Island) was developed, workers lived in company-owned cottages; in North Carolina mills, slightly later in the nineteenth century, they lived in log cabins or attached stone tenements. Each family had to supply a certain number of workers, and sometimes orphans or single adult boarders were placed in families to make up the deficit. A family was evicted and its working members fired if it could not keep up the supply of workers. Conditions were only marginally better than those of the slaves, and comparisons of "wage slavery" to "chattel slavery" were soon made. Such companies also established the "company store," which, by allowing credit, kept families in a perpetual state of economic dependency. Later in the century companies also supplied the workers with pubs and bars just outside the gates of the plants, which effectively removed the pay from the pockets of the workers and put it back into the coffers of the company. The founding of primary schools and churches for the edification of the workers, with teachers and pastors chosen by the company, was not able to overcome the demoralization of many families. Only much later, and then in only certain places and during certain periods, were churches independent of the company able to encourage the workers in organizing labor unions, credit unions, or savings-and-loan associations (of the sort made famous by the classic film It's a Wonderful Life), so that they might seek improvement of work and home conditions.[49]

Factory Girls
and Victorian Homes

The social impact of industrialization was vast and varied, and the results were not always bleak. A different industrial-residential plan was
developed by the urban heirs of the old Puritan families, the so-called
Boston Brahmans, who adopted the Waltham system. This plan, whose
name was derived from an early mill town in Waltham, Massachusetts,
centralized and integrated the manufacturing process of cloth in an early
form of the "total management" system. In this period, however, workers were in short supply and families were settling the frontiers; so
Francis Cabot Lowell established the Lowell Associates, who stimulated
the development of American industry in cities across the nation. Women
were hired to work the looms—unmarried women from the farms who
could use additional income to help their parents or to accumulate a
trousseau for their marriages (preferably to a "mechanic," a technician-
engineer who built and maintained the factory machinery). They were
offered rooms in boardinghouses or dormitories, under the supervision
of a matron who enforced church attendance, limited "improper conduct," and supervised food preparation and personal hygiene according
to the standards of the day. The exploitation of these women has been
recognized in our generation, but Wright, among others, summarizes the
experience as interpreted by the women themselves:

> Factory life provided young women with some independence and
> companionship with other women of the same age. . . . Although
> the schedule of factory work was more rigid than life on a farm,
> the labor and the house were not necessarily more arduous. A
> young woman who lived on a family farm had to contend with
> strong patriarchal control over her earnings, activities, and social
> life. Many factory girls quickly learned to ridicule the rural accents,
> dowdy clothes, and homespun ambitions of newcomers—and
> even rejected many of their parents' values, preferring to marry
> mechanics or shopkeepers and stay in town. . . . The rise of the
> New England mill . . . , especially the intense experience of female
> boardinghouses, helped shift the culture, as well as the economy,
> toward a more urbanized, industrialized way of life.[50]

Even though the pattern of industrialization in these models made
the owners and laborers appear more and more like the feudal lords and
peasants of Europe, they in fact began to shatter the patriarchal elements of the older familial traditions. What migration to this country

did for their forebears and the frontier did for those who went west, the cities did for those who stayed east. People began to define for themselves the kind of community, the kind of society, and the kind of religion they wanted. Neither the managers of the factories nor the merchants who supplied them, neither the successful farmers nor the skilled mechanics who married the mill girls, lived in the workers' cottages, the company row houses, or the dormitories and boardinghouses of the industrial towns and cities. Instead, they became the backbone of the middle classes in America, and they became owners of their own homes. They formed their own churches, developed the leadership of town and city government, demanded quality education for their children, and set the standards for the design and quality of their houses. What they began to develop many aspired to, and new industries of "housing development" and "mortgage finance" were generated to meet these new demands, as was the manufacture of durable products for the home—furniture, refrigerators, washing machines, shingles for roofs, siding, pipes for plumbing, molding for doorways, blinds and curtains and glass for windows, stoves and furnaces for heating, and gas and electricity for light.

From the last two decades of the nineteenth century throughout most of the twentieth, the suburb was the primary locus of growth, deeply committed to the valves embraced by the mill workers. They were given an enormous boost after World War II, when the profession of "developer" emerged to produce tract houses on a massive scale outside the "near" suburbs, and when the Federal Housing and Veterans Housing Administrations made loans for such houses accessible to millions.[51] Those who could afford to do so moved from the industrializing centers of the cities to their own homes. According to Irving Welfeld, "The suburban home, how it was furnished, and the family life the housewife oversaw, contributed to the definition of 'middle class,' at least as much as did the husband's income."[52] And the ideal was widely and frequently displayed, easily found then in advertisements of properties for the new houses and present today in the old neighborhoods of the near suburbs. Judge Seymour Dexter, founder of the United States League of Building and Loan Associations, commissioned a much-discussed and frequently reproduced painting in 1893 that portrays the values of the epoch. At the center is a Victorian house, with a father coming home from work to meet a child, who is rushing to greet him, and with the mother, pushing a baby carriage, also approaching. Others play croquet, on the lawn sheltered by great elms. At the side stands a school, flying the American flag, and a church with an old New England–style spire.[53] Here was the image of a new urban—now suburban—familistic culture, supported by church and school and an absent industry to which the father went. The upper half of the city population lived in patterns not unlike this by the end of the last century—although the urban population did not constitute half of the total population of the country for another quarter century.[54] This ideal brought with it a new cult of domesticity, the rise of home economics as the primary field of study for women, a redefinition of roles for men and women, and striking consequences in both religion and economics.

These developments were heatedly resisted and just as eagerly defended over the course of the nineteenth and twentieth centuries, and the nuances of the debates are many. Certain highlights, however, exemplify the range and depth of the issues. The transcendentalists sought a return to the presumed simplicity and harmony of nature, and many romantics have turned to Henry David Thoreau in opposition to industry, development, and towns and cities. Another branch of literary elites followed Ralph Waldo Emerson into a quest for subjective individuality that had resisted anything like traditional home life;[55] so did some of the communitarian experiments and radical, anarchistic movements of the nineteenth century. But both the revivalistic evangelicals on the frontier, in the black churches, and in successive awakenings and the immigrant Roman Catholics in the cities defended the family-centered developments. Even when they participated in the early efforts to form labor unions, with a heavy accent on class solidarity, their emphasis was more frequently on the right of "the worker" to earn a "family wage" than on a proletarian revolution against the capitalist, Victorian family. Indeed, the right to a family wage was celebrated as a matter of revealed and natural morality by Pope Leo XIII in his 1892 encyclical *Rerum Novarum* and by the Protestant Social Gospel.[56] Even "secular" muckrakers were ever willing to expose the venal tactics and unscrupulous motives of the industrialists, the revivalists, and the politicians whenever any of these used their influence opportunistically, covered their self-serving actions with pious moralism, pandered to the crass desires of the people, and—what was taken as the chief indicator of immorality—broke family fidelity. All of these efforts and movements were the residues or unexpected allies of the Puritan inclination to ferret out sin, to publish the punishment, and to expect that greater social discipline could contain its worst features and help bring the heart to repentance and the community to greater virtue.[57]

Anne Douglas has shown how, in such a context, much of the artistic and literary life of the period, as well as the ministry of the churches, began to focus on the role of women and families. This signaled not only a recentering of religious values on home life and a separation of church from state but a focus on moral values and religious ethics that became largely segregated from political economics and public affairs, a separation against which many have struggled.[58] The turn to the family and its idealization sometimes obscured the difficulties that were experienced inside family life, and it sometimes disconnected moral and spiritual scrutiny from matters of public justice and wider questions of civil society.[59]

Political Consequences

Increasingly, public policy was defended according to whether it supported families. The closing of the frontier began to shift government focus onto urban development, for the technologies of farming reduced the need for increasing rural populations while the technology of production and transport increased the need for cheap labor in the cities. People began to fill up the available cheaper housing, and the tenements and boardinghouses became the growth point of urban populations—a major fact of the early twentieth century in the United States, much as it is now, increasingly, in the cities around the world.

It was in the crisis of the Great Depression that economic conditions made domestic action necessary, and the rising threats of both Nazism under Adolf Hitler in Western Europe and communism under Joseph Stalin in Eastern Europe made action possible. People wanted to preserve community and help "the common man," as was often said at the time, and they did not want to turn to state fascism or state socialism to do so. Nothing seemed more obvious than to help people keep their homes. Allan Carlson summarizes the developments in housing assistance:

> The immediate goal of the New Dealers was to salvage the mortgage market and the construction industry (by defending "the home"). Toward this end, the Home Owners Loan Corporation, set up in 1933, assumed and refinanced approximately one million existing mortgages. More importantly, the National Housing Act of 1934 created the Federal Housing Administration (FHA). . . . Although not fully realized until the late 1940's, FHA innovations included development of the long-term mortgage (and several other financial and insurance arrangements) which made mass

production possible. . . . Other measures . . . included creation of
the Federal Home Loan Bank . . . and the chartering of the Federal
National Mortgage Association ("Fannie Mae," 1938).[60]

The wartime economy of the early 1940s boosted the general economic health of the nation; during this period and after World War II,
governmental economic initiatives for families were centered on the
maintenance and reconstruction of work and family life. As discussed
above, legislation aimed at returning GIs and the continued strength of
the economy provided for increased rates of home ownership and construction. Throughout the 1950s social benefit programs, beyond the
Aid to Families and Dependent Children (AFDC) and Social Security
systems established previously, had their focus in the life of working
families. As Carlson, Welfeld, Wright, and others argue, from differing
points of view, the priority of the nuclear family was stressed in virtu-
ally every discussion of housing policy and enacted in every bill passed
from 1933 until the 1960s, and the continuities with the Homestead
Act and, more generally, with the Victorian ideals and the Puritan
past—not to mention the deeper past that is suggested here—were part
of the justification for this emphasis. Yet even with these initiatives in
place, the assumption persisted on the federal level that broad-based
public assistance for the poor should remain fundamentally a state and
local issue.

Many homes and many financial institutions were saved by these
government programs, but all historians of housing now point out that
these policies were also applied in discriminatory ways in the middle of
the twentieth century. A number of minority ethnic groups, but especially black Americans, had difficulty getting access to the loans and
housing that legislation made available to others. The various developments government policy stimulated were intentionally segregated.
This policy officially encouraged neighborhood "restrictive covenants"
against Jews and Blacks. The Federal Housing Administration (FHA)
wanted its housing to be in "harmonious and stable" neighborhoods.
Thus guidelines suggested the use of "natural boundaries" to protect
racial barriers, and the restrictive covenants were a precondition to getting federally backed mortgage insurance. As Charles Abrams, one major advocate of revision of these provisions, said, "The FHA *Insurance
Manual* . . . read like a chapter of the Nuremberg Laws."[61]

If blacks could not get into the subsidized suburban housing, where
were they to live? The answer, functionally, was in the cities, in another
kind of subsidized housing—the "projects." There had been some pub-

lic housing efforts since the New Deal, and many of them showed the stamp of quests for communitarian solutions short of fascist or communist programs. The Subsistence Homesteads Division established experimental cooperative farm colonies and moved some industrial workers to rural communities, on the grounds that the ancient traditions of village life were more human. The Resettlement Administration began a similar series of government-financed communities, but later subdivided and sold them. The Farm Security Administration attempted to establish settled villages for unemployed migrant workers, on the model of the kibbutzim of the Palestinian Zionists. And the Public Works Administration (PWA) Housing Division began a program of slum clearance and the building of model urban housing complexes. In all these efforts, segregation was strictly enforced, although the PWA allocated half of its housing for blacks.[62]

But in spite of the quest for "community" and help to "the common man," the integration of public housing did not take place until 1962, when an executive order by President John F. Kennedy prohibited the use of race as a criterion in the selection of candidates. Blacks flooded into public housing forming new, racially defined areas. Ironically, that policy was defended on the basis of "individual rights," specifically against ethnic solidarities. Social policy with regard to housing tended to atomize the individual, as enforced by the national government, which mobilized to overcome resistance from any sector of the civil society. Many minorities benefited from this simultaneous individuation and national collectization. Of course, many blacks had found ways to own their own properties, and whites and other minorities also live in public housing, in greater numbers than blacks; but proportionate to the overall population, blacks in the projects quickly became more than simply a modern stereotype, and other poor populations—single mothers, drug- and alcohol-dependent people, and so forth—were soon to follow.

The reasons for this are many, including the mass migrations of people with little education and fewer industrial skills to the cities with the declining need for rural labor. Cities provided relatively more jobs at the lower end of the economic scale, just as the better jobs and better-paid workers were moving to the suburbs—a migration from farms to cities and suburbs reinforced by the decisions of thousands of soldiers who had fought in World War II and begun to experience something more of the world than what they knew on the farms, to which they were not about to return. The persistence of racism, particularly in its institutional and official forms with regard to housing, is a striking cause of the clustering of minorities in public housing as well. This was compounded by the fact that slum clearance and, later, programs in urban renewal—which some dubbed "Negro removal"—and the building of highways from the exurbs to the central city, all federally funded to "help the cities," disproportionately destroyed black neighborhoods, particularly those with the least expensive housing. Irving Welfeld, noted historian of housing policies in America, titles his chapter on this development "Perverse Programs by Prudent People."[63]

Today we bear the consequences, positive and negative, of these long-ranging developments. In several ways, they set the directions for contemporary society in contrast to those of times past, and it is likely that the stresses we feel in our society are influenced by the fact that these developments have threatened both the family and the tissues of civil society for at least a portion of the population. People put their time, energy, and money into what they believe, what they trust, and what they want, even if, as everyone knows, belief, trust, and wants can be manipulated.[64] And people do not trust programs that do not support families.

Home and Social Trust

The vital social role of the family is a central theme in the remarkable comparative study of *Trust* by Francis Fukuyama, which takes us outside our cultural tradition and helps us see some of our customs more clearly by way of contrast.[65] He shows, among other things, that every culture reveals deep connections between premodern patterns of family life and current trends. Not everything has been changed by modernity. The specific forms that "modernization" takes are channeled by deeply rooted beliefs and mediated by family practices. Indeed, what allows persons to live, civilizations to form, and economies to flourish is trust, a social virtue. And the question is, What do people trust?

To answer this question, Fukuyama turns to the comparative study of "civil society," by which he means the network of "intermediate institutions, including businesses, voluntary associations, educational institutions, clubs, unions, media, charities and churches." He argues that these are substantially dependent on, in turn, "the family, the primary instrument by which people are socialized into their culture and given the skills that allow them to live in broader society and through which the values and knowledge of that society are transmitted across the generations."[66]

Further, Fukuyama argues that a "thriving civil society depends on a people's habits, customs and ethics." These characteristics may also be mediated by schools and media without religion.[67] In other words, he seeks to study the ways in which trust, and thus civil society and peoples over time, flourish. Such flourishing is evidenced in the kind and quality of people's material development, in accord with the degree to which the moral qualities of life are generated and sustained. Fukuyama thinks that we are facing, around the world, both a convergence of common structures—patterns of constitutional democracy, technological and communication interchange, and corporations as primary actors in economic life—and a greater awareness of cultural differences. The Italians, the Japanese, and the Americans simply do not conduct their politics, their media, or their management in the same ways, and much is misunderstood if these cultural differences are not recognized.

Yet cultures are not totally self-enclosed, conflict between them is not inevitable, and differences are not forever surmountable. Cultures can develop the latent possibilities within themselves and borrow or resist elements from other cultures, and we can learn much from how distinctive cultures support or inhibit the trust that allows them to interact with greater ease. The capacity to learn and compare cultures is itself revealing, for it reflects both a deep, common humanity behind the very serious differences and certain common structures present in every society, which allows us to recognize similarities beyond the differences and to catalog the differences.

The decisive clue to the differences and the similarities between cultures can be found in family structure and its relationship to economic life. Family can become a center of loyalty to its own members or a place for nurturing values that allow family members to interact with others beyond the family itself; and if all other institutions are seen as a threat, then it is likely that certain family-based institutions will become the primary network of economic activity, and any other institution will evoke little commitment of time, energy, and money. People do not share resources with people or groups they do not trust. The range of trusting and trustworthy interaction can be contracted or expanded by the family and the family's relationship to other institutions in society.

Fukuyama develops much of his argument by giving attention to East Asian cultures, but he argues that southern Italy and historical France share a great deal with traditional China (with modern Korea as a mixed example, quite possibly because of the rapid conversion of Koreans to Christianity—more than 25 percent of the population in a generation).

All these have familistic traditions, with a grave distrust of nonfamily relationships. Deeply rooted in the religious and cultural history of these lands (although the religions differ), paternal authority is seen as the model for political and economic authority. While southern Italy preserved many of the ancient Greco-Roman traditions and France developed quite specific bourgeois forms of familism, each developed a kind of filial piety that allowed nationalist dynasties to play noble family against noble family and to achieve a degree of stable, hierarchical authority that is rare elsewhere. Simultaneously, they prevented guilds, corporations, unions, parties, and other forms of intermediary institutions from developing and thereby challenging or limiting the political hegemony, although they defended families. China, of course, rooted in the relationship of Confucianism to sacred family genealogies and imperial dynasties, developed a structurally similar civilization, not much transformed by the Maoist revolution. Fukuyama calls these "low-trust" societies, although obviously there is a kind of confidence in family connections to governmental authority. Under conditions of modernization, such societies tend to produce "smaller private [family] firms that constitute the entrepreneurial core of their economies and a number of very large, state-owned firms at the other end of the scale."[68] Ties between family and state are often corrupt.

In contrast, he claims that Japan, Germany, and Britain (with the United States as a mixed case) have "high-trust" societies, although each works in a distinct way. Although Japan has had few voluntary associations, it has had religious groups that have "members" not unlike American church membership, which may be joined or left on a voluntary basis. It also has the omnipresent *Iemoto* (self-cultivation) groups, which, while not democratic in the western sense, are not based on kinship or birth status. Further, in Japan the feudal structures involved binding relationships between leaders and people that surpassed family loyalties, and this pattern has been transmuted into the workings of modern corporate institutions, with a very distinctive shape and sense of obligation between worker and management.

Distinct but comparable forms of group loyalty outside the family can also be traced in German history, from the guild memberships and the city oaths to the loyalties to the various regional identities that persist even today, as well as those that bind workers and managers and consumers and suppliers in a web of obligation beyond the family. Such loyalties can also be found in parts of the Anglo-Saxon heritage and, even more, in the Protestant traditions, evident in the phenomenon that de Tocqueville identified as "spontaneous community" to designate the constant forming and reforming associationalism in American social, political, and economic life. This constructive communalism is the basis of the capacity to form associations that include people of many backgrounds and that are relatively free of nepotism or subservience to state control.[69]

American culture is often said to be highly individualistic, but Fukuyama argues that in comparative perspective, that judgment is questionable. While this culture protects human rights and civil liberties, it is not individualistic, familistic, or statist—at least, not historically so. It is, above all, associational. Americans are remarkable joiners. It is not quite "communitarian" in the sense of fixed solidarities based on ethnic, linguistic, class, or national backgrounds, although when groups become trapped in these, jarring low-trust features of society appear in an otherwise high-trust context, further widening gaps of understanding and economic participation. Fukuyama suggests that America may be tempted by its view of itself as individualistic to become more so, and then, to assure the sovereignty of each individual, to demand a strong central government to enforce its individualism. Yet this would further destroy the genius for the associational engagement and renewal of civil society by the forming and repeated reforming of intermediary organizations, from the inside out and from the bottom up, that the nation has shown in the past.

In the next chapter, we shall see that the American associational tradition is, in certain ways, under threat. Taking the debates over welfare as the prism of investigation, we will see all the issues we have thus far discussed—sexuality and marriage, household and work, homemaking and religion. Further, we will examine their implications for the relationship of state and civil society and note that when the moral and spiritual foundations for the structures of civil society break down, the results are devastating. The children, and the civilization, lose.

4

Welfare and Children:
The Family in State
and Society

In the first three chapters, we saw some of the key debates about sex
and marriage that center in the issues of spirituality and materiality,
of the changing shape of households and work as they affect the family
and the role definitions of male and female in them, and of the historical shifts in the place of the home in civil society. In each area, we noted
the inadequacy of several interpretations of these aspects of life and the
impact of highly influential individualist and collectivist theories that
could lead to a breakdown of civil society. In contrast, we found that a
religiously informed view that deals with covenantal relationships may
be necessary to grasp the dynamics of social history. We turn again to
these issues in chapter 5.

We turn now to the analysis of complex modern situations that develop when covenantal relationships break down in civil society and the
state begins to take on the roles that other institutions, previously decisive for the well-being of the family, have played. We shall see that, on
the one hand, a just and stable state is indispensable to the well-being
of children; children suffer in times of war, chaos, lawlessness, or total-
itarian domination. On the other hand, if nongovernmental institutions
break down, it is increasingly clear that the state makes a poor parent
and a poor source of both income and values. In fact, we are discovering on a worldwide scale that the state does not do well in these areas,
and both civil society and individual persons (particularly children) are
damaged when the state programmatically and directly tries to assume
or control the historical roles of the family: production, reproduction,
consumption, and nurture. The state better serves humanity when it
protects and supports the nongovernmental institutions that do these
things well. Thus it is a question not of state or no state but of how a
state does what must be done when things fall apart.

This is the great and valid insight of postsocialist economic analysis, and it has become the chief source of reaction against government programs of all kinds—from Thatcherite-Reaganite and neoconservative political movements to "New Democrat" and neoliberal ones. It is also the basis of many current slogans about "family values," which no one opposes as long as he or she can define "family" and "values."[1] The dispute is about what we should do when we learn that state programs simultaneously help some people in great need when no one else can and damage families and civil society over time when the government tries to do directly things that it can better do indirectly. It is doubtful if we can or should abolish all of the government social programs enacted since the welfare programs established by Prince Otto Eduard Leopold von Bismarck in Germany in the 1880s, by David Lloyd George in England in the 1910s, and by Franklin D. Roosevelt in the United States in the 1930s; but it is likely that we shall have to redesign the relationship of state to the institutions of civil society if we are to maintain a viable civilization in the next century.

Many state programs were enacted because certain key functions of the family were removed from the family. The modern corporations, as the chief instrument of economic production, removed first the father and then the children and now, increasingly, the mother from the household. Schooling, as a major part of nurture, also has been increasingly removed from the household (and church), leaving the home as a place of reproduction and consumption—the place that most people leave to develop their economic or intellectual life.

In this context, especially in times of distress, such as depression or war, the state was called upon to step in: to regulate industry so that it would serve the national purpose and allow workers to support their families, and to support education so that as many as possible could prepare to contribute to the common life. But when these efforts are wedded to national engagement in several world wars, conditions change again. The state is legally sovereign, but it is also functionally enmeshed in international social, economic, intellectual, and technological developments. The way in which the state has intervened is under debate. For one thing, the erosion of civil society below the state has continued, unabated by government actions. For another, the rapid growth of a global society beyond any and every nation state has altered the possible roles of the state in the lives of its citizens, without assuring us that a civil society with a viable and stable family life can be reconstructed. Indeed, many have become unsure about the role of the family in society, and some suspect that state welfare programs designed to help those in greatest need have exacerbated the decline of civil society and left portions of the population less able to face the problems of the global future.

We shall not treat here the indispensable role of public funding for schools and the impact that this has on the lives of children, families, and the society in general, although the issue of wider public support for private, independent, and parochial schools is likely to be on the horizon for some years.[2] Nor shall we explore the many laws that have been designed to protect children—by requiring schooling, by limiting child labor, by overriding parental authority in cases of abuse or neglect, by providing school lunches, by prosecuting sexual mistreatment, and so forth. But we should note that the state, under the reigning sense of responsibility that the government has for its citizens, plays other roles in family life. The modern state everywhere involves itself, in various degrees, in marriage, reproduction, childcare, divorce, and custody, precisely because these matters are subject to dispute or even violence, which it is the duty of legitimate authority to restrain, and because children (who are citizens as well as family members) are often the most vulnerable victims. When all goes well and the values of the society are clear to all and everyone follows them without fail, law may be unnecessary. But because this has never been the case for all, an organized form of "law and order" is always required; and law is administered by the state, even if the state is, in a constitutional democracy, under law. The state is the institution in society that is given the authority to use legitimate force to constrain illegitimate forms of exploitation and coercion.

In the United States, the state is involved in marital law mainly through the granting of marriage licenses, the registering of the events of marriage.[3] The state also records facts of birth, adjudicates divorce, and supervises any division of property and responsibility for the care of children when ordinary forms of family care have broken down. The regulation of adoption is attended with more stringent scrutiny. But the state is also involved in matters of reproduction—through the funding of medical procedures involving fertility, contraception, abortion, and prenatal and infant care, especially for poorer segments of the population and for all government employees. The state also has some involvement in issues of paternity and parental responsibility in cases of abandonment or the absence of a parent. While efforts to enforce child support are increasing, often legal enforcement of parental responsibility to offspring occurs only in cases of crisis. Individual state agencies are also involved.

Through its social and economic policies the state may also affect the availability of jobs, opportunities for education, and incentives for mobility. The government's involvement in the lives of families also occurs in the case of income transfers through taxation and benefits, whether through the compulsory savings programs, such as Social Security, or the provision of benefits to those who are most economically vulnerable: the elderly, the disabled, the poor, the handicapped, the ill, and the homeless. It is this set of issues that we shall take as the touchstone of this chapter, for the questions it raises can point to the general theory of the relationship of family, civil society, and state.

Poverty and Welfare

In every known civilization there have been poor people. And in every recorded society, the religious virtues of sacrifice, sharing, alms, and compassionate aid are honored, and those rulers who helped make provision for those in need are celebrated. Every civilization and society has established charitable institutions. The massive changes brought about by industrialization and the episodic experience of depressions, however, began to overwhelm the capacities of charitable institutions in the United States. The Protestant Social Gospel movement and the Catholic Social Encyclicals, coupled with Victorian efforts to help those in need, which date from the turn of the century, set in motion the moral movement that resulted in increased government spending programs and a system of agencies that moved public assistance from charity to entitlement programs in attempts to eradicate poverty and support families, especially children. The current debates over welfare reform involve efforts to adjust that system of government provision to deal with the persistence of poverty, to respond to the explosion of changes in family formation, to prevent the government from going broke over the expense of these programs, and, often, to bring about an alteration in the relationship of civil society to both state power and individual life.

The key issue that current movements identify is this: while the government has unavoidable responsibilities in regard to its citizens who are in difficulty, programs that have only two agents—one representing the state and the other the individual—simultaneously collectivize and atomize those persons they attempt to serve. They are seen as part of a "class" with entitlements, and they are seen as a "case" with claims. Neither part of this equation perceives a person in a matrix of relationships—familial, social, economic, political, cultural, communal, or religious. Indeed, the equation may even erode these matrices or the perception of their importance. Yet these networks of relationships constitute civil society, on which responsible human living and the viability of the state itself depend. The ability of individuals and families to support themselves and to flourish is bound up with the strength of civil society, the interlocking social institutions and social habits that shape communities and civilizations.

Yet the belief, widespread in the last several decades, that every caring arrangement results in equal social stability or equal outcomes for children, has simply proven to be untrue. We cannot ignore the breakdown of families and the negative effects on children. Increases in out-of-wedlock births, marital dissolution, and the vulnerability of single-parent families to persistent poverty and social disconnection have occurred, despite massive infusions of money and effort through state programs. Some, indeed, have argued that the system of state assistance that exists in most developed countries has contributed to social breakdown in substantial measure, because it did not seek to sustain families and other indispensable institutions of civil society but attempted to establish state agencies to assume many of the functions of society and to treat each person as an isolated set of needs.[4]

Another crucial issue is that the basic context for families and society has changed significantly over the past few decades. Traditional notions of political boundaries that contained a common culture, a civil society, and a national economy have become inadequate to describe the complexity of the international political, cultural, social, and economic trends we now face. Contemporary technology, electronic communications, transnational corporations, and the transferability of finances, among other examples, have created global rather than national markets for goods and labor. The increasingly routine encounter with the world's religions and the constant interchange of ideas, educational resources, cultural modes of expression, and information and strategies, as well as shared medical and ecological peril, has fostered this transnational development and further altered the shape of the economic sphere and of the civil society in general.

The move toward globalization has also been furthered by political changes throughout the world. With the fall of fascism in Western Europe and, more recently, of communism in the nations of Eastern Europe and of nationalist socialisms in the former colonial lands, the political divisions of West and East, and even of North and South, no longer stand as primary demarcations for world affairs.[5] Every "we" grows more and more difficult to identify as international interdependencies compound, multicultural consciousness grows, and new patterns of economic stratification increasingly define our social affinities.

It is not hard to see some of the prospects if this movement is not arrested. As political institutions become less capable of defining the boundaries of society, they could easily become little more than the instruments of social control—centered in police powers and prisons at home and military power for international use—over those left out of the global-technological-corporate society. And those who are active in the cosmopolitan political, social, and cultural life could easily form walled or gated communities, with private security systems, private schools, private social services, and private healthcare systems, all serving themselves as they lead the emerging international corporations, the media, and the political systems (as discussed in chapter 2).

There is a third crucial issue that must be attended to in assessing our ability to care for children and families: How can we understand, and renew, the common life, and on what terms, since the common life is no longer only national in scope? How may we understand our responsibilities to one another when the other is, on the one hand, everyone everywhere and, on the other hand, sometimes "other" in respects with which we have—and think anyone should have—little in common? This is, finally, a religious and ethical question beyond the power of the state to solve.

Governments have a duty to children, and state intervention certainly has an effect on the lives of children. But the underlying values, structures, and institutions that form and sustain government, and that are the locus of a common life that has constantly changing boundaries and contours, are not themselves creations of the state. They exist prior to the state; they are cultivated by organizations that the state cannot itself construct; they constitute the fabric of civil society; they are what forms the public before it gives rise to and sustains the republic. These include the institutions that shape social interaction and loyalties—the communities, parties, professions, unions, and especially the families, businesses, and churches. The state without these institutions cannot procreate, generate wealth, or form the habits and patterns of ordered and disciplined behavior that constitute the mores and the ethos of a society. Yet these are required for the conduct of the state and the state can protect the conditions under which these institutions are sustained.

While civil society is not a construction of and cannot be sustained by the state, the state can either encourage or undermine the flourishing of civil society. The changes in global organization and in economic reorganization that we noted above have brought us to a point where civil society must be both renewed and reconstructed, if a viable family formation is to be sustained in and by it. But that possibility is bound up with the question of what can transcend immediate self-interests. Civil society is always, if adequate, interlocked with a religious understanding that points us beyond ourselves to some ultimate center of meaning and loyalty. Whether or not we acknowledge it explicitly, religion exists as a fundamental social reality; the shape of that religion, in turn, forms the shape and the expectations of the common life. Religion stands as a suprapersonal, supranational force. Without consideration of its constitutive role, any assessment of the health of or any effort to reform civil society or the social order will be incomplete.

The fundamental role of religion may seem counterintuitive in a culture where dogmas about a romantic communitarianism (of the liberationist sort) and a rational choice individualism (of the libertarian sort) compete as the dominant interpretive paradigms among the intelligentsia, including among religious leaders. This may seem so especially since both perspectives have ruled religion out of court and embrace the division between church and state as a way of avoiding religious issues in public discourse and political policy. The interrelation of religion and society may be more obvious when viewed from afar: Few would doubt the formative role of Hinduism in South Asian culture, Islam in the Arab nations, tribal religions in Africa, and Buddhism and Confucianism in the Far East. But, as we have repeatedly shown throughout this book, religious traditions, particulary forms of the Judeo-Christian heritage, have shaped American culture, and civil society can be neither understood nor altered if religious realities are not grasped.

Caring for the Vulnerable

As discussed in earlier chapters, the provision of social services and support to children and other dependents has usually been the work of the family itself. In Puritan and early colonial society, those in need were generally boarded with a family in their town, under an arrangement overseen by the local government. Inclusion within a family circle was so highly valued as to be considered mandatory. This practice persisted into the nineteenth century, supplementing—or in some areas, supplanting—provision through workhouses or poorhouses in towns. These "houses" formed part of the early institutionalization and professional-

ization of public assistance and coincided with the rise of asylums, or-
phanages, and training schools, all aimed to reform and repair social
ills.[6]

In her study of Victorian care for the poor, Gertrude Himmelfarb argues that the late nineteenth century saw the "discovery" of poverty and
unemployment: These social conditions became urgent concerns at a
time when the actual standard of living, measured in wages and the
availability of basic goods, paradoxically had risen for many people
across social classes.[7] Yet the earlier century's reorganization of work in
cities and industry created rising expectations, dense populations of
poorer classes (rather than scattered poor through the countryside), and
thus increased perceptions of relative deprivation.

The new awareness of poverty led to the development, during the
late nineteenth century, of social service and social welfare organizations, often run by religiously motivated women. They took up the task
of attending to the broader needs of the poor, particularly among the
influx of immigrants into the cities, by establishing voluntary agencies
and settlement houses. As these private charities grew, relief for the
poor gradually came to be funded through a combination of public and
private resources. In many cases, the cost of providing services to poor
families in their homes was significantly lower than that of sending the
family members to appropriate institutions, since for many, the assistance needed was supplemental rather than total. This "outdoor" relief,
in contrast with the "indoor" relief of institutions such as poorhouses,
was the precursor of modern social work and the "helping professions."

The interdependence of state and local municipalities and private
agencies in helping the poor was impressive. One historian of these
public-private partnerships estimates that at the end of the nineteenth
century, nearly two-thirds of the support of private agencies in some
states came from state or local government.[8] Both public and private
assistance, however, shared the goal of rehabilitating those who would
not work, for whatever reason, and assisting those who could not work
to achieve "respectability." Himmelfarb argues that in this era "there
was a strong consensus that the primary objective of any enterprise of
reform was that it contribute to the moral improvement of the poor—
at the very least, that it not have a deleterious effect."[9] Aid, in any case,
was reserved for "the deserving poor," those of good character who
were truly unable to support themselves, and was to be conducted according to strict standards of moral development and reform. This concern for morality and the development of character and responsibility

was central to public and private assistance, both out of societal concerns and out of a concern for the formation and flourishing of individuals. There was no demand that moral or spiritual values be kept separate from the evaluation of need; indeed, they were, and are, part of human need.

Thus the emerging professions of social work and casework and the settlement house movement were concerned not only with offering tangible resources but with helping people live respectable and whole lives in viable communities. It is also notable that this work became identified as a particular "calling" for women in the late nineteenth and early twentieth centuries. In this way, values that had become stereotyped as "maternal" or "feminine" were reintroduced into the public sphere, in the interest of all families and children and as a way that women could fulfill religious duties to the neighbor in need. Social work was, along with nursing, teaching, and missionary work, a means by which women developed public skills and began to develop professional roles in society.

The late nineteenth century was marked by an intense optimism among Christians about the repairing society's ills.[10] Yet the level of need was also intensified by economic depression. In 1893 financial panics drove factory production down and unemployment up across a wide spectrum of industries; overall, about 18 percent of the workforce was unemployed.[11] Public and private relief surged to meet the needs of former wage earners and their families who had been dependent on industrial jobs. For many the issue was not the lack of a desire to work but the instability of job availability for the "working poor" and the burgeoning flood of new migrants willing to take the jobs at the bottom at lower pay—a forecast of what is now a global situation.

By the early twentieth century, assistance to the poor was joined with the concept of assistance and protection for workers, and restrictions on immigration became more stringent. Workers' compensation legislation was enacted in forty-three states to provide some provision for injured workers or for the families of workers killed on the job.[12] Attempts to protect the family through governmental policy took several directions. A series of child labor laws were enacted, with laws requiring school attendance. Legislation protecting women in industry both prevented exploitation in the factories and prompted women to spend their time at home with the children. And the minimum wage laws attempted to enforce a "living wage," whereby a man would earn enough by his labor alone to support his wife and children, a goal embraced by the growing labor unions, such as the United Mine Workers; by industrialists such as Henry Ford; and by many Roman Catholic and Protestant advocates.[13]

Modern Programs

While many legal initiatives aimed at assisting the employed, the system of poor relief evolved as well, with continued refinements of "welfare." Theda Skocpol shows in her history of veterans' and widows' pensions that these were the first modern social assistance policies to operate on the federal level.[14] In Europe, earlier industrialization, more fully centralized political authority after centuries of kings, greater ethnic senses of nationhood, stronger socialist movements, and the tradition of established churches had spurred the extensive development of welfare and labor initiatives; but in America, the local-private partnership model remained well into the twentieth century. The first program in cash assistance was for veterans of the Civil War. Skocpol points out that U.S. courts continued to turn down federal attempts to broaden government assistance to unemployment insurance or old-age pensions, for they were afraid to encourage dependency or adopt socialist policies. But state programs, which offered financial assistance to widows, were established in all but two states by 1931.

Nevertheless, public welfare expenditure nearly doubled from 1903 to 1929.[15] Despite the continuing presence of private charities, public relief spending in the early twentieth century was three times that of private relief. Still, little effort was made to develop federal strategies to intervene in the lives of families or to offer widespread aid. Privately administered charity remained the rule for families and the very poor until the Great Depression of the 1930s. The financial collapse of 1929 created pervasive unemployment, reaching nearly 25 percent by the summer of 1933.[16] The need for welfare and other forms of public assistance, still handled by states and local governments, soon exceeded the resources available from state, local, and private sources. Some reluctant efforts were made by Herbert Hoover, but it was Franklin Delano Roosevelt's New Deal programs that first developed massive federal responses to the problem, along with work programs and the first direct federal payments to support families. In tandem with the programs to build housing and to protect mortgages, some federal family benefit programs were instituted that persist to the present. In 1935, Aid to Families with Dependent Children (ADC, later AFDC) was inaugurated, which provided cash supplements to poor widows to allow them to stay home with their young children. The first Social Security Act was passed in 1935, providing not only pensions for the elderly but broader assistance to dependent children and disabled adults.

These programs were designed to provide a safety net for crisis situations, and it was presumed that everyone knew the causes of the crisis: They were social and structural. The response to the Great Depression thereby detached poverty from issues of morality. It rendered poverty or economic hardship a function of broader economic forces, uncontrollable by individuals and families. Those in need had a claim on the national economy that the economy itself could not meet but to which the government, as the comprehending instrument of society, had a duty to respond.

From Casework to Entitlement

The broader federal assistance programs of today that are the center of political dispute are based in the New Deal, but they found their modern, expanded form in the 1960s. During the 1960 presidential campaign, John F. Kennedy and Lyndon Johnson noted the extreme variations in American living standards. Especially striking were pockets of poverty in the Deep South and Appalachia, as well as in certain urban areas, despite the continued economic strength the country enjoyed after the Second World War. The problems of these areas were compounded by racism. Under Kennedy, substantive gains were made in terms of legal access and integration. But after Kennedy's death, Johnson expanded the New Deal vision with his Great Society and War on Poverty initiatives. Rather than responding to temporary or isolated severe problems, these programs of the 1960s were broadly reconstructive in their aim to eliminate the systemic causes of poverty, especially for minority Americans. It was taken as a purpose of government to redesign the society by equalizing opportunity and changing forever the social and economic fabric of civil society. It was a grand, noble vision; but the unintended consequence was the demoralization of those most directly affected.

Programs to promote job training, such as the Comprehensive Employment and Training Act, and early childhood education programs, notably Head Start, were developed to meet the aim of equal opportunity. Funding levels in existing programs were substantially increased during the 1960s, and economic development initiatives were made through block-grant programs to bring renewal, and jobs, to inner-city communities. New benefit programs were also established. Food stamps were introduced in 1964 and Medicaid in 1965. A host of programs appeared in a comprehensive plan to attack poverty through provision of increased benefits and economic development.[17]

In their recent text on welfare policy, Mary Jo Bane and David Ellwood contend that these early comprehensive attempts at addressing poverty were based on a quite traditional "casework" model.[18] They point out, however, that federal and state governments had never before attempted such a model without a link to private agencies. Yet from 1962 to 1967, social workers were mandated to visit poor families in their homes, develop relationships with them, and determine what they needed to move out of poverty into self-sufficiency. Just as the Peace Corps, also founded in this period, was a secularized "foreign missions" program dedicated to democracy and development, the War on Poverty was a secularized "home missions" program for the socially excluded and morally underdeveloped. Both persons and societies were to be transformed by social workers.

Bane and Ellwood argue that in this early stage of welfare reform, more relationships between caseworkers and clients were developed than actual services provided to which clients could be referred. This approach also required a larger number of caseworkers than were graduating from social-work schools, in spite of a surge of status for this profession, and massive unanticipated administrative costs. Further, the caseworkers, stretched thin, found it impossible to maintain the frequent and sustained contact with their clients that the model required.

What social workers did was to transfer benefits or purchase social services for those who qualified, thus transforming the effect of the programs. Within a decade, social service purchases rose nearly 43 percent and medical care payments rose 37 percent, while cash payments (for disabilities, work injuries, etc.) declined by around 5 percent. Increasingly, the recipients of welfare were treated less as moral agents than as problems to be serviced. Much of this shift was fueled by the costs of maintaining and administering the spectrum of programs. By the late 1970s, administrative costs would absorb as much as 50 to 60 percent of total welfare spending in some cities.[19]

In addition, questions were posed about the values held by the social workers. Some wondered if they were compatible with the values of those they tried to help. Others suspected that they were unable to address their clients' situations in any enduring way. And still others pressed for the "destigmatization" of welfare, to make it more an entitlement than a charity and to lessen the ability of caseworkers to make decisions based on their observations of recipients' homes, habits, and lives. Welfare rights organizations grew in number and force, flooding welfare offices with applications. Some programs, such as AFDC, had been designated "entitlements" under the legislation of the 1960s, meaning that anyone who fulfilled the application requirements was entitled to receive benefits. Thus AFDC caseloads, which grew at an annual rate of just over 6 percent from 1962 to 1967, grew nearly 17 percent each year from 1967 to 1972. This massive increase in caseloads and services shaped a new operational model for the provision of benefits in the 1970s and early 1980s. Bane and Ellwood characterize this as a shift from casework and care to eligibility and bureaucracy. Others, such as Lawrence Mead, note the escalation from "need" to "entitlement" to "right," a development that obscured and sometimes almost discredited concepts of human or civil rights.[20]

While eligibility requirements were loosened, the discretion of caseworkers to make decisions individually according to the specific needs of families was diminished in the interest of equity and ease of administration. By the 1980s, the focus of interaction between benefit recipients and administrators had been substantially reduced to proving one's eligibility to receive benefits, with little scope for dealing with interlocked, multiple difficulties or for devising particular solutions. Both cash benefits and other, more specific services were handled in the welfare office setting, each service having its own particular set of requirements for eligibility. Recipients came to live in an increasingly Kafkaesque world of documenting their needs for the sake of receiving government benefits, but without anyone taking an interest in their lives—contrary to the intent of the programs, the wishes of the social workers, and the objectives of the client organizations.

How effective were these programs? In a 1994 analysis, Sheldon Danziger and Daniel Weinberg argued that the poverty rate remained essentially constant despite increased spending, though they suspect that economic recessions were also a factor in this.[21] Most observers agree that parts of the War on Poverty and its successor programs did bring some changes for the better to the lives of poor people. Head Start prepared thousands of children to enter school. Nutrition programs, through schools and through food stamps, significantly reduced the incidence of malnutrition. Poverty among the elderly was considerably reduced, and the rate of reduction continues.

Yet many of the ills that the Great Society programs were designed to address continue, and some were exacerbated. Between 1962 and

1992, AFDC rolls swelled from 3.7 million persons to 14 million.[22] The poverty rate, which stood at 19 percent in 1964 (at the beginning of the War on Poverty), declined to about 11 percent in 1973; by 1982 it had risen again, to just over 15 percent, and in 1992 it stood at 14.5 percent, with modest fluctuations since.[23] Despite the downturn in poverty and the successes of some programs, the Great Society did not emerge, especially not in the cities. Indeed, in urban areas, the very institutions that were necessary to foster work and the movement of families out of poverty had been supplanted by the government. Marriage and work were replaced by a welfare check. Parental approval and guidance were replaced by that of a social worker, now deciding matters on the basis of eligibility. Housing and healthcare became the responsibility of state agencies. Unattached, unemployed, and undereducated young men came under the supervision of the schools and the police, while stores, factories, unions, and community organizations looked elsewhere for members.

The results of this trend have often been intense: Anomie develops, individuals fall into "drift"; the expansive government support system and freedom from both parental and social worker guidance do not result in focused lives, enduring relationships, social commitment, or solid roots. Indicators of social distress—rates of alcoholism, drug use, suicide, and crime, especially among those who have been "nurtured" longest by this society—have all risen sharply. Changing social mores brought the increased approval of premarital sex, one consequence of which was more single women with children who had or were able to substitute the government for a husband or a job as a source of financial support. Indeed, in the United States, changing mores became the focus of efforts to liberate sexuality from family life and from all the residues of "puritanical" moralism, "Victorian" inhibition, and "bourgeois" values and institutions. *Playboy, Ms.,* and *Jet* celebrated every breakthrough; rock and roll and then rap exhibited the effort to liberate sexuality; John Updike portrayed them for those of literary taste.[24]

The work ethic was not, however, entirely lost, and in the late 1970s, stricter work requirements were attached to public assistance. Family assistance was linked to employment through the 1975 introduction of the Earned Income Credit, which allowed poorer families to keep a larger share of their employment income. But recessions in the 1970s decreased the relative value of benefit payments, and inflation rates rose at a faster pace than benefit increases did. While the Earned Income Credit, stronger work incentives, and inflation should have provided disincentives for relying on public assistance, the number of people on public assistance continued to rise. Arguments that the costs of the programs themselves were at least part of the cause of the "stagflation" seemed more persuasive than they had been since the 1930s.

During Ronald Reagan's administration in the 1980s, work and eligibility requirements became more stringent, while benefit levels decreased. The Family Support Act of 1988 continued this trend. AFDC required mothers with no children under age three in the home to be employed in order to receive benefits. In addition, states were given wider latitude in child-support enforcement, including the power to garnish the wages of noncustodial parents in order to cover some of the costs of public assistance for their children.

Attacks on Welfare

The moves to limit and restructure public assistance benefits in the 1980s were fueled by a growing conviction, in government and among voters, that the programs designed to help the poor had gone awry. Criticisms of welfare became widespread. Poverty was not eradicated, family dissolution was increasing, and the links between these marital trends and poverty became apparent to any who would study the data. From 1960 to 1992, the proportion of families in the United States headed by single parents (overwhelmingly single women) rose from 8 to 24 percent among whites and from 21 to 62 percent among African Americans[25]—this in spite of wider knowledge of and availability of birth control. Further, as Lawrence Mead has shown, the percentage of children born out of wedlock rose, between 1960 to 1987, from 2 to 17 percent for white women and from 22 to 62 percent for African-American women.[26] These percentages have continued to increase, with the rate of increase for white women now surpassing that for African-American women. These trends have a significant effect on the lives of children; in 1991, nearly 36 percent of all female-headed families lived below the poverty line, in contrast to only 6 percent of married-couple families.[27] Similar patterns are appearing, to a greater or lesser extent, in other nations with developed welfare programs—the same inability to create long-term change through these programs and the same patterns of family dissolution, unmarried childbearing, and increased poverty among those without stable families.[28]

The 1980s were marked by a growing conviction that welfare exacerbated the problems it was intended to solve, creating a culture of dependency that provided strong economic and psychological disincentives for seeking work. No one has maintained this view more strongly than Charles Murray, whose 1984 book *Losing Ground* argued for the virtual elimination of cash-transfer programs. According to Murray, welfare payments make it attractive for recipients to remain in the conditions that make them eligible.[29] Further, he holds that the less likely it is that unwanted behavior will change voluntarily, the more likely it is that a program to induce change will cause net harm.[30] Murray's assessment is that the broad structure of benefit programs in the 1960s and 1970s actually hurt the poor by rewarding unemployment, by providing incentives for unmarried motherhood, and, incidently, by subsidizing these programs through the tax dollars of the lower middle classes, who bore the brunt of the tax increases to pay for these programs and who were thus punished for their industriousness. He proposes forcing people to support themselves and their families:

> The proposed program . . . consists of scrapping the entire federal welfare and income support structure for working-aged persons, including AFDC, Medicaid, Food Stamps, Unemployment Insurance, Worker's Compensation, subsidized housing, disability insurance, and the rest. It would leave the working-aged person with no recourse whatever except the job market, family members, friends, and public or private locally funded services.[31]

Other researchers also have been critical of the welfare system, although few have followed Murray's "cold turkey" lead. Lawrence Mead argues that the poor do indeed need help and should certainly be expected to work, but a more intensive sort of assistance is often required to make this possible. Mead explicitly regards work and participation in other forms of public life as both formative for individuals and part of fulfilling one's civic obligations to the broader community. Consistent with this, he argues that while the threat of dependency for the poor has traditionally been cast in economic or structural terms, many of the actual issues of need and dependency are "social and personal" in character.[32] He sees tremendous social costs incurred in the politics of dependency; much welfare advocacy presumes that the recipients are incapable or weak, in contrast to earlier progressive movements that demanded support for the poor as a matter of equity and reparation, or to the even earlier views that a moral or spiritual transformation may enable the recipient of aid to become a moral agent in and an active member of civil society.

Mead contends that jobs are available, although because of their low pay or low status they may seem less attractive than receiving welfare benefits. Nevertheless, work is more than the earning of money:

> Employment is the best single indicator of competence. People who work steadily are more likely to marry and stay married, and to function well as parents; employment either fosters these abilities or results from them. If the adult poor were commonly employed, rather than jobless, it would be difficult to imagine an underclass. It is workers, not nonworkers, whom government has much the most power to help, and who also have the most power to help themselves. [33]

The issue of an "underclass," a segment of society cut off from employment, family life, and civil society, is also the focus of William Julius Wilson. In his 1987 work *The Truly Disadvantaged,*[34] Wilson claims that cycles of deprivation have marked the lives of many minorities, especially African Americans, in the inner cities of America. Wilson cites the interaction of historical discrimination and economic changes to argue that the jobs which traditionally were available to urban dwellers, factory and industrial jobs, have moved to the suburbs in the past few decades (if they have not moved abroad), beyond the reach of poor urban populations. Moreover, deterioration in the infrastructure of cities, rising crime rates, and the removal of jobs to other areas drove many employed, middle-class city dwellers to the suburbs. Wilson argues that this has left a gap within the inner city. Young men lack extensive role models for employment or realistic expectations for change and, in desperation, engage in antisocial behaviors. This, in turn, reduces their attractiveness as permanent partners, and women take over the responsibilities of childrearing, often with the support of other women, especially grandmothers, and welfare checks.

These factors, Wilson believes, account for much of the extraordinary rise in female-headed families and out-of-wedlock births among young African-American women in the 1970s and 1980s. Given the alternatives, raising a family alone on public assistance has offered a better prospect than becoming tied to a husband who will not offer support. Wilson believes that the culture of dependency is not the result of innate flaws in welfare or directly a result of the provision of social benefits; rather, the provision of social benefits has made possible a way of life that economic change and racism have largely fostered. Instead of calling for the end of welfare, Wilson advocates government intervention in increasing the job supply (which, contrary to Mead, he does not see as available) and in the maintenance of some transfer programs. He also believes that racism makes targeted programs impractical, and that political consensus can be reached only on programs that apply to all. He wants to spur job creation in cities and reverse the prospects of "unmarriageable" males.

Economist Glenn Loury agrees with Wilson on several key matters, including the importance of job creation and the persistent problem of racism. Unlike Wilson, however, he does not look to government to supply the intervention. It is a major error, Loury says, to attribute "*our* (Black) lack of achievement as evidence of *their* [white] failure, hoping to wring from their sense of conscience what we must assume, by the very logic of our claim, lies beyond our individual capacities to attain."[35] In some ways, he thinks bureaucratized government can be only marginally helpful in touching the deeper sources of despair. He also agrees with the perspective, taken in one way by Lawrence Mead and in another way in this book, that many analyses of poverty seem to have little idea of what it takes to alter the human situation, precisely because they overlook religion and morality as primary causes in personal and social change. For all the good government programs can do and economic participation entails, it simply is not the case that the external manipulation of social conditions can alter fully the essentially moral and spiritual dimensions of the human situation or the ethical and social-bonding dimensions of civil society. Substantive change here will, above all, require a transformation of human motivation and of the resolve to solve the inner psychological and motivational crises that attend people, some of whom live in situations of despair. Although Loury is an overtly active Christian Evangelical who disagrees vigorously with Minister Louis Farrakhan on a great many issues, he agrees with the leader of the Nation of Islam (for example, in his Million Man March Speech) that only a transformation of heart, involving repentance and a resolve to take responsibility for family, economic, and community life, joined to reconstructive social strategies, can restore the life of the inner cities.

Obviously, there is no widespread agreement on most of these matters. Further, none of these authors discusses long-term cultural changes, the impact of the globalization of the economy, or the influence of technology on prospects for employment and on urban culture generally. Yet, at certain levels, we can find indicators of convergent opinion. All recognize the problem of the detachment of persons from familial, work, and community involvements and from the very programs that were designed to help them. In consequence, dependency is compounded, and people are trapped in situations where they are unwanted, not needed, unloved, viewed as problems, and doubted as moral agents capable of contributing to the common life. This is dehumanizing; and what is worse, it drives people to have children simply so they can be needed, wanted, loved, in authority as moral agents, and contributing to the ongoing life of humanity. But without a stable family in a viable civil society, difficulties are perpetuated from generation to generation. What is also emerging as an agreement of substantial importance is that the well-being of the children and of their children is very much at stake in this process.

Kids Need Parents

Mary Jo Bane and David Ellwood found that married recipients of benefits required much shorter spells on AFDC—under two years—and were less likely to undergo repeated cycles of receipt than were never-married recipients, who had far longer first spells of receipt (approximately six years); further, 50 percent of those unmarried recipients who left the rolls returned.[36] Nearly 80 percent of those starting AFDC began either because a wife became a female head of a family through the dissolution of a marriage or because an unmarried woman became a female head of a family through childbirth.[37] Changes in earnings or work status, though more common as a reason for married-couple AFDC starts, accounted for less than 10 percent of total new applications.

Bane and Ellwood's study confirms what Alan Tapper found in his analysis of the welfare situation in Australia, with comparative references to Europe and Japan. But Tapper also argues that many of the economic pressures faced by families are specific to particular parts of the family life cycle. For example, families with children can experience significant economic stress in the early years of a marriage, when the costs of raising children and paying for housing (either through mortgage or increased rental costs for a home that can accommodate children) and the frequent reduction or elimination of income for one spouse (in order to provide care for children) combine to strain the family budget. In contrast, Tapper holds, the years before children are born—often extended years of work as young adults delay marriage—and the years after children are grown offer the opportunity for the accumulation of income or a higher standard of living. Any program of family subsidies or family assistance that affected all families with children, including two-parent families, would, in effect, constitute a transfer from one part of the life cycle to another.[38] He posits that for young working people, whether not yet married or married and parents, such a program of family subsidies would actually be a form of compulsory savings, which would have its precedent in old-age insurance structures such as Social Security in the United States. For older people, the transfer of income through taxation to fund such a subsidy program would largely function as a way of paying back the subsidies they would have received during their early family formation and childrearing years.

Tapper argues that any form of assistance given to families as families, intended for the purpose of assisting with the costs of children, must be given to all families rather than only to single-parent families. He wants to avoid penalizing single parents, yet he is mindful that the costs of raising children are often an economic strain on two-parent families as well. Tapper considers that a system of cash assistance to single parents only, funded in part by transfers from two-parent families, is unfair to those families in which parents have married and stayed together. Overall, he sees the decision to dissolve a marriage or not to marry at all as a free, adult choice, and he argues that single or divorced parents are "only victims of injustice if they suffered an injustice in becoming a single parent.[39]

Part of his reasoning here stems from his reading of trends in family formation and dissolution since the 1950s. Divorce rates soared in the 1970s, with the majority of marital breakups occurring early in the course of people's marriages; these trends continued internationally into the 1980s. Yet rates of teen marriages, which are more vulnerable to breakup, declined; indeed, the age of first marriage for women and men climbed. Opportunities and rights accorded to women expanded. Living standards also generally rose in the post–World War II decades, despite the recessions of the 1970s. These factors should have combined to make marriages more stable rather than less so. It turns out, then, that arguments attributing marital decay primarily to economic pressures are difficult to sustain.

Tapper suggests that expectations of marriage have become unrealistic. People divorce, under this theory, generally not because of economic pressures or youthful mistakes but because of dissatisfaction with the level of emotional rewards they found in marriage.[40] Rising social acceptance of divorce and single parenting, expanded options for women, and the possibility that marriages fail to meet intensified expectations all seem to explain parts of the picture of increased divorce and unmarried parenting; but, more important, Tapper points to the need for a viable, wider civil society in order for marriages to remain stable. A marriage cannot be the center of all of a person's needs and wants under contemporary conditions. Yet single-parent families show not only striking reductions of income but also lower levels of participation in other institutions of society. They are plunged not only into poverty but also into loneliness. Divorced and unmarried families are generally poorer than others, and poorer than they would be if the couple stayed (or joined) together. Such parents pay a quite measurable economic and social price. Their kids pay more.

In their work *Growing Up with a Single Parent,* sociologists Sara McLanahan and Gary Sandefur suggest the link between family form, poverty, social isolation, and other types of vulnerability:

> Children who grow up in a household with only one biological parent are worse off, on average, than children who grow up in a household with both of their biological parents, regardless of whether the parents are married when the child is born, and regardless of whether the resident parent remarries.[41]

Working with data from four major longitudinal studies,[42] McLanahan and Sandefur examine the differences among distinct family forms in three areas: children's educational achievement (comprised of school attendance, grades, attitudes toward school and future college attendance, as well as actual rates of high school graduation, college enrollment, and college graduation); young adult labor-force attachment; and early family formation (teen childbearing). Each of these areas is critical in preparing for adulthood. In each area, the risks and outcomes for children in single-parent families are, on average, worse than for children living with both biological parents.

What causes these differences? Many social programs assume that the income difference is the decisive factor. It is true that income loss was responsible for many of the differences observed in child outcomes. The overwhelming majority of single parents are single mothers who experience a sharp reduction in family income after divorce. For never-married mothers as well, income levels are lower than for two-parent families. If the issue were income alone, then subsidies or child-support enforcement might alleviate these differences completely. Yet, after controlling for income, the outcomes for children in one- and two-parent families still differed, with differences remaining as well between children living with two biological parents and children living with one biological parent and a stepparent. Income alone was not the answer.

Socially Involved Parents

To explain the remaining differences, McLanahan and Sandefur turned to the concept of "social capital," an idea first developed by James Coleman and increasingly adopted throughout the social sciences.[43] Social capital refers to the fabric of community and social connections that is conveyed, generation to generation, by parents' involvement in the lives of their children, and by children's involvement in the life of their parents as they introduce the child to wider networks of friends and acquaintances and, beyond these, to the larger and more enduring institutions of society. Parental resources are decisive in these matters and are mediated by the amount of time parents spend with their children (meals together, helping with homework), as well as by the rules, aspirations, and expectations that parents set for children and the modeling of how to cope with wider social realities. In these areas, children in single-parent families, on average, lose out: Across many of these indicators, single parents were less involved with their children and had narrower ranges of social experience to mediate to the children, both according to parental reports and the reports of the children, in spite of the heroic efforts of some.

This could well be the result of the sheer volume of demands on a single parent's time. Yet when a custodial mother remarries, theoretically adding the involvement of the stepfather, the mother's involvement with the children typically declines. The ability of children to maintain bonds with and learn from the noncustodial biological parent declines radically after divorce as well; approximately 30 percent of the children of divorced parents have contact at least once a week with their fathers, while only 8 percent have such contact with their fathers after their mothers remarry.

The combination of income loss and decrease in parental involvement accounts for a great deal of the difference in outcomes between children in single-parent and children in two-parent families. McLanahan and Sandefur argue that diminished parental involvement is a function of decreased time available (single parents carry a double load of responsibilities) and that these differences are independent of income.

Yet the difference in outcome between children in families with two biological parents and children in stepfamilies, in which income differences are not a significant factor, still remains.

McLanahan and Sandefur then turn to the issue of community resources, which, of course, includes educational services available in the community as well as school quality. Children in two-parent families were more likely than those in single-parent families to live in communities with lower dropout rates, more likely to attend schools with high per-pupil spending, and less likely to have friends in school with behavioral problems (as well as less likely to have behavioral or truancy problems themselves).

More significant than these issues of school quality, however, were issues of community involvement. McLanahan and Sandefur examined residential mobility rates—the average number of times a family moved in a year—to determine the potential for social connections and knowledge of a community's resources. The authors point out that while residential moves are not necessarily a bad thing, each move weakens or severs children's ties to the other adults in a community, as well as families' links with other institutions in the community. It is here that the authors find the basis for the worsened outcomes for children in stepfamilies; these children averaged between 2 and 3.5 residential moves per year, compared with 1.5 moves per year for children living with two biological parents. While single-parent families experience fewer moves per year than stepfamilies, their moves are more likely to be involuntary (through eviction or economic constraint). McLanahan and Sandefur found that controlling for residential mobility and school quality eliminated much of the difference in outcomes between children in stepparent families and children with two biological parents in the home.

The choices parents make, then, affect children deeply, often with unintended results. Children whose parents divorce or never marry generally have their affective bonds with at least one parent profoundly weakened. They lose the resources of that parent, and, to a lesser extent, of the parent who is present, in the day-to-day events through which children learn—help with their homework, playing with a parent, listening to stories—and in the modeling of understanding their gifts and skills and building enduring relationships. Single parents, in many cases, do an extraordinary job of meeting their children's needs and being present for their children, often in the face of significant time and financial stresses. Yet the idea that all family forms do an equally effective job in raising children, given enough money, is simply wrong.

Some government programs for the poor and families have done very well within highly focused areas. McLanahan and Sandefur agree with other observers that Head Start and nutrition programs are among these; they have served many children well and continue to do so. Thus they argue for the preservation of such programs and for the government to take on tougher paternity identification and child-support enforcement provisions, to ensure at least that both parents fulfill the ongoing financial responsibilities to their children.[44] They also suggest that residential stability, which constitutes a significant challenge for children in single-parent and stepfamilies, might be encouraged through properly structuring custody awards and tax incentives.

A viable society will always need some governmental supports to provide emergency services and intervention in cases where children are caught in damaging situations they did not create and cannot easily survive. But it is at just such points that care must be taken, for we now know that helpful government initiatives may also have unintended effects. As we saw in chapter 3, housing programs designed to assist working families, single parents, and the poor generally contributed to inner-city problems. Nevertheless, even more clear is that if we identify state programs only as the source of the problems or as the means of solution, we will miss certain significant factors. It simply may be the case that both the causes and the cures for the problems lie elsewhere than with government, and that the chief role of government is to constrain those forces that destroy civil society and to support those that constitute and enhance it—that is, to serve institutions beyond itself and to work less directly with citizens as individuals than with the multiple institutions of civil society that might draw persons into creative participation and membership.

What Might Help?

When the state becomes the provider of care for people in need on the basis of eligibility and entitlement, and when the casework model fails, all other institutional networks that could become involved are seen as irrelevant. But what this overview shows is that it is the interlocking of moral, social, and material factors that seems to make the difference. The organizations and relationships that might well be able to support and aid people in their communities—families, voluntary organizations, churches, potential centers of employment—must be drawn into, and not be shut out of, the processes of decision making that determine the fate of individuals. At present, these organizations have no influence, morally, socially, or materially, in how people in need are treated. Moreover, many private or religious agencies that maintain involvement with people in need focus their attention on patching the cracks in the system of government provision or on mobilizing federal support recipients to become political advocates of more and more services, rather than assuming a deeper formative or reconstructive role in people's lives—whether ethically and spiritually or socially and economically.

All the historical state efforts to help those in need have been driven by good intentions and a desire to find a compassionate, effective way of helping people in the face of disruptive social change. Yet each of the successive stages of government acting alone in this regard has failed to catch the complexity of what social well-being and flourishing institutions require, as well as the importance to the lives of families—and specifically, to the lives of children (which, of course, means for generation after generation)—of viable social context.

If the reconstruction of civil society is beyond the ability of government alone, then we must attend to those institutions that shape persons and form networks of associated life. For instance, some problems of poverty and family stress are related to changing work configurations and transitional needs, as economies adopt to new global or regional conditions. This may well be the situation of many of the "working poor," whose jobs are made obsolete. Being willing to work and to seek work in order to support a family may not be enough. New attention must be given to those institutions that might best sustain motivation in times of economic transition, when jobs are not easily found and discouragement and self-doubt are frequent. New attention must be given to those networks of acquaintance and trust that seek to discern vocational options and that encourage the will to become participants in new ventures, since it is not clear that opportunities will be created by others. New attention must be given to the resolve that is required to stay with and help partners and children in times of difficulty, and to the deliberate commitments to wider human associations and memberships that generate viable friendships, neighborhoods, towns, cities, and civilizations. In other words, new attention must be given to religion and religious institutions and to their role in the reformation of civil society.

It is unlikely that we will ever see a day when government does not have a role to play in protecting the exercise of religion; but it is not at all clear that the state can or should attempt to create or control these generating sources of moral will and motivation, social organization and commitment. Nor is it likely that states can, today, create the jobs and deliver the goods, services, and even the training that people need to live decently in the material sense. Indeed, evidence suggests that people are plunged into isolation and anomie if the state attempts to fulfill such roles, even if certain material needs are temporarily met. Thus not only government but religion must attend to those institutions that can and do create jobs, namely, business corporations and enterprises.

Religious traditions have largely ignored the potential contributions of corporations and hence have ceded their own ability to be a shaping force for or a check on corporations through church members who manage or work in them. Religious traditions have also, in recent years, turned almost exclusively to political institutions to shape and sustain civil society and to aid in providing help to distressed populations.[45] Despite the traditions' skepticism, transnational and local corporations serve as means to remake local economies and bring areas out of abject poverty through the creation of jobs and linkages with the broader world economies. Indeed, even political leaders have begun to think in these more constructive terms. What the most recent Republican administration called "enterprise zones" and what the current Democratic administration calls "opportunity zones," barely distinguishable in operation, involve tax and other benefits to corporations that work in underdeveloped urban areas. And in zone after zone, it is para-church organizations that are developing the new possibilities, encouraging the people, finding the paths to participation and creative cooperation. The alternatives are few.

The history of public assistance in the United States has been marked by increasing shifts of responsibility to government and increasing professionalization and routinization of services. The shifts are quite understandable, given the levels of need that compassionate people attempted to address and the relative stability of an emerging world power in the process of developing confidence in its unity as a nation-state. Much good was done by these programs, and it would be tragic if they were entirely dismantled, as some today advocate. But certain things were lost by them, and certain side effects on the fabric of civil society were entirely unanticipated. The flexibility to respond to particular situations and the ability to see the whole person, in his or her broader context, were largely lost. These were among the strengths of late-nineteenth-century assistance to the poor, for all its condescendence and failings in other respects. These features, however, remain a vital strength of religiously motivated institutions that are filling small niches in assisting those in need today. Of course, historically, religious interventions were moralistic in the worst Victorian senses, and they sometimes tended too quickly to demonize other groups in society. And even today, some religious organizations have been guilty, through their silence, of allowing the debate over welfare and social provision to miss the broader issues at hand. But nothing else is able to comprehend the fullness of our dilemmas in society. Nothing else is able to call people out of their immediate concerns so that they may attend to the needs of others and to seek to order institutional life justly, naming sin where it appears. Nothing else is able to help people see themselves as beloved creations, as more than merely their social location or present situation, and to give hope to individuals and communities.

In encyclical *Centesimus Annus*,[46] Pope John Paul II argues that the two key forces likely to have the most direct bearing on the future are corporations and religion. Corporations are the instrument of economic productivity for the foreseeable future, and religion is the bearer of those decisive and universal values by which we guide our production, distribution, and consumption of wealth. Those who are not involved in the economic processes of life will find development taking place "over their heads," tragically to be left in perpetual poverty. And those who are not rooted in the moral demands of profound religion are likely to be consumed by consumerism and led to an emptiness that will further destroy family and the community life of civil society.

We have identified several different streams of need that welfare programs address: transitional help for the working poor; assistance for the very poor; support policies for two-parent family life, with both parents involved in the life of society; and policies that are willing to work with corporations to create and sustain viable economic resources. As far as we can see, such efforts are more likely to be indirectly affected by the constructive influence of religious and corporate institutions as supported by government than directly affected by state action. Yet the ultimate inclusion of all within the structures of work and social institutions depends on the reconstruction of civil society and the availability of jobs within the poorest communities. If resources or institutional access are not made available through the influence of religious or corporate life, then opportunities for formation and learning through disciplined work habits, higher expectations, and participation in the common life will not exist. The reconstruction of formal institutions in poorer communities will also have a significant impact on the working poor in those communities, offering structure and support for their efforts in the midst of decaying and often dangerous neighborhoods.

Some religious and material institutions, when present and strong among the people, have a deep impact on the ability of families to envision a future in which families can establish viable patterns outside these protected environments—ones in which children will be able to grow and learn and work, in which spouses will have the support and incentives to remain together and form enduring bonds, and in which temporary difficulties do not necessitate a rapid slide into poverty but can be countered through small-scale assistance, offered through community relationships marked by trust. The importance of these institutions does not eliminate the role of government in social provision and welfare. Government is a necessary ordering force and institution as well, but not the only such institution. We have seen that assigning government the role of chief provider for those in need tears at the fabric of relational and societal life. It undercuts the context in which persons and communities flourish and leaves only isolated individuals and state authority.

To identify this need to turn to religious resources is not necessarily to repeat the mistake of some critics of the current systems of welfare, who want to use religious passions to force government to legislate a narrow moral agenda that fails to attend to the very real needs and pain of many people.[47] Religion is transforming, but it is not magic. Nor is faith a matter to be legislated: the days of a national faith were gone even before the days of a national economy, and properly so. In addition, the days of a strict, national definition of a political border in every area of life are gone as well. Part of the work of government—and of religious institutions—must be to attend to the complexity of human life throughout the globe and to participate in assisted development to foster the alleviation of poverty outside this country's borders. Again, the task becomes a cooperative venture, fostering the relationships between families, governments, corporations, and local communities to shape a new, viable civil society.

What religion can do that? In what alliance with what material forces, and in accord with what sort of architecture for society? That is the set of questions to which we now turn.

5

Covenant and Love:
What Have We Done?

We have explored a number of dimensions of family life that stand on the boundary of economics and faith. We began with observations about the traditional marriage ceremony, in which a man and a woman celebrated a covenant before God "for richer, for poorer; for better, for worse," in what was both a legal act and a moral confirmation of a loving and just bonding as honored by a community of faith. The wedding signified the legitimacy of sexual intimacy and the formation of an independent unit of mutual support and care, which had the moral right to procreate and nurture children and the duty to become a decisive, responsible unit in civil society. We noted the connection between those sacred vows and the ethical and economic dimensions that are stated in them, and we pointed out that each of these dimensions is presently under challenge.

We turned then to the most intense contemporary intellectual and social challenge to this tradition: the gay and lesbian advocacy movements, which call for the celebration of same-sex marriage, the ordination of homosexual persons, and the legal, ethical, and theological equality of homosexual and heterosexual orientations and behaviors. We examined the arguments for these advocacy positions and found them deficient, as nearly all of the churches have; and we suggested that the covenantal traditions entail onto-theological aspects of divine-human and human-human relationship, the presence of which doubtful in enduring relationships between consenting, same-sex adults (although we also argued that the latter should not be criminalized and may be morally superior to loneliness or promiscuity). We concluded that the advocates who thought they were being prophetic by overthrowing classical standards on this matter are, in fact, likely to be judged as false prophets by most ecumenical and catholic, as well as most orthodox and evangelical, traditions.

The homosexuality debates, it turned out, proved to be substantially dependent on competing theories of anthropological history and political economy and on specific theories of the relationship of spirituality to materiality and of the past to the future that are more widespread than the issues of ordination or gay marriage. Competing assertions about the relative moral superiority of various social relationships and of a particular kind of society, which are, in fact, what are embodied in these several issues, have shaped the reigning ideologies of sexuality and family and of the place of the family in production and reproduction, consumption, and the nurture of the young.

Hence we turned to two predominant theories of modernity, based on notions of political economy, that bear on household and work as well as sex and marriage. One is the liberationist view, often rooted in the thought of Hegel and Marx and given to various communal views of social solidarity; the other is the libertarian view, often rooted in Adam Smith's notions of the free market as modified by Darwinian theories of competition. Both views claim to be modern and scientific, but they actually restate ancient philosophical traditions, and both are laden with materialist assumptions. We found, however, that neither theory could account for the fabric of civil society that constitutes the network of life in which the modern family actually lives, a context with a partial, if fragile, moral framework that partially contains and channels liberationist and libertarian tendencies. We also found that neither view accounts for the place of schools, corporations, community organizations, and churches that are independent of both family and state in the life of people. Above all, these theories could not account for the fact that people pray about these matters (school, corporations, etc.) and discuss them with a moral earnestness that seeks to discern the right way to live and the good worth living for. The inadequacies of the liberationist and libertarian theories, in spite of their influence today, force us to explore different directions.

When we looked at what people actually do with their money, we found that the home is most often a center of cooperation and mutual sacrifice; but we also quickly found that this depends on the kinds of social channels that are at hand to guide the modes of cooperation and sacrifice, and that these, in turn, depend on the kind of religion that guides the culture. The liberationist and libertarian theories do not turn out to be wrong because they hold that there is conflict between various classes and competition for resources, sexual partners, and prestige between individuals, both of which, these theories maintain, can be overcome only by state power. They are wrong in their understanding of what it is that is able to overcome these realities and generate a viable civil society, a network of humane institutions, and a constitutional government under law, in which the family, the school, the corporation, and the church can thrive to form the kinds of persons able, in turn, to become responsible builders of the common life for generation after generation.

In tracing the long history of the development of the household, we noted that various models of society and family have come to dominate various epochs, and that each is rooted in one or another idea of what is holy, of what is the divine unit of loyalty. And we found that, in contemporary life, revised divisions of labor have taken much of production outside the household, locating it in corporations, and new patterns of education have taken part of nurture out of the household, locating it in schools and colleges. These changes may open up the family to the further sharing of affection and intimacy, as well as to a wider sharing of consumable material goods. We also found that a great number of public policy efforts designed to help people in need ignored the decisive role of religion in life and of independent institutions in civil society, increasingly defining social reality in terms of dependent, needy, incompetent individuals and a sovereign, providing, and wise state.

These policies have introduced major changes to the entire fabric of civil society. They have brought with them continually changing internal and external divisions of labor and changing definitions of both sex roles and household, home, and housing. Yet, more recently, the influences of education, technology, multinational corporations, and international political conditions began to reduce the influence of the state and its capacity to continue its social policies. Indeed, doubts about the effectiveness of such social programs and their costs—financial, moral, and social—will make it very difficult to extend or rebuild them in the foreseeable future. The political will is simply not at hand, even if some people suffer as government programs are reduced.

Throughout these explorations, we suggested that the Christian tradition contained a quite different understanding of the relationship of family, society, citizen, and state from those that dominated earlier pagan and modern secular theories. Christianity has viewed the divine-human relationship as the center of meaning, morality, and society and considers that the basic design of familial, economic, political, and cultural life flows from that central relationship. Religion is what establishes the possibility of a bonded association that lies under a higher law and a greater purpose than any natural solidarity or contractual agreement and that is both more stable and more true to the human condition than either the (presumedly) altruistic communitarianism of primal hordes or the felt needs, rationally calculated, of the competitive individual. Indeed, it is proper to intellectually honest social theory, as well as to theological claims that familial, economic, and political institutions be understood and formed on nothing less than an understanding of God that spells out the foundations for a viable, pluralistic, complex civil society, governed by a faith that seeks justice and love. Social analysis and social history ought therefore to turn to a perspective that is unavoidably theological.

The Christian tradition offers at least three possible versions of that perspective: catholic, covenantal, and communitarian. It is the covenantal version that we shall explore the most extensively, although with frequent reference to the catholic and occasional reference to the communitarian. This last one is, as we shall see, most deeply rooted in the Hebraic tradition, and it has echoes both in tribal traditions, where ethnic groupings are taken as the decisive mark of community, and in those Christian, Islamic, Hindu, Taoist, and Buddhist traditions that accent voluntary monastic or sectarian impulses. This perspective tends to identify an in-group against all other out-groups. The catholic and the covenantal views, however, seek to provide a general theory of the relationship of God and humanity that is valid for all. We turn to the covenantal tradition for the following reasons:

1. Although it is the least acknowledged of the traditions in regard to faith, family, and social life, the covenantal tradition stands near the roots of each of the topics here treated, and failure to understand it is a source of considerable contemporary difficulty.

2. It is the most pertinent to our present condition and to the needs of a modern civil society and political economy, for the most creative and sustaining contemporary institutions are sufficiently covenantal that they can be revised from within.

3. It is more able than the others to render a view of justice that is fair to all, for it is universalist and sensitive to ontological realities, as is the catholic tradition, but antihierarchical and reformist, as is the communitarian approach.

4. It is "exportable." It can be both understood and adopted by those who are not Christian, primarily because it is grounded in what is present in all humans, even if the fuller consciousness of it grows out of a particular religious history and tradition.

5. It allows us to recognize the plurality of obligations that we have to form and sustain complex societies, for it invites us to recognize that each person has a vocation to live in multiple networks of relationship, each one of which may be covenantal.

6. It gives the most adequate account available of the structure and dynamics of love for each area of life; and love, the Christian tradition says, is the law of life. While familial economic, social, and political forms are not always loving and are never purely loving, they may relatively embody love's graces.

What Does Covenant Mean?

The sociotheological idea of covenant is so rich with ethical content that it gives moral meaning to all it touches. This very complex richness needs to be explored in several ways. Here we use three approaches: First, we focus on the linguistic issue, particularly as it is drawn from biblical words and their translations. Second, we consider the institutions and social practices to which the covenant was applied in religious and social history; here, of course, we touch on a number of the themes we have already treated from other perspectives. Third, we identify systematic attempts to state the enduring theological and ethical meanings of covenant, especially as these were developed by scholars of the Reformed tradition but that are now more widely accepted by philosophical and non-Reformed thinkers.

The Hebrew term *berît* (or *brt*) is found in the Old Testament 286 times and is regarded by some to be the guiding idea, the organizing principle, of the highly diffuse and historically changing world of biblical thought.[1] Most authorities agree that the term is likely derived from, or at least related to, the Akkadian word *biritu,* which these ancient neighbors of Hebrews used to mean "to bind together" or "fetter." This binding, however, involved a voluntary acceptance of terms by those who were bound. Thus it involved simultaneously a passive and an active element: Free parties agreed to be bound into an ordered re-lationship that both limited their autonomy and guaranteed a degree of liberty in mutuality, in accord with terms that were adhered to but not constructed by them. No one is so free that he or she can avoid being drawn into normative relationships, and the attempt to claim unfettered freedom leads to destruction.

This idea is also similar to the Hittite term *ishuiul,* which had directly political connotations. It refers to the case of a powerful ruler binding himself to a lesser one in an alliance, with both parties acknowledging duties to the other. This relationship was, to be sure, one that the lesser power could refuse only at a cost. Yet, if the lesser power agreed and honored the terms of the agreement, a kind of "protoconstitution" was established—a formally stated and legally binding understanding of common purpose, of what counted as right and just, and of the range of limited autonomy that would be guaranteed by the fabric of mutual obligation. "Covenant" thus, in these deeper roots, could take a binary, mutual form; a pluralistic, federated form; or a hierarchical-subsidiary form. All entailed a "constituted" moral and legal association.[2]

In one of the most important new treatments of the idea of covenant and its ethical and social implications, Daniel J. Elazar points out that all these forms are related to the key term for making a covenant, *likhrot brit*—literally, "to cut a covenant"—and may take place between those of more or less equal status (*bnai brit*), where the covenant is basically a partnership of equals, or between those of superior and subordinate authority (*ba'alei brit*), as when a king and a people pledge themselves to each other or when parents and children are bound together. The us-age of "cut" derives from a ritual meal—one that sees covenant making in the context of the sharing of material resources in a sacrificial and cel-ebrative rite that invokes the presence or witness of God and establishes a system of justice by stipulating a framework of duties and rights. What is thus intended in the rite is the recognition that what is at stake is not merely an opportune human agreement or a power ploy but the estab-lishment of a more righteous social order than would otherwise be pres-ent, under the standards of holiness. In a covenant, something is at stake in the material sharing that is sacred, life-giving, enduring, and transcendent (that is, beyond the boundaries of creation and hence not subject to physical, biological, or sociohistorical determinants alone).

All sorts of deals may be made between people; many processes and dynamics may be active in the struggles to survive in hard conditions; and various forms of domination and control have been known from time immemorial. But a covenant shifts the terms of these relationships. It is not cut casually, for it entails not only celebration and sacrifice but also the incorporation of new shared duties and rights that nourish life with other meanings, and thus a sense that these duties and rights are based on an enduring law and purpose as established by a higher authority.[3]

In key traditions, a sacrificial animal was cut in half and the human parties passed between the blood—a sign of *ruach,* the divine, animating spirit of life—being shed by the sacrificed creature. An old order of life was ended, a new one begun. As Elazar says:

> It is significant that cutting (dividing) and binding, are the principal elements in the terminology and early practice of covenant-making since a covenant both divides and binds, that is to say, it clarifies and institutionalized both the distinction between or separate identities of the partners and their linkage. This is, of course, precisely what covenants are about. In other words, the covenant is . . . [like Martin] Buber's I-Thou relationship. . . . Through covenants, humans and their institutions are enabled to enter into dialogue while maintaining their respective integrities within a shared framework.[4]

Whatever its historical or primitive cultic origins, the biblical prophets, priests, and kings recognized in covenant a basic feature of human life, something central to the formation and preservation of community, personal identity and, indeed, the moral life of humanity. Not only did they apply the term to the relationship of God to chosen persons, who were called to specific vocations in the world, and to Israel as a chosen people, but they also saw in the very fabric of this association an ordered liberty that interwove righteousness and power, law and promise, and thus a form of structured accountability that allowed all people to deal justly with one another and to manage scarce resources and competing loyalties with the greatest possible harmony. Those called into covenant were to be a light to all.

This biblical idea of covenant involves a multiplicity of dimensions, in terms of both the norms involved and the relationships to which it refers. It is applied to friend-friend, husband-wife, parent-child, tribe-tribe, king-people, kingdom-kingdom, employer-employee, teacher-disciple, judge-accused, and redeemer-humanity relationships. The common feature of these is that each may represent an ethical outworking of the divine-human relationship, for each not only is constituted but may be measured by a God-given framework and purpose for human life.

Further, covenantal thinking has been adopted and adapted in a variety of cultural settings beyond the biblical and ancient Near Eastern societies. "Covenant" is variously read in terms of the Greek *diatheke*, which has the overtones of being joined together rightly because the parts belong together, or (rarely) *syntheke*, which also includes a joining but in a "constructed" or "synthetic" sense, usually with an implication of artificiality. It is also read in the Latin *testamentum*, the term that is used for the "new covenant" of the New Testament as well as for a promised and witnessed plan for the future, as in "last will and testament," and *foedus*, the term from which we get the word *federation* and, later, the entire idea of a federated civil society.

The Hebrew and Greek terms have sometimes also been translated into Latin as *pactum* and *compactum*, which imply binding agreement but may also suggest a pact of political convenience or a commercial contract. When any of these terms are used, they are often associated with or set in the context of *institutio*, with its overtones of a settled or required practice or of an organization set aside for a practice (such as a school for teaching), and of *religio*, which has the notion, in at least one major etymological tradition, of "binding" spiritual and ethical obligation. These classical translations are historically related to the French *promettre, contrat*, and, in one sense, *alliance*. The concept of covenant is also related to the German *Bund* or *Vertrag*, the former of which refers to "ties" and the latter to agreement or pledged trust. However, the idea of "compact" can also refer to an outlaw agreement, against institution or religion—and especially against "institutional religion," as we see in the literary references to a "compact with the devil."

All this leaves English, which draws on several of these linguistic traditions, with an embarrassment of riches. Covenant may be understood as sacred *promise, oath, contract, bond, troth*, or, more quaintly, *bounden duty*. The rich and complex overtones of these various terms make the concept of covenant baffling to any who think that a concept can and should mean only one thing, if it is to be worthy of attention. But this linguistic richness may more nearly approximate both the character of theological discourse and the ethical realities of human existence than does the "flat" language that requires a singularly "clear and distinct" idea at every point, and which so often leads ethical theory to a reductionism of one or another sort—*the* categorical imperative or *the* divine command, *the* greatest good for the greatest number or *the* cultivation of virtue, *the* contextual discernment or *the* existential decision. Indeed, the concept of covenant may include these as criteria that illumine dimensions of a valid covenant, but it weaves them into a larger sociotheological whole.

In fact, rich and complex symbolic concepts may be necessary to treat the kinds of issues raised in this book and may be preferred over simpler ones, not because they obscure or mystify but because they more accurately illuminate the multifaceted dynamics and structures of moral life, as this life necessarily involves the processes of coming to judgment and resolution, shaping a polity and policy, and forming interpersonal, social, cultural, economic, or political institutions. The most subtle, complex symbolic concepts point to these several levels all at once, for it is in the multidimensionality of moral life that we can find an accurate understanding of the nature of every serious ethical issue.

In citing appearances of covenant-like phenomena outside those of the ancient Near East, Elazar also refers not only to the old Hungarian national covenant, the Scottish seventeenth-century one, and the American Declaration of Independence, all of which are surely influenced by the biblical tradition, but also to Scandinavian oath pacts, Native American tribal confederacies, and selected "pacts" in South Asian, Chinese, and African traditions. But not all examples are political. We have already noted Francis Fukuyama's treatment of the various patterns of covenantal trust found in family life in several cultures of Europe and Asia,[5] and we have suggested the possibilities of economic covenants at a number of points.

In all these traditions we see a "constitutionalization of relationship," one that has analogues in the Hebraic tradition. The significance of such cross-cultural references is high, for it helps clarify a key implication of covenant thinking for understanding the nature of revelation as it bears on ethics and the common life. It may be that God reveals to some people highly specialized ethical insights, for which there is no possible warrant except the insight itself; but if that is so, then those who do not have the insight are not required to take it seriously for themselves or in public life. But the presence of covenant-like possibilities in many, perhaps all, cultures suggests that in the very structure of human relationships we find traces of what God has graciously revealed to humanity in the fabric of creation, even if we have come to know about that reality primarily through unique, historically conditioned insights. Humans may look around in the world and see only imperial relations and imposed heteronomy, or they may see only individuals competing for dominance and calculating pleasures and pains. Or they may see through the eyes of faith the traces of right and good that preserve a modicum of justice and peace, even a measure of love and hope, in spite of the fact that these seem everywhere disrupted. If this last is so, then we can recognize nomic patterns and purposive ends that seem to appear perennially in human cultures, and by which everyone knows enough of the right and the good to have no excuse when they betray them, even if every code and policy is distorted by the attempts of the powerful to form it in the image of their own interests.

To approach theology this way makes it less a privileged dogmatic assertion than a public claim about the basic texture of the common life. It suggests that in the special disclosures of God—in the covenant with Moses that forms Israel, in the new covenant in Jesus Christ that forms the church, and in those wonderful and rare friendships, marriages, and work teams or voluntary associations we sometimes experience—certain aspects of the eternal and universal relationship of God to humanity are made manifest. Believing people thereby gain the capacity to clarify and actualize what is, in fact, already present as a universal possibility at the deepest levels of existence. They may then help all peoples see what is there, even if it is obscured by the raw corruptions of life and thought, by the frequent thin flatness of things, or by the willful repudiation of any notion of a divine self-disclosure.

Some key elements of this covenantal approach have been summarized by Delbert Hillers:[6]

1. A prologue that identifies the parties involved. The historical identity of each person, of each people, or of the sovereign (divine or human) establishing this covenant is not only preserved but also honored. Covenant making does not demand a repudiation of self-understanding or of past experience, even if both of these are reconstituted by new relationship.

2. Identification of the purposes of the new relationship and of the principles that are to guide it. Every such agreement thus has both teleological and deontological elements that bind the parties with a promise toward the future and an acknowledgment that all parties live under context-invariant standards, which no one can break with impunity.

3. Implicit or explicit operative clauses, which indicate the likely conditions that make the relationship durable and specify the contextual conditions to

which these clauses are to be applied—or, more often, a statement of the deeper context that disallows
willful invalidation of the relationship.

4. A body of sanctions, positive and negative, that on
   the one hand detail what benefits may be realized if
   the bond is kept and on the other hand define what
   is likely to happen if one or the other of the parties
   fails to fulfill the promises or live up to the standards. Blessings and woes are specified.

5. Sworn oaths or solemn promises that make the
   covenant binding. Covenants thus involve an inner
   commitment as well as an external validity. Indeed,
   if it can be shown that the will was coerced, that
   consent was not freely and truly given, the covenant
   may be declared as never having been made.

6. A public and permanent record of the covenant-
   making event, often with stipulated provisions for
   periodic "covenant renewal." What is done in
   covenant is of public as well as private import, of
   theological significance for social, even world, history, and is to be so recognized.[7]

The two great covenantal events that are remembered as the foundation points of Judaism and Christianity exemplify these features. God established a covenant with the children of Israel through Moses at Sinai
by revealing God's own identity and by reminding the Israelites who they
were, as those who were rescued from slavery; by the giving of the laws;
by establishing the terms for right and regular worship; and by citing the
hope-filled promises of blessings if these terms were kept, so that the
warnings of woe would not have to be invoked. Further, provision for
remembering the event was established, including the "cutting of sacrificial offerings" (Ex. 24:3–8). And Matthew, the first and most widely
used Gospel in church lectionaries over the centuries, recalls all these elements, in a different order, in the Sermon on the Mount. There the
blessings are stated first; then the meanings of the laws are restated, intensified, universalized, and personalized; and finally, the character of
God and the disciples and their relationship are foretold through the life,
message, death, and resurrection of Jesus Christ, as later signified also by
the symbolic sharing of shed blood in a communion meal (Matt. 26:28).

Historical Developments

It is sometimes argued that the idea of covenant disappeared in the early church and in most of medieval history, only to be resurrected by the Reformation. If one followed certain lines of the linguistic argument alone, that might seem to be the case. But it is also quite possible to see three distinct pre-Reformation developments as a manifestation of the covenantal tradition in church history. First is the development of the doctrine of the Trinity, second is the development of the sacrifice of the mass, and third is the formation of a political polity. We cannot deal with the Trinity here, but the development of the mass points to sacramental theory and marriage liturgies, which we treated in chapter 1, and the issue of polity has to do with the formation of a pluralistic, federal theory of civil society, in which the family has a distinct place. It is this last issue that we treat here.

It is also possible to see, in the development of the ecclesiology of the Catholic and Orthodox traditions, patterns of covenantal order that are rooted in the biblical view of covenant, as it is interpreted by the royal traditions. Not only did these traditions long ago sense what modern scholarship has also concluded—that Saul was conceived of as a "conditional appointment or covenant," to be honored "so long as the 'Spirit of God' was upon him, and so long as he did not violate the legal traditions or constitution of the league"[8]—but they also recognized that when David was anointed as Saul's successor, he made a covenant "before the Lord" with Israel and was installed as one who would exercise a "limited kingship," "under God's law," that involved the establishment of dynastic rule and hierarchical priestly governance.[9] To be sure, the prophetic tradition rose up, following Nathan, who had called the kings to account for violating marriage vows, for exploiting the poor, for waging unjust wars, and for introducing pagan priests. The prophets established the idea that there was one covenant with several manifestations—familial, economic, political, and prophetic. They supported rulers when they followed the covenant in various areas but opposed them when they did not. Just prophetic protest demanded covenantal integrity in each area of life.

It is to the political part of this precedent that the kings of Christian royalty and the medieval church appealed. Rulers of the Holy Roman Empire, from Constantine until Napoleon, and the czars from Constantine up to the Bolshevik Revolution in the East claimed to be in the line of David and sought to establish integrated societies by the coordination of the body of Christ and the body politic, which also protected wealth and family.[10] In these histories the church served, sometimes as society's priests and sometimes as society's prophets, in vast, fateful, and often-forgotten struggles of *regnum* and *sacerdotum* over the shape of God's *compactum* with humanity in time and space.[11] The Reformed tradition radically revised these developments, both in social history and in theory.

Covenant in Society

In 1521 the Scottish scholar John Major wrote a *History* which asserted that the people made kings and thus could dethrone them—an idea that had been debated in certain Roman scholastic circles for some years and that reflected the practices of several councils of the church with regard to the pope but that was deeply opposed by royalty and many clergy.[12] Such ideas were eventually to find fertile ground in Great Britain, for the Magna Carta had already established the principle that royal authority was under the constraint of law and accountable to plural "lesser" authorities. The ideas were refined and extended by several thinkers, including George Buchanan, who published his *De Jure Regni* in 1579. Such texts gained a large audience for the notion that the just laws, purposes, and common practices of society—its covenants—are formed under God and thus are prior to kingly authority. They are neither derived from nor identical with political power. As David was not king until he was anointed by the spiritual leader of the people of Israel, Samuel; exceeded his authority when he presumed to be both priest and king; and was subject to prophetic protest, so leadership is to be the servant of the God-given institutions of society, constituted as a federation of covenantal communities.

At the center of this federation stands the church—not one that accedes, bows, or serves as chaplain to political power but one that interprets to the people what the just laws, purposes, and agreements of society may be. The people, so instructed, then elect the custodians of political power and remove them when they misuse their power. Indeed, the people's proper representatives are to elect their clergy and to remove them also when they do not sustain either the laws and purposes of God or the covenantal structures that constitute society. Ecclesiology, rooted in covenant, is thus the mother of democracy; the church is the model for family, political regime, and the commonwealth.

These ideas stand at the root of what was later to be called "civil society" by political philosophers.[13] Such views found precedent not in the Davidic or Solomonic dynasty but in the prophets who railed against unjust rulers in the name of God's covenant. The heirs of the prophets did not attempt to abolish regimes or to have the church withdraw from engagement with them, but they did attempt to found them on just principles. It was on such bases that the movements for Congregationalism and Presbyterianism and political parliamentarianism began to rise against the ideas of episcopacy and the "divine origin of royal power," as King James was to write to his son Charles in the seventeenth century. This set in motion the trajectory that would take Scotland—and later, England and Ireland—toward the "Puritan Revolution."[14] The "Covenanters" of nearly a century later were those who publicly subscribed to a "confession and covenant" that protested tyranny of all kinds. Although the movement was relatively short-lived, the ideas on which it was based were graphically illustrated and generated convictions that spread throughout the Protestant world, bringing movements for "democratic" order in many spheres of life.[15]

Covenantal Confessions

The creedal-doctrinal side of this Reformation-influenced movement is the one that gave rise to "covenant theology," as it was most often called in the Anglo-American Puritan traditions, or "federal theology," as it became known in Reformed circles on the continent, especially after the rise of Dutch pietism at the hands of Johannes Cocceius, who wrote the famous *Summa doctrinæ de fœdere et testamento Dei.*[16] Parallel movements were afoot under the influence of William Ames in England and Holland and James Ussher in Ireland and Scotland, but the core ideas that were gaining ground were deeper and related to the pervasive Reformed understanding of the story of salvation.[17]

In an important new work, David Weir has traced the origins of this doctrinal development to the key questions of the Swiss Reformers, as can be seen, for example, in the First Helvetic Confession, written by Heinrich Bullinger in 1536, regarding the relationship of Christ to Adam, that is, the relationship of God's gracious gift of redemption to human nature as it was before the Fall and as it is after the Fall. The issue was taken up by Martin Luther and Desiderius Erasmus in some ways and, more systematically, by Theodore Beza in his 1555 *Summa* and by John Calvin in his 1559 *Institutes,* as is well known.

But it was Zacharias Ursinus of Heidelberg, Weir notes, who, building on these sources, expanded the range of the issue "against a background of re-examination of the meaning and translation of the words *berîth, diatheke,* and *testamentum.*"[18] For Ursinus, and in the Heidelberg

Catechism of 1562, which he penned, the "covenant" (*foedus, Bund*) was not first given to political authority through Samuel to David, through Moses to Israel, or even through Noah to humanity "after the Flood," as claimed by some.[19] Rather, it was given by God to Adam in the very fabric of creation. By implication, this means that it was in the very nature of God, and thus of those made in the image of God, to be covenantal. Various historic "covenants" may be given by grace in the midst of time, but these are possible because the primal relationship of God to humanity is covenantal, and the cosmic story of salvation is to be told in terms of the covenant of God with Adam, broken in the Fall, and the redemptive covenant of God with the second Adam, Christ, who points toward the promised covenant of a new heaven and new earth, a New Jerusalem, where all is perfected. In between are many covenantal possibilities of preservation or renewal, as is shown not only in book of Exodus but in the covenant of God with Abraham well before that and in the histories (Kings, Chronicles, etc.) thereafter. We do not know if Ursinus spelled out all these implications, for little of his other work survives; but the logic is already clear, and many clergy preached just this.

In the same period Bullinger, who had already developed the idea, was asked to aid Frederick the Elector in defending himself against the charge of heresy (at the hands of the Lutherans) for endorsing the Heidelberg Catechism.[20] Bullinger penned the Second Helvetic Confession, which contained extension of the concept of covenant, one that he believed was also implied by scripture and the logic of theology based on it: Not only are the Trinity, the church, and its sacraments and rites to be understood covenantally but also (paralleling Calvin's argument in the *Institutes* 4.14–20) our responsibilities in regard to wealth and property, sex and the family, and politics and power.[21]

The latter point is critical, for while the Reformed heritage only rarely adopted Luther's notion of the "orders of creation," an idea drawn from the medieval idea of the "estates," it generated a great interest in the vocations humans have to engage the multiple arenas of social and historical existence and to transform them to the glory of God, and it recognized the interdependence of the institutions of society and thus of an adequate theological-ethical approach to them. Under the influence of the idea of covenant, a range of "spheres" is seen not only as functionally necessary to the preservation of human life as created by God but also as arenas in which the grace of God's covenant might be made manifest. The true believer will attend to each of these areas with constant support, continued care, and repeated reformations. The life of faith is thus not only to be cultivated in the church but to be cultivated in and by the church for actualization in these other areas. In human terms, this attentiveness assures the refinement and renewal of valid previous agreements and a rededication to the imperfectly actualized new covenant, "already" established in Christ but to be fulfilled in the "not yet" of social life provisionally and in eschatological life ultimately.[22]

This is the doctrine—indeed, the theology of history and of society—that came more and more to predominate in Christian thinking over the seventeenth century, especially among thousands of practicing clergy, as manifest both in its more established European forms, as seen in the Westminster Confession of 1648,[23] and in its "free-church" Congregationalist forms, as seen in the Cambridge Platform of the same year.[24] Further, this heritage entered into an intellectual and social-ethical alliance with the parallel developments of "natural rights" theory, developed in the work of Reformation-influenced lawyers from Johannes Althusius, Hugo Grotius, and Samuel von Pufendorf to John Locke, and antiauthoritarian, pro-todemocratic parliamentarianism, as sketched above in regard to the Covenanters, to form the basis of modern constitutional democracy and human rights theory.[25] It is likely, in this regard, that the much-celebrated idea of "contract" as developed by the Enlightenment tradition, deriving from such figures as Hobbes, Locke, Rousseau, and Immanuel Kant, is fundamentally dependent on interpretations of the covenant idea (Davidic, Mosaic, federalist, and Adamic) as these theorists attempted to state it in terms drawn from the traditions of Roman legal theory.[26]

The philosophers thought, after all, that religion seemed to bring war and that philosophy could bring peace. As we shall shortly note, they were mistaken. But certain integrations of the two rendered a second "Christian social philosophy," as Ernst Troeltsch called it,[27] beyond the combination of Augustine and Aristotle that Thomas Aquinas had developed, one that engendered a distinctive "character" that has come to establish in much of Protestantism around the world an enduring "emphasis on diligence, duty and discipline" in personal life and a pluralistic, constitutional ordering of society in the common life.[28] It is on this foundation that a number of major authors have continued to build, in the face of many objections, over the last four decades.[29]

Continued Implications

If the noted scholar Jon Levenson is correct, it is precisely these ideas, rooted in scripture and written into the discourse of contemporary political life, that are again at the center of current disputes, as "Newt Gingrich promotes a Contract with America, and President [Bill] Clinton speaks of a New Covenant."[30] The problem is that both politicians know that they are using powerful symbols, but they do not know what these concepts entail or what to do with them. Thus these terms appear empty of moral and spiritual power. Yet the ideas did not die in the Enlightenment, even if they have become somewhat confused by manipulations of terms that carry more weight than the manipulators recognize or can control. Nevertheless, the alliance of the one with the "new religious right" and the dependence of the other on obvious biblical reference and the renewal of the family suggests that the reputed "secularization" of the twentieth century is a fraud.[31]

We do not need to agree with everything currently proposed by Republican or Democratic leaders to acknowledge what we have seen in every chapter of this analysis of family life: that it was presumed by several generations in our century that society could and should be organized, that governments should and could be constituted, and that personal relationships could be conducted on the basis of either historical communal solidarities or of voluntary, no-fault "contracts," and that these have no need of God or of theology. Both the socialisms and the individualisms of this epoch that dispense with God, however, have proven disastrous. One led to the terrors of National Socialism, with its neopagan nihilism, and to proletarian socialisms with their programmatic secularizations, both of which impoverished the people and deconstructed the moral fiber of civil society by means of state dominations seldom matched in human history. And individualism, as often as not, led on the one hand to neopagan theories of the solitary self, with all that is divine within the individual, or on the other hand to the antitheological *homo economicus* theories of possessive "rationalism," both of which destroyed families, undercut communities, and savaged civil society. Indeed, even a number of religious leaders became enamored with Marxist or Nietzschean ideas on one side or with existentialist or utilitarian ideas on the other, although what they frequently had in mind was, on the one hand, a protest against sentimental idealism in the analysis of society or, on the other, a protest against the erosion of the value of the human person at the hands of false collectivisms.[32]

But it is doubtful that antitheological, postreligious, or merely protesting views can guide us. They do not see humans as living under God, in covenanted communities, and thus necessarily under a higher law, for a larger purpose, and in the midst of a host of providential networks given for our well-being. Instead, they think only of a historically conditioned, totally contingent, artificially constructed context that is thought to determine all that people are and think, want and need. The failure of these views has triggered a host of efforts to retrieve the deeper foundations of faith and the common life.[33]

For those nurtured in or who (like the present author) are converts to this understanding of the biblical tradition and of the importance of theology for ethics, there is a more reliable option that can be retrieved and reconstructed on the basis of the covenantal, trinitarian heritage. It is surely, at the very least, one promising element in the reformation of an orthodox, catholic, evangelical, and ecumenical interpretation of ethics for the new global civilization that shall unavoidably be part of our common future.

What, Then, Can Guide Us?

We need, above all, a rebirth of the biblical understanding of covenant, refined by two thousand years of Jewish and Christian reflection in multiple cultures; by the recognition that we face a new global civilization, where the dialogue on every point will have to be refined once more in the face of a new international, multicultural civil society; and by the contemporary awareness that certain definitions of "natural law" and "orders of creation," rooted in preindustrial cultures, that defined and limited gender roles have to be changed. The reconstruction of a theology of covenant for family life will, of necessity, have several features. As we draw this book to a close, we can identify these several dimensions and invite all to join in their refinement.

The Federal Character of Civil Society

The family is one of the key institutions that constitute civil society; but it is only one of several, and it is interdependent with the others. It does not fare well when the others falter, and its own internal fabric does, and must, shift when the fabric of civil society shifts. In most traditional societies, and in nearly all of the classical theories of society, life was organized according to household and regime, and production, politics, reproduction, education, and religion were conducted in the context of, for the sake of, and under the control of these two institutional orders.

The differentiation of religion from these spheres by Christianity began a long process in which, in alliance with certain insights of the Greek philosophers, education also became substantially independent of the household and regime and gradually became centered in the "scientific" university or, in the case of medical education, the hospital. Similarly, Christian theologies of covenant, using aspects of Roman law, developed the notion of constitutional order, in which the courts are, in considerable measure, independent of and constraining of both regime and family, along with definitions of human rights. At the local levels, the church, the school, the clinic, and the police officer intervening in family disputes replicated these changes and altered the structure of traditional familial and political life. Although the church nurtured these changes, it also has periodically resisted its progeny by opposing science, "the medical model," the "depersonalization of politics" as kings were abolished, and the individualizing effects of human rights.

In our time, an even more dramatic transformation has taken place. The long and slow development of the corporation, based also in the intellectual and legal influences of the church, came to triumph over both traditional, family-based subsistence economies and state-directed political economies, a success that, indeed, has made a great number of political efforts to constrain these corporate units impossible. The corporation is now, without question, the center of production, and increasingly, with the rise of complex technology media, dominates most aspects of culture and communication.[34] Again, parts of the church have resisted these developments, although the church has increasingly turned to contractual models of marriage and human relationships.[35]

Our interest in these questions lies in the fact that the actual structure of social life and the necessity for a sound theory of that life require that we recognize that the "estates" or "orders" of life are at once more simple and more complex than was earlier thought. They are more simple in that each order is less a complete design for living than a basic, skeletal structure that indicates what is functionally indispensable in the development of a viable design. It does not tell us how to build a house, how to make a house a home, or how to allocate the roles and relationships between the members of the household; but it can tell us that if certain support systems are not in place, if the house is built on sand and not on rock, then it will fall, no matter how grand the design or how complicated the agreements between those in the house. Each order, thus, requires a covenant that acknowledges the demands of the order and then fulfills its possibilities in a distinctive, graceful way that points to patterns of justice and love, which the order itself does not indicate and cannot supply.

But these orders are more complex in that each is only relatively sovereign, and between the individual and the state stands an enormous, interactive network of social institutions that themselves alter even as they change, in ever new ways, the fabric of family and regime. Modern civil society now knows itself to be a complex federation of partly interdependent and partly autonomous social institutions, each of which may be formed by covenantal traditions. The failure to recognize this complexity, and indeed, the fact that many of these orders seemed simple to the point of being identical, brought patriarchal-hierarchical structures, on the one hand, and short-term, contracted interpersonal deals and relationships, on the other, into predominance. Males and females, parents and children, in our time thus find themselves participants in an enormous—indeed, through indirect influences, worldwide—network of relationships that require covenantal ordering but bear residual marks of both patriarchal domination and contractual egoism. It is likely that nothing less than an understanding of and a commitment to covenantal mutuality under God can bring moral and spiritual coherence to what is otherwise experienced as a seething, chaotic mass of dominations and arbitrariness.

Our Vocations to Multiple Covenants

It is further the case that no two people experience the complex in exactly the same way. The people we live with, the people we work with, the other parents and the teachers we discuss our children with, the people who vote as we do, the people we play sports or see movies with, the people we shop with, and even the people with whom we worship may differ from us in racial, class, ethnic, and cultural backgrounds, and will be woven into a network of interdependent familial, economic, educational, recreational, political, and religious commitments that are distinct from our own—except in the area where our activities overlap. And each may have agreed, in the midst of multiple pressures, to join that particular area for reasons different from the ones we hold most dear.

In this context, many have tried to be "supermoms" or "superpops" and have fallen victim to careerism on the one side and exhausted resentment on the other. The only way to negotiate our way through the mazes is to recognize that each of us is made in the image of God, and on that basis we are called to be persons of integrity in the midst of a pluralism of vocations. One may, for example, be called to be accountant by day, parent in the mornings and evenings, choir member at church on weekends, decorator and cook during holidays, volunteer during selected political campaigns, jury member in certain trials, and lover and partner throughout. Or one may be called to be store manager by day, homework supervisor and Little League coach in the evenings, usher at church, sports fan on weekends, debater over zoning regulations at a town meeting, gardener and house painter on holidays, officer in the National Guard, volunteer fire department member during crises, leader of family prayers at the table, and lover whenever both partners can find time and privacy and energy.

Something must give integrity to these multiple activities, each of which is necessary to the sustaining of civil society, each of which involves potentially covenantal relationships, and each of which is demanding of attentive excellence. Without an integrating center of identity, without a sense of being called and empowered by God to fulfill one's gifts and serve God, the neighbor, and the community, these activities become only a whirl, a drudgery of socially imposed activities with no sense of purpose or vision. Or they become something that others do—in which case one either becomes a dependent, living as a leech off the social capital others create, or is excluded from the skills, networks of interaction, and informal information flows that define the boundaries of societal inclusion or exclusion.[36]

It was not long ago that the doctrine of vocation was applied first to those who were called to the religious life as priests or nuns. The Reformation extended the idea and applied it to all believers. That extension converged, by a hundred indirect channels, with ideas of covenant, and together they influenced the church, democracy, education, the corporation, the family, and now the whole federation of covenanted institutions that constitute civil society.[37] At times it was thought that the father had a vocation to earn the money to sustain the family by having a job of a particular kind and to tend the politics of the common life (in some periods, by being a soldier), whereas the mother had a vocation to raise the children and tend the household (and, in some periods, to keep religion vital: *Kinder, Kirche, Küche*). It is clear that the transformations brought by the convergence of vocation and covenant demand a revision of the way we think of both our vocations and our covenants.[38]

We now know that we have multiple vocations, and this very pluralism can be maintained only by a centered relationship with God. That is the core of the calling to be and to live with energy, dedication, grace, and creativity in all areas of life, ever and in all things being a witness to and an agent of God's covenantal justice and love, that allows us to gain a contextualizing perspective on the multiple jobs, roles, and talents we have; to accept with serenity the limitations we find in ourselves and in our situations when they clash; and to accept with gratitude the gifts we are given to fulfill the multiple demands we face to the best of our ability.

Each covenant ought to be seen as a means of grace. In many of the world religions, it is not only the marriage that is celebrated as a sacred moment, with prayer and special music and high rhetoric, but also the coronation of a king or the opening of Congress (a political event), the opening of a school year in a convocation or the closing of it in a commencement (educational events), the dedication of a hospital (a medical milestone), the planting and the harvest or the blessing of the fleet (critical economic moments), and even some sporting and artistic performances (cultural events). In Christian circles, the Catholic, Orthodox, and Anglican traditions have a deeper and more profound understanding of the place of liturgy in the life of society than do many Protestants. But it may not be necessary to develop an entire set of dogmas about sacramental life to recognize that these rites and rituals correctly acknowledge that something holy is potentially at stake in each department of life. We have no justifiable grounds for thinking that the moments of society listed above can be carried out without a full sense of their dependence on God and without the kind of attentiveness to excellence, care, and graciousness that derives from lives lived under the consciousness of God.

When we suggest here that each of the multiple areas of life may be a means of grace and that we have a calling to live rich, full, and complex lives, we are not implying that these areas are beyond breakdown, distortion, failure, and even destructive impact. Every demon, according to the tradition, is a fallen angel; every hell on earth is a promise of paradise gone crazy and become self-absorbed. Each of these areas, and each segment of our diversified lives, can curve in on itself, begin to worship its own powers, deify its own potentialities, and conspire with others to monopolize its own benefits, as if it were self-sufficient. When that happens, evil possesses the individual life and wickedness begins to characterize the culture. Civil society is deconstructed, politics becomes but an orgy of power, stupidity is celebrated, sickness besets many, businesses fail, the arts do not inspire, marriages fall apart, and prayer ceases.

But these trends are all reversible, and in sometimes long and slow processes, life can be reconstructed. The turning point is a matter of theologically guided religious renewal. And the center of religious renewal in the community of faith is tested first of all on the basis of how it relates to the two areas that are, of necessity, most directly and personally physical and material: family and economics. It is these areas that political, cultural, educational, medical, and legal institutions must protect; and if they do not, then they will be abandoned, overthrown, or changed as the covenant is renewed.

It is not that these various covenanted areas of life can, in the ultimate theological sense, bring salvation. Only God brings that, and only in times and seasons of God's choosing and only for those who are chosen, matters which no human knows with certainty. But in the proximate sense of ethical living in this life, where a little more or a little less justice and love can make the whole difference between joyful living and miserable existence, the sustaining of graceful and thus viable tissues of religious, family, economic, and civil life is a blessing.

How, Then, Ought We Live in Families?

What is most pertinent to our topic, in this context, is what is appropriate to the sort of creatures we are at our deepest levels—physical, social, and willing beings, in relationship to God and made for just relationships between persons in all areas of life that sustain and enhance life over time. Love, therefore, ought to have a form suited to the religious center of our existence, one already present in the teachings of our tradition, because that tradition touches the very core of who and what we really are. And this means that while all are fully human at a primary level, we are secondarily male *or* female—neither of which can be both or neither or play the part of the other without a distortion of that sex's nature. All are bound together in communities of love and duty under God, in religious communities of faith and in civil communities of justice when those communities recognize the God-given dignity of each person and rightly order themselves in covenant to meet the physical and material needs of each. When our love is actualized, it is understood to be a call to be faithful to our humanness in the context of the whole web of blessings—biophysical, social, moral, economic, and religious.[39]

The covenanted marriage affords the best answer yet discovered to human distortions of relationships and to loneliness. Some remain lonely because they do not find a suitable spouse. Some remain lonely in what looks like a marriage but may be plagued by abuse, hostility, injustice, or exploitation. These are tragedies with which many wrestle.

In all cases, communities of faith, who know that God is in relationship with each person and that no one is ultimately alone, need to establish contexts in which loneliness is reduced. Further, all people in these conditions of loneliness should be encouraged to reach out, through community organizations, personal charities, and tax policy, to those who are not like themselves and to assume concrete forms of responsibility for coming generations.

We are created for community with the divine Other and with the human other. We have already seen something of the place of the family in the network of required institutions that allow a civilization to exist; no society can survive without an economy, a political order, a cultural-linguistic system by which to communicate, a family system, and, above all, a religion. Further, a society can be said to flourish best when it also has well-developed legal, educational, medical, and technological systems.[40] But we can here note again that how these "orders" are formed under the impact of covenant has quite profound implications for how persons find channels for their personal relations. Through covenant they become interlocked structures by which our human propensities to egoism, selfishness, short-sightedness, and carelessness are constrained and the possibilities of altruism, generosity, long-range vision, and engagement are evoked. These call us to contribute to the whole of life by making us concretely involved in forming a loving, just, and sustainable society that anticipates the new Jerusalem for which we hope.

The family, while it inevitably involves a division of labor and a structure of authority (as, for example, between parents and children), best flourishes when it is governed by principles that recognize the rights and needs of each, when it measures out duties and responsibilities with equity and rewards and punishments with compassion, and when it constantly schools all members in the necessity of mutuality, responsiveness, and duty to the commonwealth.[41] This model necessitates a sustained commitment, built into our daily lives, that involves the constant forming of others to have regard for these structures of civility. Even personally, a covenanted marriage is a *healing* bond in which the sinful impulses, tendencies, and pathologies present in all are disciplined, restrained, and repaired, and in which—with God's help—we pursue a path toward holiness, the true pattern of wholeness that alone saves life from the emptiness and terror of death. In marriage we begin to learn the meaning and difficulty of committed love, in which there are no guarantees of success or triumph, only a pledge of mutual support as the uncertain future is faced in sickness and in health, for better or for worse, for richer or for poorer. We pledge fidelity to the spouse as we make ourselves physically, socially, emotionally, and spiritually vulnerable to and before each other. This revealing and giving of the self calls for faithfulness in response, and it demands trust, forgiveness, and acceptance on the part of both partners.

It is true that a good measure of healing and wholeness can be found elsewhere than in marriage—most notably in communities of faith, but also in many close companionships. Wherever the possibilities of healing occur, fidelity, trust, forgiveness, mutual edification, and acceptance are both necessary ethical principles and means for that healing, and at least some of the subjective effects of covenantal living become manifest. The very graciousness of such living takes us out of ourselves and makes alive in us a consciousness of the mystery of another realm of being, which we come to know in love.

The proper form of gratitude for these gracious gifts is to develop—in the arts, in the art of lovemaking, and in the covenants of mutual responsibility in which these occur—the most holy embodiments of these mysteries we can find. We offer, in other words, the best that humanity *can* offer to the source from which our humanity comes, and even as we acknowledge the relative inadequacy of our gift, we seek to conform it to the highest, widest, deepest, broadest model available to humanity. In brief, it may well be that ecumenical and, specifically, covenantal ideas of marriage more accurately grasp and guide human condition and understand the promise and perils of human love in the context of contemporary social and, especially, economic institutions than any known alternative.

Notes

Notes to Introduction

1. James Q. Wilson, *The Moral Sense* (New York: Free Press, 1993), 176.
2. Some may be puzzled by the distinction implied here between theology and religion, but this is one of the key reasons that a definition of theology as distinct from religion is used in this volume. Generally, theology may be understood in one of two ways. One, sometimes called the "confessional" or "dogmatic" definition, focuses primarily on the articulation of the assumptions or implications of a particular religious faith. The other, more "philosophical" or "apologetic" approach involves the critical and comparative analysis of religions, which are present in every culture, according to the ultimate standards that humanity can grasp—that is, God and reason, *theos* and *logos*. The second view is the one generally used here.
3. In the present study, I draw on essays that I developed while working on this book. Portions of the first chapter were offered at a conference at Brown University by Martha Nussbaum and Samuel Olyn in March 1996; portions of the second chapter are drawn from "The Moral Roots of the Corporation," *Theology and Public Policy* 5, 1 (summer 1993): 29–39; several themes in the fourth chapter appeared in "Beneath and Beyond the State," in *Welfare in America,* ed. S. Carlson-Thies and J. Skillen (Grand Rapids: Wm. B. Eerdmans Publishing Co., 1996); and sections of the fifth chapter will appear in "The Moral Meanings of Covenant," *Annual of the Society of Christian Ethics* (1996), 249–64.
4. C. Wright Mills, *The Power Elite* (New York: Oxford University Press, 1957), 6.
5. See Charles Lemert, *Sociology after the Crisis* (Boulder, Colo.: Westview Press, 1995), 3 and passim.
6. Edward O. Laumann, John H. Gagnon, Robert T. Michael, and Stuart Michaels, *The Social Organization of Sexuality* (Chicago: University of Chicago Press, 1994).
7. Lawrence Stone, "On Family Values," *New York Review of Books* (March 1989): 15.
8. This is the view, for example, of E. Barna, *The Future of the American Family* (Carol Stream, Ill.: Intervarsity Press, 1991), 33.

9. Alan Tapper, *The Family in the Welfare State* (Sydney: George Allen & Unwin Australia, 1990), chap. 7.

10. See Roderick Phillips, *Putting Asunder* (Cambridge: Cambridge University Press, 1988).

11. See David J. Garrow, *Liberty and Sexuality: The Right to Privacy and the Making of Roe v. Wade* (New York: Macmillan Publishing Co., 1994).

12. The first known text of this wedding formula of voluntary consent is in the Sarum Manual, probably dating to 1330–1340. See Kenneth Stevenson, *Nuptial Blessing: A Study of Christian Marriage Rites* (New York: Oxford University Press, 1983), 79–80 and 226n. 49. This formula also provides for the mutual exchange of rings, with all the sexual symbolism involved, in the name of the Trinity, a tradition possibly developed as early as the seventh century (136).

Notes to Chapter 1.
Sex and Marriage: An Intense Debate

1. See J. Gordon Melton, *The Churches Speak on Sex and Family Life* (Detroit: Gale Research Inc., 1991); and idem, *The Churches Speak on Homosexuality* (Detroit: Gale Research Inc., 1991). Cf. Mary McClintock Fulkerson, "Church Documents on Human Sexuality and the Authority of Scripture," *Interpretation* 49, 1 (January 1995): 46–58; Mark Ellingson, "Homosexuality and the Churches . . . " *Journal of Ecumenical Studies* 30, 3–4 (summer–fall 1993): 354–71; and the early analysis by Don S. Browning, "Homosexuality, Theology, the Social Sciences, and the Church," *Encounter* (July 1979): 223–43, which anticipates many of the issues.

2. This includes most Protestants, Catholics, and Orthodox Christians, but it excludes Baptists, who, with Mennonites and others, practice adult baptism. For the most part, the latter denominations deny a place in the church to homosexual persons. See Melton, *Sex and Family Life,* on the General Baptists, 132ff.; the Free Will Baptists, 143ff.; and the Southern Baptists, 200ff. The American Baptists now have the question under study, although some congregations have been "disassociated" for ordaining homosexual pastors.

3. The ambiguity in the United Church of Christ arises because statements by the General Synod are viewed as recommendations to local congregations. In fact, most congregations follow the ecumenical consensus, although national statements are more permissive. In the Episcopal Church, some bishops have ordained openly homosexual candidates for ministry; however, these bishops and the practice are sharply criticized by other bishops, and procedures are under way to condemn them.

4. Few doubt that gender stereotyping has deprived many women of equal opportunities in society and has supported patriarchal structures in much of human history. These matters demand redress in the name of justice.

More doubtful is whether gender is entirely a social artifact, constructed by males who use religion (and law, medicine, etc.) as a tool to oppress and control women, and whether gender analysis can honestly explain both biblical texts and theological affirmation. The 1993 consultation of feminist Christians, the "Re-Imagining Conference," involved efforts to invalidate key motifs in faith and theology by the use of gender analysis. The outrage and resistance in many churches was enormous.

5. Debates about artificial means of procreation and about adoption, especially in lesbian partnerships, are under way. As we shall see later, Protestants tend to be more open to technology than some other Christians when it comes to "responsible parenthood" and birth control, yet most are quite doubtful about lesbian artificial insemination and gay adoption. No definitive statements exist, and no official approval of the marriage of same-sex partners exists in any Christian church except the overtly gay congregations (e.g., the Metropolitan Community Churches), although some pastors unofficially bless them on the ground that it helps stabilize otherwise fragile relations. Others resist on the ground that such reasoning turns religious ritual into a psychosocial manipulation of sentiment and popular legitimacy. No reservations exist about the baptism of the child.

6. My colleagues Thomas Gillespie, Ulrich Mauser, and Charles Bartow have argued this point in Choon-Leong Seow, ed., *Homosexuality and Christian Community* (Louisville, Ky.: Westminster John Knox Press, 1996). Other contributors to the book are not fully convinced by their arguments or base their own arguments on quite different considerations, frequently on historicist or contextualist grounds that are suspicious of the continuing normative character of this "creational" order.

7. Two contrasting views are, I think, most suggestive in their summaries of the great interpretations of the past and in their fresh insights for today: Leon R. Kass, "Man and Woman: An Old Story" *First Things* (November 1991): 14–26; and Phyllis Trible, *God and the Rhetoric of Sexuality* (Philadelphia: Fortress Press, 1978).

8. To be sure, some Christian hermits held that this pattern was set aside by New Testament texts, such as 1 Corinthians 7, that tend to commend celibacy; but the associative implications of Christian theological anthropology very quickly demanded that they organize into monastic communities, and the Protestant churches doubted the place of celibacy except for those with special apostolic callings, for missiological purposes.

9. See the commentary on these matters by Richard Whitaker, "Sexuality and Creation," in Seow, ed., *Homosexuality*, 3–13.

10. Walter Brueggemann, *Genesis: An Interpretation* (Atlanta: John Knox Press, 1982), 47.

11. As far as I have been able to discover, every creation myth has a division of male and female linked with an ethic of order and fertility, but this is often found among the gods. Humans stay home and honor the god's generative activities. The biblical story is distinctive in that it locates sexuality in

creation and calls for humans to leave home and to create new institutions. Historically, a major debate about this new community has revolved around the priority of fidelity or fecundity to the right order of things, or as Thomas Aquinas wrote, of *fides* and *proles,* but some have argued that this third factor, the formation of new community and institutions, is central to the biblical record and decisive for the formation of the nuclear family. See Otto A. Piper, *The Christian Interpretation of Sex* (New York: Harper & Brothers, 1941).

12. In Prof. Seow's contribution to the book he edited (*Homosexuality and Christian Community,* 14–27), he argues for the importance of the wisdom tradition of biblical material, which, he suggests, points to the necessity of including experience and social-scientific perspectives in our understanding of moral issues and not only depending on Torah or the Prophets. I fully agree, although it is not clear that the wisdom literature should override these entirely or that the appeals to experience and social-scientific theories most frequently used by advocates of the ordination and marriage of homosexual persons are valid.

13. This suggests that marriage is to be "covenantal," a matter considered more extensively in chapter 5. In covenantal theory, particular judgments or policies ought, I believe, to include a synthesis of the three basic modes of discourse often called deontology, teleology, and ethology (or sometimes contextuality). See Max Stackhouse, "The Trinity as Public Theology," in *Faith to Creed,* ed. M. Heim (Grand Rapids: Wm. B. Eerdmans Publishing Co., 1991), 162–97.

14. However, the city that welcomes all peoples and is planted for their healing is "adorned as a bride" (Rev. 21:2).

15. Many Christian theologies depend on "natural law" theory to explain this knowledge of common morality. However, many Protestant scholars are skeptical of natural law insofar as it tends to suggest that the knowledge of God and of the biblical witnesses to God are quite unnecessary in matters of ethics, including the ethics of sexuality and marriage. Thus they insist on "common grace" or "general revelation" to identify this aspect of human moral knowledge, an emphasis that both allows recognition of the potential moral wisdom of nonbelievers and offers a theological, and not merely a naturalistic, account of the roots of that knowledge.

16. See John T. Noonan, *Contraception* (Cambridge, Mass.: Harvard University Press, 1965), which is as yet unsurpassed as a general study of the institutions guiding marriage in the early church.

17. I am much indebted to James T. Johnson, whose *A Society Ordained by God* (Nashville: Abingdon Press, 1970) remains one of the best treatments of the contrasts between Protestant and Catholic teachings on this matter.

18. This view is not held by all Protestants equally. Some quite "conservative" views hold that a great deal can be known about God's creational intent by studying nature, and some quite "liberal" Protestants have almost identified "creation" with "nature," as understood in the Enlightenment or even

in romanticism, and thus take whatever is found in nature as what God intended. We shall see later that some confusion in Protestant thought about nature, specifically in regard to homosexuality but also in regard to ecology and technology, has contributed to contemporary debates.

19. See Mark Ellingsen, *The Cutting Edge: How Churches Speak on Social Issues* (Geneva: Institute for Ecumenical Research, 1993); Ronald H. Preston, *Confusions in Christian Social Ethics: Problems for Geneva and Rome* (Grand Rapids: Wm. B. Eerdmans Publishing Co., 1995).

20. In this area there is some difference between "confessionalist" approaches to public theology, as represented by Martin Marty, Ronald Theimann, and Robert Benne, and the more "apologetic" approach seen in the work of Robin Lovin, James Skillin, Christopher Mooney, and myself, each in distinctive ways. For summary perspectives, see Robert Benne, *The Paradoxical Vision: A Public Theology for the Twenty-first Century* (Minneapolis: Fortress Press, 1995); and Max Stackhouse, *Public Theology and Political Economy* (Lanham, Md.: University Press of America, 1991).

21. See Noonan, *Contraception;* cf. Kenneth Stevenson, *Nuptial Blessing: A Study of Christian Marriage Rites* (New York: Oxford University Press, 1983).

22. See Christopher Brooke, *The Medieval Idea of Marriage* (Oxford: Oxford University Press, 1989); cf. Stevenson, *Nuptial Blessing.*

23. Quoted from Erasmus in Margo Todd, "The Spiritualized Household," in *Christian Humanism and the Puritan Social Order* (Cambridge: Cambridge University Press, 1987), 99. Todd's whole chapter is pertinent. Later, John Calvin made the same argument on biblical grounds. See his various references to the synecdochic meanings of Deut. 5:18–21 ("Thou shalt not commit adultery; . . . Neither shall you covet your neighbor's wife"); of Hosea 1 and 2 and of Prov. 2:17 (the adulteress who commits adultery, even by smooth words, forgets "her sacred covenant"); and of Eph. 5:25 ("Husbands, love your wives, just as Christ loved the church and gave himself up for her").

24. The best treatment of this reorientation can be found in John Witte, Jr., "The Transformation of Marriage Law in the Lutheran Reformation," in *The Weightier Matters of the Law: Essays on Law and Religion,* ed. John Witte, Jr., and Frank S. Alexander (Atlanta: Scholars Press, 1988), 57–97.

25. See Walter Kasper, *Theology of Christian Marriage* (New York: Seabury Press, 1980); and Stevenson, *Nuptial Blessing,* 134–40, especially in regard to the Reformers' influence on the *Prayer Book of 1549:* "It is at root a service which is thoroughly Reformed in theology, but in postmedieval dressing, with a dash of Luther and Henry here and there" (139).

26. However, Charles J. Reid, Jr., following Noonan, writes of the principle behind contract that "neither Roman law nor Germanic law made free consent central to the formation of marriage, and Gratian (who first codified church law on the matter, *Decretum,* in 1140) himself was forced to rely on rather meager authority to conclude in favour of freedom." See Charles

J. Reid, Jr., "The History of the Family," in L. Cahill and D. Mieth, *The Family* (London: SCM Press, 1995), 14; and John T. Noonan, "Power to Choose," *Viator* 4 (1973): 419–34.

27. We can see this rather dramatically in the widely read treatise by John Milton, "The Doctrine and Discipline of Divorce," in *The Complete Poetry and Selected Prose of John Milton* (New York: Modern Library, 1950), 615–62. But here we begin also to see the distinction between a theology of covenant and a legal arrangement based on contract.

28. See Johnson, *Society Ordained by God;* cf. F. W. Dillistone, *The Structure of the Divine Society* (Philadelphia: Westminster Press, 1949). Both authors accent the contrast between sacramental-organic and covenantal-associational modes of human interaction in church and in civil society. Both theories included the idea of "contract," which gradually became more distinct from both sacrament and covenant, with fateful implications for marriage. One can see this, for example, in the difference between a U.S. Supreme Court judgment at the end of the nineteenth century and one at the end of the twentieth. In 1888 the Court spoke of marriage as "something more than a mere contract. . . . It is an institution . . . , for it is the foundation of the family of society" (*Maynard v. Hill,* 125 U.S. 190 (1888), 210–11). But in 1972 the Court ruled that "the married couple is not an independent entity . . . , but an association of two individuals" (*Eisenstadt v. Baird,* 405 U.S. 438 (1972), p. 453). These changing views are treated in Carl Anderson, "The Supreme Court and the Economics of the Family," *Family in America* 1 (October 1987): 1–8. The former ruling includes the personal and voluntary element in the latter but the latter denies the bonded element in the former.

29. See Max Stackhouse, *Creeds, Society, and Human Rights* (Grand Rapids: Wm. B. Eerdmans Publishing Co., 1986).

30. A key historiographic treatment of these themes is John Witte, Jr., "Blest Be the Ties That Bind: Covenant and Community in Puritan Thought," *Emory Law Journal* 36 (1987): 579–601.

31. A very helpful treatment of these themes is Joseph L. Allen, *Love and Conflict: A Covenantal Model of Christian Ethics* (Nashville: Abingdon Press, 1984).

32. Historically, the term *compactum,* from which we get "contract," signals a voluntary agreement, but it also includes the notion that the terms of the agreement were pre-given and can be morally or legally voided if these terms are not met. See John Witte, "From Sacrament to Contract: The Legal Transformations of the Western Family," *Criterion* (Fall 1996), 1–12. A later distinction between *covenant* and *contract* begins to suggest that "social contracts" are wholly constructed by human will and voluntary, mutual actions between adults are exempt from theological-ethical evaluation. Similar ideas can be found in Rousseau but became influential in ecumenical circles, with regard to sexuality, at the hands of the Quakers. See *Towards a Quaker View of Sex* (London and Philadelphia: Friends Home

Service Committee, 1963). Cf. P. Ramsey, "On Taking Sexual Responsibility Seriously Enough," in *Deeds and Rules in Christian Ethics* (New York: Charles Scribner's Sons, 1967).

33. See Stevenson, *Nuptial Blessing*, 153–66, for the genealogy of marriage rites from Calvin in 1542 through John Knox in 1555, Thomas Cranmer in 1559, and Richard Baxter in 1661 to the Methodists, Presbyterians, Congregationalists, Baptists, and, eventually, Unitarians.

34. Stevenson points out that in the mid-nineteenth century, the Reformed Episcopal Church reproduced the rite that became most famous in the United States, but one phrase, which had been debated since 1555 yet used in this tradition for centuries—"with my body I thee worship"—was excised from the rituals (*Nuptial Blessing*, 148, 153).

35. At the popular level, one thinks of Hugh Hefner's "playboy philosophy," developed in his *Playboy* magazine in the 1960s; at the scholarly level, one thinks of the work of Michel Foucault, especially his *The History of Sexuality*.

36. See especially the superb study by Edmund Leites, *The Puritan Conscience and Modern Sexuality* (New Haven, Conn.: Yale University Press, 1986). It is fascinating that such an emphasis with regard to sexuality in marriage should occur simultaneously with the relative reduction of the focus on the sacraments in worship. It is quite likely that this development parallels what Max Weber proposed with regard to economics, namely, the movement of the ascetic ethic from the monastery to the world of work. Hence the "foretaste" of heaven is found as much in the disciplined ecstasies of the marriage bed as in the transubstantiated elements at the altar.

37. As far as I can see, it is protest against this loss and against the Victorian denial of the religious significance of sensuality that prompts some today to press in the opposite direction, although some do so in the extreme. See, e.g., *Sexuality and the Sacred*, ed. James B. Nelson and Sandra P. Longfellow (Louisville, Ky.: Westminster John Knox Press, 1994).

38. As we will see in later chapters, church, state, family, and economy became closely interwoven in the American colonies. In this connection, Edmund S. Morgan notes that weddings were performed by civil magistrates until 1686, and ministers began to perform them only after the colonial charters were revoked and royal sovereignty was proclaimed (*The Puritan Family: Religion and Domestic Relations in Seventeenth-Century New England*, rev. ed. [New York: Harper & Row, 1966], 32). But Morgan does not seem to see the significance of this. Before rule by the king, government was seen as a secondary, covenanted body politic, informed by the structures of the covenanted community of faith. When that could no longer be assured, the clergy assumed the responsibility of aiding the theological formation of the "little church," the "little commonwealth," that was the family.

39. Edmund Leites, "The Duty to Desire: Love, Friendship, and Sexuality in Some Puritan Theories of Marriage," *Comparative Civilization Review*, no. 3 (fall 1979): 40–82. See also Mary S. Van Leeuwen et al., *After Eden* (Grand

Rapids: Wm. B. Eerdmans Publishing Co., 1991), for what may be the best feminist treatment of many of these themes.

40. John Cotton, "A Meet Help: Or, a Wedding Sermon . . . " (Boston, 1699), cited by Morgan, *The Puritan Family*, 29.

41. See Morgan, *The Puritan Family*; and the striking new study by Stephen Innes, *Creating the Commonwealth: The Economic Culture of Puritan New England* (New York: W. W. Norton & Co., 1995).

42. This is, in some vocabularies, a distinction between private and public; but that distinction can obscure as much as it reveals, for it presumes that "public" has to do with law and government or sometimes with economic matters, whereas religion is public and much of economic life is quite private.

43. Very few studies of this matter seem to exist; but these accents can be seen in the attitudes of the most "liberal" heirs of the Puritans, when they met to discuss these matters and were surveyed by Yoshio Fukuyama in *The Views of General Synod Delegates on Human Sexuality* (New York: United Church Board for Homeland Ministries, 1977).

44. See Melton, *Homosexuality*.

45. H. Richard Niebuhr, *The Kingdom of God in America* (New York: Harper & Brothers, 1937), 193.

46. Todd, *Christian Humanism*.

47. See, for example, *Human Sexuality* (Philadelphia: United Church Press/ Pilgrim Press, 1977). Cf. also a recent manual for ministry, *Created in God's Image*, by M. E. Haines and B. Stackhouse (New York: United Church Board of Homeland Ministries, 1995), and two study volumes under the same title by Eleanore S. Morrison and Melanie Morrison.

48. I fear this is the temptation of Mark Burrows, "The Pluralism of Grace: Homosexuality and Communion in the Church," *On the Way* 12, 1 (summer 1995): 5–25, the best paper on the topic in this UCC journal.

49. Noted UCC pastor Herbert Davis offered this formulation in criticism of the direction of the UCC and its tendency to approximate the Unitarian Universalist Association (UUA). See his "The World May Need More Than Love," *Unitarian Universalist Christian* (spring–summer 1994): 37.

50. Quoted in ibid.

51. See World Council of Churches (WCC), *Consultation of the Department on Cooperation of Men and Women in Church, Family, and Society* (Geneva: WCC, 1963); and idem, *Consultation on Developing Relations of Men, Women, and Children* (Geneva: WCC, 1968).

52. On the relation of freedom to holiness, see Max Stackhouse, "The Vocation of Christian Ethics Today," *Princeton Seminary Bulletin* 16, 3 (1995): 284–312.

53. See the summary and critique of this study by William H. Lazareth, "ELCA Lutherans and Luther on Heterosexual Marriage," *Lutheran Quarterly* 7, 3 (fall 1994): 235–67.

54. See Melton, *Homosexuality*. Cf. also Wunibald Müller, *Homosexualität, eine*

Herausforderung für Theologie und Seelsorge (Mainz: Matthias-Grunewald-Verlag, 1986).

55. Thomas C. Oden, *Requiem: A Lament in Three Movements* (Nashville: Abingdon Press, 1995), has caused a lively debate by suggesting that most ecumenical seminary faculty members agree with the minorities.

56. Beverly Wildung Harrison, "Misogyny and Homophobia," in *Making the Connections* (Boston: Beacon Press, 1985), 135–36.

57. Ibid, 136.

58. See James Nelson, *Embodiment* (New York: Pilgrim Press, 1978), 180–235.

59. These are themes in many of his works, but this is a paraphrase of James Nelson, "The Liberal Approach to Sexual Ethics," in *Between Two Gardens* (New York: Pilgrim Press, 1993), 45–65.

60. Patricia Beattie Jung and Ralph F. Smith, *Heterosexism: An Ethical Challenge.* (Albany: State University of New York Press, 1993).

61. Ibid, 19.

62. David Greenberg, *The Construction of Homosexuality* (Chicago: University of Chicago Press, 1988), chap. 9, especially pp. 409–11.

63. This view is the key to the very influential study by Michel Foucault, *History of Sexuality,* 3 vols. (New York: Vintage Books, 1980), especially vol 1.

64. Pim Pronk, *Against Nature? Types of Moral Argumentation regarding Homosexuality,* trans. John Vriend, foreword by Hendrik Hart (Grand Rapids: Wm. B. Eerdmans Publishing Co., 1993).

65. This is so in spite of the fact that many use medical and theological references. The basic logic of practical reasoning selects the evidence. See, e.g., Task Force to Study Ministries to Gay and Lesbian Persons, "Faithful Inquiry" (report presented to the Annual Conference of the United Methodist Church in Minnesota, 1993).

66. The use of amniocentesis to reveal the sex of a fetus, the prospect of genetic engineering, and the possibility of determining the sex of child by selective abortion introduce a necessary qualification at this point. The preferences for a male child that have led to practice of the last option on a massive scale in India and China, according to repeated press reports, mean that parental intentionality is already shaping the sex of a generation. Still, a person does not intend his or her *own* sex, although we have some choice as to how we live out what is given to us, both personally and in our accommodation to or resistance to culturally defined gender roles. Sex comes to us as a given, even if some feel strange to what is given, especially when reinforced by strong gender definitions and role stereotypes. What is not clear is whether all three medical breakthroughs—amniocentesis, genetic engineering, selective abortion—are equally subject to programmatic alteration, as some of the research on sex-change operations suggests.

67. One possible exception in regard to women is the nursing of infants. Nothing like that obtains for racial groupings, which, as Jon Gunneman recently wrote, are "simply a moment in the evolutionary drama, [in which] . . . the intermingling, conjoining and eventual unity of the species is an ineluctable

destiny" ("Alchemic Temptations," *Annual of the Society of Christian Ethics* [1995]: 15). With the exception of a few lesbians who artificially inseminate and thereby seek to imitate heterosexual reproductive behavior, homosexually oriented persons participate in neither of these activities—procreation and nursing of infants—as they form the future.

68. In May 1995 the U.S. Court of Appeals for the Second Circuit in Cincinnati, Ohio, issued a judgment that is likely to be reviewed by the U.S. Supreme Court, namely, that homosexuals "do not constitute a distinct, identifiable group that can be singled out for special protection. Gays, lesbians, and bisexuals are not a special group that can be identified as persons of a given race can be. Homosexuals might be defined by their special conduct, but that conduct is not protected by the Constitution." See "Cincinnati Court Rules Against Gay Group," *The Witness* 16, 2 (fall 1995): 10.

69. I have argued this point also in relation to some contemporary ecological arguments. See Max Stackhouse, "Can 'Sustainability' be Sustained? A Review Essay of John B. Cobb, *Sustainability,*" *Princeton Seminary Bulletin* 15, 2, n.s. (1994): 143–55.

70. See Allan Carlson, "The Religious Possibility," in *From Cottage to Work Station: The Family's Search for Harmony in the Industrial Age* (San Francisco: Ignatius Press, 1993), esp. 98–102. Cf. also the writings of John Boswell, Peter Coleman, John H. McNeill, Robin Scroggs, and the extensive bibliographies mentioned in Jung and Smith, *Heterosexism,* and in Pronk, *Against Nature?* On the other side, see James Skillen, "The Political Confusion of the Christian Coalition," *Christian Century* (August 30–September 6, 1965): 815–21.

Notes to Chapter 2. Household and Work:
On Sex, Economics, and Power

1. It is widely recognized in the West that the Hebrew *bayît* and the Greek *oikos* may mean house, home, estate, or property. Similarly with the Latin *familia,* although *domus* is usually used for home or house. Clearly, *oikos* is the root word for both economics and ecology. Similar, if not identical, meanings can be found in the Sanskrit *grhya,* the Chinese *jia,* and the Japanese *ei.* See Francis I. K. Hsu, *Iemoto: The Heart of Japan* (New York: Schenkman Publishing Co., 1975); and F. L. K. Hsu, *Caste, Club and Clan* (Princeton, N.J., and New York: D. Van Nostrand Co., 1963).

2. See Talcott Parsons's summary of the evidence a generation ago in "Part Two—Introduction," in *Theories of Society* (New York: Free Press of Glencoe, 1961), 1:240.

3. The view of early matriarchy was first set forth by John F. McLennan, *Primitive Marriage* (1866); that of the transition to patriarchy by Henry Maine, *Lectures on the Early History of Institutions* (1975). Both are now seriously doubted. Of matriarchy, the *Dictionary of the Social Sciences,* ed.

Julius Gould and William Kolb (New York: Free Press, 1964), now says, "Anthropologists now agree that there is no evidence to substantiate the claim that any society has ever been under such control"; and of patriarchy it says that the term has "now nearly disappeared from the vocabulary of the social scientist." However, the terms have been widely adopted in literary, philosophical, and political circles to refer to preferred or opposed institutionalized gender roles.

4. See Lewis H. Morgan, *Ancient Society* (New York: Holt, Rinehart & Winston, 1877), and idem, *Systems of Consanguinity and Affinity of the Human Race* (Washington, D. C.: Smithsonian, 1979); Baldwin Spencer and F. J. Gillen, *Native Tribes of Central Australia* (London: Anthropological Institute, 1904).

5. For obvious reasons this theory was attractive to Marx, and he quotes Morgan in the *Manifesto*. The rebirth of the nineteenth century's love for communitarian theories during the 1960s and 1970s was not limited to Marxism, however; see Raymond L. Muncy, *Sex and Marriage in Utopian Communities: Nineteenth Century America* (Bloomington: Indiana University Press, 1973).

6. McLennan, *Primitive Marriage*. Cf., for example, Herbert Marcuse, *Eros and Civilization* (Boston: Beacon Press, 1955).

7. Stephanie Coontz, *The Social Origins of Private Life: A History of American Families, 1600–1900* (London: Verso Press, 1988).

8. Ibid., 46.

9. Ibid., 52–57.

10. Ibid., 73.

11. C. N. Starcke, *The Primitive Family* (London: Kegan & Paul, 1889); and Edward A. Westermark, *The History of Human Marriage* (London: Kegan & Paul, 1891).

12. See Max Stackhouse, "The World Religions and Political Democracy: Some Comparative Reflections," *Religion and Society* 29, 4 (December 1982): 19–49.

13. See Max Stackhouse, *Creeds, Society, and Human Rights* (Grand Rapids: Wm. B Ferdmans Publishing Co., 1986), especially chaps. 7 and 8.

14. See Peter van der Veer, *Religious Nationalism: Hindus and Muslims in India* (Berkeley: University of California Press, 1984).

15. There are many treatments of these basic matters. See, for example, John O. Voll, *Islam: Continuity and Change in the Modern World* (Boulder, Colo.: Westview Press, 1982); and Mark Juergensmeyer, *The New Cold War: Religious Nationalism Confronts the Secular State* (Berkeley: University of California Press, 1991).

16. See Stackhouse, "World Religions," 19–49; John Esposito, *Islam: the Straight Path*, expanded ed. (New York: Oxford University Press, 1991), esp. 94–101; Bruce Lawrence, "Woman as Subject/Woman as Symbol: Islamic Fundamentalism and the Status of Women," *Journal of Religious Ethics* 22, 1 (spring 1994): 163–88; and Jane I. Smith, "Islam," in *Women*

in World Religions, ed. A. Sharma (Albany: State University of New York Press, 1987), 235–50.

17. J. Spencer Trimingham, *The Sufi Orders in Islam* (London: Oxford University Press, 1971).

18. The Mahayana traditions have to be seen in the context of Confucian influences, and the Tibetan tradition is unique. Thus one gets a clearer picture from the Theravada traditions in Sri Lanka, Myanmar, Thailand, and, to a degree, Cambodia. These matters, however, are extensively debated by specialists, and each region and subtradition has distinctive features. My view of the decisive features of the various traditions is best summarized in "Politics and Religion," in *Encyclopedia of Religion,* 16 vols., ed. M. Eliade, et al., (New York: Macmillan Publishing Co., 1987), 11:408–22.

19. See Stackhouse, "World Religions," 19–49. Cf. Russell F. Sizemore and Donald K. Swearer, eds., *Ethics, Wealth and Salvation: A Study in Buddhist Social Ethics* (Columbia: University of South Carolina Press, 1990).

20. See the striking new book by Francis Fukuyama, *Trust: The Social Virtues and the Creation of Prosperity* (New York: Free Press, 1995), which treats the relationship of familial, political, and economic institutions.

21. We return to these motifs in the last chapter, when we trace how the covenantal tradition modulated and transformed them.

22. See C. Bailey, *The Greek Atomists and Epicurus* (London: Oxford University Press, 1928).

23. Phillip H. De Lacy, "Epicurus," in *Encyclopedia of Philosophy,* 8 vols., ed. Paul Edwards (New York: Macmillan Co., 1967), 3:5.

24. See Phillip H. De Lacy, "Lucretius and the History of Epicureanism," *Transactions of the American Philosophical Association* (1979): 12–23.

25. R. E. Latham, "Lucretius," in *Encyclopedia of Philosophy,* 5:101.

26. The connections of classical and Renaissance thought that run from Bernard de Mandeville in Holland through Adam Smith in Scotland to John Stuart Mill and from Herman Heinrich Gossen in Germany and William Stanley Jevons in Britain to Alfred Marshall and contemporary neoclassical economics are traced by Robert G. Simons, *Competing Gospels: Public Theology and Economic Theory* (Alexandria, Australia: E. J. Dwyer, 1995), chapter 2.

27. No one has drawn the connection for the modern period quite so clearly as Edmund Leites, *The Puritan Conscience and Modern Sexuality* (New Haven, Conn.: Yale University Press, 1986).

28. See, especially, G.W.F. Hegel, *Reason in History: A General Introduction to the Philosophy of History,* trans. R. S. Hartman (New York: Library of Liberal Arts, 1953).

29. This paragraph is a restatement of the table of contents of G.W.F. Hegel's *Philosophy of Right,* trans. T. M. Knox (New York: Oxford University Press, 1967). Each step of this argument has direct references to Plato's *Republic* and to Aristotle's *Politics,* which this book intends to supersede.

30. See Gertrude Himmelfarb, "From Marx to Hegel," in *On Looking into the Abyss* (New York: Alfred A. Knopf, 1994), chap. 3, esp. 64–69. See also idem, *Marriage and Morals among the Victorians* (New York: Alfred A. Knopf, 1986), and her commentaries in idem, *On Liberty and Liberalism* (New York: Alfred A. Knopf, 1974).

31. See Max Stackhouse, "Religion and Society in a Marxist Land" and "The Socialist Creed," in *Creeds,* chaps. 5 and 6.

32. In spite of my appreciation of Fukuyama's work (see *Trust,* cited in n. 20, above), he misses this implication in his *The End of History and the Last Man* (New York: Free Press, 1992).

33. The efforts of many, such as Erich Fromm, ed., *Socialist Humanism* (New York: Doubleday, 1965); Michael Harrington, *Socialism* (New York: Saturday Review Press, 1970); Gustavo Gutiérrez, *A Theology of Liberation* (Maryknoll, N.Y.: Orbis Books 1971); and Paul Tillich, *The Socialist Decision* (German ed. 1933; New York: Harper & Row, 1977) almost persuaded me and an entire generation that Marx's thought could go in other directions; but the evidence against that conviction is now overwhelming. Marxism's incapacity to sustain family life and civil society is a key part of that evidence.

34. Marx's most extensive comments about the family appear in the works he wrote with Engels: *The German Ideology* (1845–1846) and *The Manifesto* (1848).

35. Among the many treatments of these ideas and their influence, see the particularly concise one by J. P. Diggins, "Feminists and Black Intellectuals," in *The Rise and Fall of the American Left,* rev. ed. (New York: Harcourt Brace Jovanovich, 1992), 124–44.

36. We have already seen some of this in the challenges to the theological traditions treated in chapter 1.

37. Gary S. Becker, *A Treatise on the Family* (Cambridge, Mass.: Harvard University Press, 1981; enlarged ed., 1991).

38. Richard A. Posner, *Sex and Reason* (Cambridge, Mass.: Harvard University Press, 1992).

39. Becker, *Treatise on the Family,* 8–9, summarizing chaps. 5–7.

40. Ibid. This is his summary of a major theme of chap. 8.

41. Ibid., 15.

42. Posner, *Sex and Reason,* 23–30.

43. Ibid., 30.

44. See ibid., 17; and for his varied references to Christian thought, especially chaps. 2 and 6, where he sometimes draws distinctions among these.

45. Ibid., 55–6.

46. Ibid., 181, and passim.

47. Ibid., 86.

48. Ibid., 324.

49. See Himmelfarb's remarkable essay on Mill's confusions, "Liberty: One Very Simple Principle?" in *Looking into the Abyss,* chap. 4, and note the contrast

with other forms of liberal theory—as found, for instance, in John Locke—in Leites, "The Political Meanings of Constancy," in *Puritan Conscience,* chap. 2.

50. Alan Wolfe, *Whose Keeper? Social Science and Moral Obligation* (Berkeley: University of California Press, 1989); David Popenoe, *Disturbing the Nest: Family Change and Decline in Modern Societies* (Berlin and New York: Walter de Gruyter, 1988). A fuller analysis of the pertinent data on this point will be presented in chapter 4.

51. Michael J. Piore, *Beyond Individualism* (Cambridge, Mass.: Harvard University Press, 1995), 23.

52. See William Everett, *God's Federal Republic* (New York: Paulist Press, 1988), esp. chap. 4, "Federalism: The Covenantal Heritage," and chap. 5, "The Covenanted Public"; and idem, *Blessed Be the Bond* (Philadelphia: Fortress Press, 1985), esp. 101–50 on "Covenanted Communion" and "Marital Vocation: A Societal Covenant."

53. This is the warranted assessment of Fukuyama, *Trust,* 45, as he treats the legacy of Weber's theory in the context of current comparative and historical studies that seek to understand social and economic development.

54. See G. P. Davis, *The Corporation* (New York: Harper & Brothers, 1908).

55. Stanley Lebergott, *The Americans: An Economic Record* (New York: W. W. Norton & Co., 1984), 45.

56. Nancy Cott, *The Bonds of Womanhood* (New Haven, Conn.: Yale University Press, 1977).

57. Ann Douglas, *The Feminization of American Culture* (New York: Alfred A. Knopf, 1978); Max Stackhouse, *Public Theology and Political Economy* (Grand Rapids: Wm. B. Eerdmans Publishing Co., 1986), esp. chaps. 4–6; and George Weigel, ed., *A New Worldly Order* (Washington, D.C.: Ethics and Public Policy Center, 1992).

58. Allan Carlson, *From Cottage to Work Station: The Family's Search for Harmony in the Industrial Age* (San Francisco: Ignatius Press, 1993), 37.

59. Quoted in Martha May, "The Historical Problem of the Family Wage: The Ford Motor Company and the Five Dollar Day," 8 vols., in Nancy Cott, *History of Women in the United States* (New York: K. G. Saur, 1992), vol. 5, part 1.

60. See Julie A. Matthaei, *An Economic History of Women in America* (New York: Schocken Books, 1982).

61. U.S. Bureau of the Census, *Work and Family Patterns of American Women,* Current Population Reports, P23–165 (Washington, D.C.: Government Printing Office, 1990).

62. Marianne A. Ferber, Brigid O'Farrell, and La Rue Allen, *Work and Family: Policies for a Changing Work Force* (Washington, D.C.: National Academy Press, 1991).

63. Ruth Schwartz Cowan, *More Work for Mother* (New York: Basic Books, 1983), 26.

64. Ibid., 45.

65. Juliet Schor, *The Overworked American* (New York: Basic Books, 1991), 87.

66. See Ferdinand Mount, *The Subversive Family* (New York: Free Press, 1992).

67. See Charles L. Glenn, *The Myth of the Common School* (Amherst: University of Massachusetts Press, 1988). The purpose of this move was, in part, to inculcate the values thought to be proper to a democratic, industrializing society.

68. See Robert L. Griswold, *Fatherhood in America: A History* (New York: Basic Books, 1993).

69. See Edward O. Laumann, John H. Gagnon, Robert T. Michael, and Stuart Michaels, *The Social Organization of Sexuality* (Chicago: University of Chicago Press, 1994).

70. Schor, *Overworked American,* chap. 1.

71. I have treated many of these factors in Max Stackhouse, "Reforming Protestant Views," in *Christian Social Ethics in a Global Era* (Nashville: Abingdon Press, 1995), 11–74.

72. E. Galinsky and D. Hughes, *The Fortune Magazine Child Care Study* (paper presented at the Annual Convention of the American Psychological Association, New York, 1987), cited in Ferber, *Work and Family,* 44.

73. D. Hughes, E. Galinsky, and A. Morris, "The Effects of Job Characteristics on Marital Quality: Specifying Linking Mechanisms," *Journal of Marriage and the Family* 54 (February 1992):31–42.

74. L. White and B. Keith, "The Effect of Shift Work on the Quality and Stability of Marital Relations," *Journal of Marriage and the Family* 52 (May 1990):453–62.

75. Barbara B. Bunker, Josephine M. Zubek, Virginia J. Vanderslice, and Robert W. Rice, "Quality of Life in Dual-Career Families: Commuting versus Single-Residence Couples," *Journal of Marriage and the Family* 54 (May 1992):399–407.

76. Dana Vannoy and William W. Philliber, "Wife's Employment and Quality of Marriage," *Journal of Marriage and the Family* 54 (May 1992): 387–98.

77. Elizabeth Menaghan and Toby Parcel, "Parental Employment and Family Life: Research in the 1980s," *Journal of Marriage and the Family* 52 (November 1990):1079–98; see also idem, *Parents' Jobs and Children's Lives* (Berlin and New York: Walter de Gruyter, 1994).

78. Harriet Presser, "Can We Make Time for Children? The Economy, Work Schedules, and Child Care," *Demography* 26 (November 1989): 33–42.

79. U.S. Bureau of the Census, *Who's Minding the Kids?,* prepared by L. Casper, M. Hawkins, and M. O'Connell, Current Population Reports, P70–36 (Washington, D.C.: Government Printing Office, 1994).

80. Ellen Galinsky, James T. Bond, and Dana E. Friedman, *The Changing Workforce* (New York: Families and Work Institute, 1993).

81. Ibid.

82. Phyllis Palmer, *Domesticity and Dirt: Housewives and Domestic Servants in the United States, 1920–1945* (Philadelphia: Temple University Press, 1990), 157–58. See the discussion, citing Palmer, of current views about the household services available on the commercial market by

David Cay Johnston, "The Servant Class Is at the Counter," *New York Times,* August 27, 1995, B–1.

Notes to Chapter 3.
Home and Religion: Sharing and Home Life

1. U.S. Department of Commerce, Economic and Statistic Administration, Bureau of the Census, "Current Business Reports," *Combined Annual and Revised Monthly Retail Trade* (Washington, D.C: Government Printing Office, January 1985–December 1994). I am grateful to economist Alden Sears for preparing a memorandum on this.
2. Leigh Eric Schmidt, *Consumer Rites: The Buying and Selling of American Holidays* (Princeton, N.J.: Princeton University Press, 1995), 4.
3. It is also quite remarkable that, for the most part, the social roles for performing these tasks are quite clearly defined. With some exceptions, it is frequently the women who know how, where, and for whom to shop, holding in their minds an enormous quantity of information about what is a good, fair, or exorbitant price and what the arts and proprieties of gift wrapping and holiday decoration are. The men, in turn, are expected to be sure not only that the resources for these festivities are at hand but that certain mechanical accoutrements—Christmas-tree stands, colored lights, materials for toy assembly, and so forth—are working properly. Nor are these definitions confined to this culture. I have observed non-Christian festivals in Indian, Chinese, and Indonesian cultures and recognized roughly comparable role divisions. This suggests that, for all the cultural and historical variation, some residual "creational" distinctions between men and women may exist, beyond than the biological differences in the procreational process, and account for some portion of stereotyped sexual behavior.
4. Alden Sears, "The Relative Importance of Housing in the Economy and for Individual Spending Units," memorandum prepared for this book, November 4, 1995. See also Elaine T. May, *Homeward Bound* (New York: Basic Books, 1988), who argues that nearly all of the increase in the gross national product recorded in the mid-1950s came from family-related spending.
5. Irving Welfeld, *Where We Live: The American Home and the Social, Political and Economic Landscape from Slums to Suburbs* (New York: Simon & Schuster, 1988), 15–16.
6. Ibid., 144–47.
7. Ibid., 16.
8. Numa Denis Fustel de Coulanges, *The Ancient City: A Study on the Religion, Laws, and Institutions of Greece and Rome,* trans. W. Small in 1873 and published several times in English (Garden City, N.Y.: Doubleday Anchor, nd). It has recently been republished with a new introduction by S. C. Humphreys and Anoldo Mornigliano (Baltimore: Johns Hopkins University Press, 1980).

9. One wonders if the authors of the Southern Baptist Convention's publication *Home Life,* which features a section titled "Altar Fires" with devotional reading for family prayers, are alert to how ancient the practice they are echoing is. See William Leonard, "Southern Baptist: Family as Witness of Grace in the Community," in Phyllis Airhart and Margaret Bendroth, eds., *Faith Traditions and the Family* (Louisville, Ky.: Westminster John Knox Press, 1996).

10. Fustel, *The Ancient City,* books 1–3.

11. Ibid., 63. Cf. book 3, chap. 1, "The Phratry and the Cury: Tribe."

12. Ibid., 120–21.

13. Scholars who argue that the distinction between private and public is caused by modern, bourgeois patterns of life, such as Stephanie Coontz (*The Social Origins of Private Life: A History of American Families, 1600–1900* [London: Verso Press, 1988]), may know well how these matters are perceived today, but it is doubtful that they know the root causes of this separation.

14. Common to both, interestingly enough, were Hestia (Vesta, in Latin), who was the goddess of the hearth. In household worship, however, she was often connected with fertility. In city worship—city councils were held around the public cult hearth of Hestia—she was a virgin. Vesta, however, had relations with Mars, and their twin sons, Romulus and Remus, were raised by a she-wolf. They were the founders of Rome, according to legend, although Romulus also defeated Remus in a fight and Romulus captured and raped the Sabine women in order to populate the new city. The empire, in other words, wedded sexual and military aggression and violated both household and city sacredness. The new sacred fires were protected by the vestal virgins and by the Roman armies—each quite gender- and role-distinct.

15. See Alan Soble, *The Structure of Love* (New Haven, Conn.: Yale University Press, 1990), especially chap. 5, "Aristophanic Love," and passim; see chap. 2 of his book for a synopsis of how this theme has entered contemporary life.

16. The attribution of the fall of Rome in part to this by Edward Gibbon, who became a Roman Catholic and was pressured by his father to become again a Calvinist Protestant, had no small effect on American thought. His famous *The History of the Decline and Fall of the Roman Empire* was first published in six volumes from 1776 to 1788.

17. Paul Veyne, ed., *A History of Private Life,* vol. 1: *From Pagan Rome to Byzantium* (Cambridge, Mass.: Harvard University Press, 1987), esp. 51–70.

18. Georges Dumézil, *The Destiny of the Warrior* (Chicago: Chicago University Press, 1970).

19. It is not possible here to treat the several directions in which this development led. One was toward feudalism, as we shall shortly see. Another was toward federated communities under common law, a matter we discuss in chapter 5. But some of the *comitati* evidently established traditions

of radical enclaves of resistance to all imperial and federal authority—traditions still quite alive in sectarian, racist, and survivalist groups.

20. Fustel wrote, for example, "There is some analogy between the client (the dependent servant, included in the wider household) of ancient times and the serf of the middle ages. The principle which condemned them to obedience was not the same . . . , [but] the subordination of the client and of the serf was the same; the one was bound to his patron as the other was bound to his lord; the client could no more quit the gens [public] than the serf could quit the glebe [private]" (*Ancient City,* 257). The noted contemporary medievalist Georges Duby has traced the definitions of the terms *public* and *private* from classical Latin through the Middle Ages to nineteenth-century Europe and concludes that "it remained essentially unchanged in the interim" (See Georges Duby, ed., *A History of Private Life,* vol. 2: *Revelations of the Medieval World* [Cambridge, Mass.: Harvard University Press, 1988], 4–5.

21. See Garth Fowden, *Empire to Commonwealth: The Consequences of Monotheism in Late Antiquity* (Princeton, N.J.: Princeton University Press, 1993).

22. See Kathleen McVey, "Christianity and Culture, Dead White European Males, and the Study of Patristics," *Princeton Seminary Bulletin* 15, 2, n.s. (1994):103–30.

23. I have treated his claims in this regard elsewhere; see C. N. Cochrane, *Christianity and Classical Culture* (New York: Oxford University Press, 1957); and Max Stackhouse, *Ethics and the Urban Ethos* (Boston: Beacon Press, 1972).

24. Many of the key themes and some of the early documents can be found in Paul A. Holmes, "Betrothal: A Liturgical Rite" (*Dissertatio ad lauream,* Pontificia Studiorum Universitas, Rome, 1991).

25. Christopher Broke, *The Medieval Idea of Marriage* (New York: Oxford University Press, 1989), especially chaps. 3 and 6.

26. See Max Weber, *Economy and Society,* vol. 3, *The City,* trans. G. Roth and C. Wittich Berman (1918[?]; reprint, Philadelphia: Bedminster Press, 1969); and Harold Berman, *Law and Revolution* (Cambridge, Mass.: Harvard University Press, 1983).

27. Avihu Zakai has conveniently summarized the changing reputation of the Puritans in American historiography in his "Epiphany at Matadi: Perry Miller's *Orthodoxy in Massachusetts* and the Meaning of American History," *Reviews in American History* (December 1985): 627–41. He shows how a generation of historians in the early part of the century depicted the Puritans as opponents of liberal and democratic traditions and as preoccupied with repressive religious ideologies; how Perry Miller revolutionized the study of the Puritans by showing that view to be false; and how contemporary scholars, refining and correcting some of Miller's ambiguous conclusions, are recognizing the enduring contributions of the Puritans.

28. See Max Stackhouse, "Peace in Church, Family and State: A Reformed View," in *Baptism, Peace and the State,* ed. R. T. Bender and A.P.F. Sell (Waterloo, Canada: W. Laurier University Press, 1991), 69–85.

29. On this speech and a major interpretation of its significance in American social life, see Robert N. Bellah, *The Broken Covenant* (New York: Seabury Press, 1978).

30. Gwendolyn Wright, *Building the Dream: A Social History of Housing in America* (Cambridge, Mass.: MIT Press, 1993), 8.

31. Ibid., 9.

32. The Puritans were not absolutely consistent in this. In his pioneering book on these matters, Edmund S. Morgan cites John Cotton's commentary on Ecclesiastes, *A Briefe Exposition . . .* (London, 1654), where Cotton seems to be speaking in terms of the developmental stages of the individual when he writes that God constituted an order in society that presupposed his "appointment of mankind to live in Societies, Firstly of Family, Secondly Church, Thirdly Common-Wealth." See Edmund S. Morgan, *The Puritan Family: Religion and Domestic Relations in Seventeenth-Century New England*, rev. ed. (New York: Harper & Row, 1966), 18.

33. Morgan, *The Puritan Family*. The tension between familial and personal membership in the church led to controversies over the "halfway covenant," by which someone nurtured in a Christian family was presumed to be a believer. When this was challenged by the greatest theologian of the period, Jonathan Edwards, he was dismissed from his pulpit. He excluded from communion those who had no mature personal experience of or commitment to Christ, since Christianity, for all its support of the family, is not familial or hereditary but associative.

34. Wright, *Building the Dream*, 9.

35. E. D. Baltzell, *Puritan Boston and Quaker Philadelphia* (Boston: Beacon Press, 1979).

36. Ibid, 35.

37. Wright, *Building the Dream*, chap. 2.

38. See James H. Cone and Gayraud S. Wilmore, *Black Theology: A Documentary History*, 2 vols., rev. ed. (Maryknoll, N.Y.: Orbis Books, 1993). These volumes, however, make no significant reference to family life.

39. I am well aware that the thesis by Will Herberg in his *Protestant, Catholic, Jew* (Garden City, N.Y.: Doubleday & Co., 1955) is under suspicion on several points, but it is not clear that he was altogether wrong in arguing that a certain commonality was formed. I think such a commonality persists, and that it does so on the basis of principles established by the Puritan wing of American religious thought, as modulated by Enlightenment liberalism in the tradition, especially that of Locke. See Max Stackhouse, *Creeds, Society and Human Rights* (Grand Rapids: Wm. B. Eerdmans Publishing Co., 1984). Regarding Catholicism, the impact of Vatican II, much influenced by American thinking at the hands of John Courtney Murray and others, is still present. And modern Judaism continues to be influenced by themes identified by Albert Gordon a generation ago in *Jews in Suburbia* (Boston: Beacon Press, 1959).

40. See the treatment of Adams's thought, as compared to that of his Southern colleagues, by David Flaherty, "Law and the Enforcement of Morals in Early America," *Perspectives in American History* 5 (1971): 247.

41. The references to nations imply not only foreign governments but the Native American peoples, whose cultures were family-, clan-, or tribe-based. Their rights were often violated and frequently revised, and their inclusion in civil society was marginal. The states, of course, had great power in the federal period and were guaranteed certain powers in the Bill of Rights. However, for quite good reason in the struggle over slavery, the actions of the slave states prompted the repeal of the Tenth Amendment. Thus nothing constitutionally stood between the individual making a contract and the strengthened federal government except the freedom of religion, and on that basis, the rights of assembly, speech, and press. See R. C. White, Jr., and A. G. Zimmermann, *An Unsettled Arena: Religion and the Bill of Rights* (Grand Rapids: Wm. B. Eerdmans Publishing Co., 1990).

42. Jan Shipps, *Mormonism: The Story of a New Religious Movement* (Urbana: University of Illinois Press, 1984); cf. Klaus Hansen, "Mormonism," in *The Encyclopedia of Religion,* ed. M. Eliade et al. (New York: Macmillan, 1987), 108–12.

43. The main lines of the tradition were altered toward monogamy by a later revelation, after sometimes violent attacks on believers by vigilante Christians, protofeminists, and the U.S. government. The familism of the tradition excluded black peoples from church leadership for more than a century, but this, too, has been reversed by revelatory insight.

44. See Richard C. Wade, *The Urban Frontier* (Cambridge, Mass.: Harvard University Press, 1959).

45. See Arthur Vidich and Joseph Bensman, *Small Town in Mass Society: Class Power and Religion in a Rural Community* (Garden City, N.J.: Doubleday & Co., 1958).

46. In recognition of these factors of human social consciousness, Gibson Winter, *The New Creation as Metropolis* (New York: Macmillan Co., 1963), and Harvey Cox, *The Secular City* (New York: Macmillan Co., 1965), find in the city the true locus of God's activity. Cf. Stackhouse, *Ethics and the Urban Ethos.*

47. I am, throughout this portion of the chapter, deeply indebted to Wright, *Building the Dream,* esp. chap. 4. Many of her themes are confirmed by Allan Carlson, *From Cottage to Work Station: The Family's Search for Social Harmony in the Industrial Age* (San Francisco: Ignatius Press, 1993).

48. Wright, *Building the Dream,* 61.

49. Although they focus more on the relationships between religion, labor, and management than on family life, two pioneering and indispensable studies of this tradition and its consequences can be found in Liston Pope, *Millhands and Preachers* (New Haven, Conn.: Yale University Press, 1942); and John R. Earle, Dean D. Knudsen and Donald W. Shriver, Jr., *Spindles and Spires* (Atlanta: John Knox Press, 1966).

50. Wright, *Building the Dream,* 67.

51. Welfeld argues that the growth of the suburbs was possible because the developers brought the factory to the fields being developed, reproducing a highly mobile industrial plant on the scene. Further, the trend was reinforced by new methods of insurance, reducing risk, and especially by the

mortgage provisions of the New Deal (1934–1938) and the Veterans Administration (1947–1949). See, especially, Welfield, *Where We Live,* 25–72.

52. Ibid., 99.

53. Wright reproduces this image in *Building the Dream,* 101, along with several others (98) and photographs of housing from the period that approximates the image (103, 105).

54. See Stackhouse, *Ethics and the Urban Ethos.*

55. See, especially, Colin Campbell, *The Romantic Ethic and the Spirit of Consumerism* (Oxford: Basil Blackwell Publisher, 1987).

56. James Dombrowski, *The Early Days of Christian Socialism in America* (New York: Columbia University Press, 1936).

57. See Campbell, *Romantic Ethic;* and Charles H. Hopkins, *The Rise of the Social Gospel in American Protestantism, 1865–1915* (New Haven, Conn.: Yale University Press, 1940).

58. Ann Douglas, *The Feminization of American Culture* (New York: Alfred A. Knopf, 1978). Cf. G. Winter, *The Suburban Captivity of the Church* (New York: Macmillan Co., 1961).

59. This is a valid insight in the otherwise highly ideological and questionable volume of Stephanie Coontz, *The Way We Never Were: American Families and the Nostalgia Trap* (New York: Basic Books, 1992).

60. Carlson, *From Cottage to Work Station,* 65–66. Cf. Welfeld, *Where We Live,* chap. 3.

61. Abrams is quoted by Welfeld, *Where We Live,* 126.

62. Wright, *Building the Dream,* 220–22.

63. Welfeld, *Where We Live,* chap. 8.

64. William Leach, *Land of Desire* (New York: Pantheon Books, 1993).

65. Francis Fukuyama, *Trust: The Social Virtues and the Creation of Prosperity* (New York: Free Press, 1995).

66. Ibid., 4.

67. Ibid., 5–6.

68. Ibid., 127.

69. Other major scholars have reached similar conclusions on the basis of comparative studies. See James Fallows, *Looking at the Sun: The Rise of the New East Asian Economic and Political System* (New York: Pantheon Books, 1994); and Dennis McCann, "Reforming Wisdom from the East," in *Christian Social Ethics in a Global Era,* ed. M. Stackhouse (Nashville: Abingdon Press, 1995).

Notes to Chapter 4. Welfare and Children:
The Family in State and Society

This chapter was written with Deirdre Hainsworth, research assistant for the entire volume.

1. See, for example, "A Progressive, Ethical Covenant with American Families" (draft document prepared for the Summit on Ethics and Meaning in

Washington, D.C., which was sponsored by *Tikkun* [a Jewish journal] and by several liberal Christian leaders, spring 1996).

2. See Charles Glenn, "Free Schools and the Revival of Urban Communities," in *Welfare in America,* ed. S. W. Carlson-Thies and J. W. Skillen (Grand Rapids: Wm. B. Eerdmans Publishing Co., 1996), 393–425.

3. In many cultures marriage is an alliance between families, ratified or enforced by the courts in cases of dispute. In other cultures, two ceremonies are common: a civil registration and a religious service. In most western countries, however, under the influence of Catholic and Reformed traditions, the clergy serve as officers of the state as well as of the church in performing the service. The pastor, priest, or rabbi is simultaneously a justice of the peace and the presiding officer of the religious community in certifying the fact of marriage and filing the license.

4. The best single study is Alan Tapper, *The Family in the Welfare State* (Sydney: George Allen & Unwin Australia, 1990). Although focusing on the Australian situation, Tapper treats the comparative data of North America, Europe, and Japan.

5. See M. L. Stackhouse, Peter Berger, Dennis P. McCann, and M. Douglas Meeks, *Christian Social Ethics in a Global Era* (Nashville: Abingdon Press, 1995).

6. Michael B. Katz, *In the Shadow of the Poorhouse* (New York: Basic Books, 1986), 11.

7. Gertrude Himmelfarb, *Poverty and Compassion* (New York: Alfred A. Knopf, 1991), 483–85; see also the introduction.

8. Lester M. Salamon, *Partners in Public Service* (Baltimore: Johns Hopkins University Press, 1995), 86.

9. Himmelfarb, *Poverty,* 7.

10. See my earlier treatments of the Social Gospel and the *Social Encyclicals* as Protestant and Catholic influences on social thought: Max Stackhouse, "Jesus and Economics: A Century of Christian Reflection on the Economic Order," in *The Bible in American Law, Politics and Political Rhetoric,* ed. James T. Johnson (SBL Centennial Series 5; Decatur, Ga.: Scholars Press, 1985), 107–52; and idem, "Liberalism Revisited: From the Social Gospel to Public Theology," in *Being Christian Today: An American Conversation,* ed. R. J. Neuhaus and G. Weigel (Washington, D.C.: Ethics and Public Policy Center, 1992), 33–58.

11. Katz, *Shadow of the Poorhouse,* 147.

12. Ibid., 191.

13. See Allan Carlson, "The Family Wage Experiment," in *From Cottage to Work Station: The Family's Search for Social Harmony in the Industrial Age* (San Francisco: Ignatius Press, 1993), esp. 38; cf. also Federal Council of Churches, "The Church and Modern Industry: A Resolution Unanimously Adopted by the Federal Council of Churches, 1908," reprinted in Max Stackhouse, *Creeds, Society, and Human Rights* (Grand Rapids: Wm. B. Eerdmans Publishing Co., 1986), appendix 3. Carlson's documentation is accurate, although he is much opposed to government interference in the market and in family life.

14. Theda Skocpol, *Protecting Soldiers and Mothers* (Cambridge, Mass.: Harvard University Press, 1992).
15. Katz, *Shadow of the Poorhouse,* 208.
16. Ibid., 207.
17. In a new study, Michael S. Sherry argues that the "War on Poverty" was one of several manifestations of the militarization of American culture in the struggles against fascism and communism, which motivated the expansion of governmental functions and legitimated the willingness to go into debt in order to accomplish good by defeating evil. Further, in a military organization, people may be identified by rank or by fighting unit, but they are not properly divided according to familial, religious, cultural, professional, or social associations: if anything, these are systematically reduced in importance. See Michael S. Sherry, *In The Shadow of War: The United States since the 1930's* (New Haven, Conn.: Yale University Press, 1995).
18. Mary Jo Bane and David Ellwood, *Welfare Realities* (Cambridge, Mass.: Harvard University Press, 1994).
19. Katz, *Shadow of the Poorhouse,* 263.
20. See Lawrence Mead, *The New Politics of Poverty* (New York: Basic Books, 1992).
21. Sheldon Danziger and Daniel Weinberg, "The Historical Record: Trends in Family Income, Inequality, and Poverty," in Sheldon Danziger, Gary Sandefur, and Daniel Weinberg, eds., *Confronting Poverty* (Cambridge, Mass.: Harvard University Press, 1994), chap. 2.
22. Blanche D. Coll, *Safety Net* (New Brunswick, N.J.: Rutgers University Press, 1995), 238, 281.
23. Introduction to Danziger, Sandefur, and Weinberg, eds., *Confronting Poverty.*
24. See Martha Bayles, *Hole in Our Soul: The Loss of Beauty and Meaning in American Popular Music* (New York: Free Press, 1994).
25. U.S. Bureau of the Census, *Population Profile of the United States,* Publication P23–185. (Washington, D.C.: Government Printing Office, 1993), 17.
26. Mead, *New Politics of Poverty,* 53.
27 Bureau of the Census, *Population Profile,* 28.
28. See those authors who have done comparative studies: Alan Wolfe, *Whose Keeper? Social Science and Moral Obligation* (Berkeley: University of California Press, 1989); David Popenoe, *Disturbing the Nest: Family Change and Decline in Modern Societies* (Berlin and New York: Walter de Gruyter, 1988); Richard A. Posner, *Sex and Reason* (Cambridge, Mass.: Harvard University Press, 1992); and Tapper, *Family in the Welfare State,* although they do not agree politically.
29. Charles Murray, *Losing Ground* (New York: Basic Books, 1984), 212.
30. Ibid., 216.
31. Ibid., 228.
32. Mead, *New Politics of Poverty,* 211.
33. Ibid., 56.

34. William Julius Wilson, *The Truly Disadvantaged* (Chicago: University of Chicago Press, 1987).

35. Glenn Loury, *One by One, from the Inside Out: Essays and Reviews on Race and Responsibility in America* (New York: Free Press, 1995), 12.

36. Bane and Ellwood, *Welfare Realities,* 51.

37. Ibid., 54.

38. Tapper, *Family in the Welfare State,* 121.

39. Ibid., 190.

40. Ibid., 160–64.

41. Sara McLanahan and Gary Sandefur, *Growing Up with a Single Parent* (Cambridge, Mass.: Harvard University Press, 1994), 1.

42. These studies are the Panel Study of Income Dynamics, the National Longitudinal Survey of Young Men and Women, the High School and Beyond Study, and the National Survey of Families and Households.

43. See James Coleman, "Social Capital and the Creation of Human Capital," *American Journal of Sociology* 94 (1988): 95–120; and idem, *Foundations of Social Theory* (Cambridge, Mass.: Harvard University Press, 1990).

44. See also Irwin Garfinkel, *Assuring Child Support* (New York: Russell Sage Foundation, 1992).

45. See Mark Ellingsen, *The Cutting Edge* (Grand Rapids: Wm. B. Eerdmans Publishing Co., 1993). This study of public church statements about social issues from the 1960s to the 1990s identifies more than 120 substantive statements by denominations and councils of churches from around the world on topics of economic life, poverty, development, and unemployment. Three of these statements gave a positive assessment of the contributions of corporations. In contrast, see Max Stackhouse, Dennis McCann, Shirley Roels, and Preston Williams, *On Moral Business* (Grand Rapids: Wm. B. Eerdmans Publishing Co., 1985).

46. Pope John Paul II, *Centesimus Annus* (On the hundredth anniversary) (Washington, D.C.: St. Paul Books, 1991). For particularly interesting commentaries on this encyclical, see George Weigel, ed., *A New Worldly Order* (Washington, D.C.: Ethics and Public Policy Center, 1992).

47. See James Skillen, "The Political Confusion of the Christian Coalition," *Christian Century* (August 30, 1995): 816–22.

Notes to Chapter 5.
Covenant and Love: What Have We Done?

1. See Walther Eichrodt, *Theology of the Old Testament,* trans. J. A. Baker, 2 vols. (Philadelphia: Westminster Press, 1961, 1967). For an artful overview of how this thesis has fared in the last three decades, see Patrick D. Miller, "Creation and Covenant," in *Biblical Theology: Problems and Perspectives,* ed. S. J. Kraftchick et al. (Nashville: Abingdon Press, 1995), 155–68.

2. G. Mendenhall, "Covenant Forms in Israelite Tradition," *Biblical Archeologist* 17 (1959): 50–76.

3. D. J. Elazar, *Covenant and Polity in Biblical Israel,* vol. 1 (New Brunswick, N.J.: Transaction Publishers, 1995), 1:86.

4. Ibid., 65.

5. Francis Fukuyuma, *Trust: The Social Virtues and the Creation of Prosperity* (New York: Free Press, 1995). See especially chapter 3, above.

6. These were adapted from G. E. Mendenhall, "Covenant," *Encyclopaedia Britannica,* 15th ed. (1975), 5:226–30, by Delbert R. Hillers, *Covenant: The History of a Biblical Idea* (Baltimore: Johns Hopkins University Press, 1969), and they are further modified here by intentional accent on ethical implications.

7. In a treatment of "covenantal renewal" in Deuteronomy, Moshe Weinfeld identifies eight parts, this last one having several features. See his *Deuteronomy and the Deuteronomic School* (New York: Oxford University Press, 1972).

8. Frank M. Cross, *Canaanite Myth and Hebrew Epic* (Cambridge, Mass.: Harvard University Press, 1992), 221.

9. Paul Hanson, *The People Called: The Growth of Community in the Bible* (San Francisco: Harper & Row, 1987), esp. 101–9. See also Michael Welcher's theological analysis of the significance of this in terms of "the fulfillment of the law," the "preservation of the people," and the grant "of prosperity," and especially in terms of the implications of the claim that the covenant of God with the house of David was "everlasting" (2 Sam. 23:4) (*God the Spirit* [Philadelphia: Fortress Press, 1984], 145–46).

10. The best single treatment of the contrast between the "organic" (integrated into one system) and the "pluralist" (differentiated into several systems) understanding of society in the West is F. W. Dillistone, *The Structure of the Divine Society* (Philadelphia: Westminster Press, 1951). However, see also William J. Everett, *God's Federal Republic: Reconstructing Our Governing Symbol* (New York: Paulist Press, 1988), which takes into account more recent critiques of this tradition.

11. See J. N. Figgis, *The Divine Right of Kings* (New York: Harper Torchbooks, 1965).

12. I have traced some of these key developments with regard to their impact on both church doctrine and sociopolitical developments in Max Stackhouse, *Creeds, Society, and Human Rights* (Grand Rapids: Wm. B. Eerdmans Publishing Co., 1985), esp. 44–49.

13. See Adam Selegman, *The Idea of Civil Society* (New York: Free Press, 1992), esp. 62–78.

14. See A.S.P. Woodhouse, ed., *Puritanism and Liberty* (London: J. M. Dent & Sons, 1938), for a remarkable collection of primary documents of this period. Cf. Michael Walzer, *The Revolution of the Saints* (New York: Atheneum Publishers, 1968). A useful contemporary treatment is D. Little, *Religion, Order, and Law: A Study in Pre-Revolutionary England* (Chicago: University of Chicago Press, 1969).

15. These spheres included family and economic life. See William J. Everett, *Blessed Be the Bond* (Philadelphia: Fortress Press, 1985).

16. Published in Leiden in 1648. See William Klempa, "The Concept of the Covenant in Sixteenth- and Seventeenth-Century Continental and British Reformed Theology," in *Major Themes in the Reformed Tradition,* ed. D. K. McKim (Grand Rapids: Wm. B. Eerdmans Publishing Co., 1992), 94–107. While helpful historically, this essay turns also to some systematic reflections and too slavishly follows Karl Barth's criticism of federal theology as set forth in *Church Dogmatics,* vol. 4, part 1, 54–66. Cf. A. C. Cochrane, "Karl Barth's Doctrine of the Covenant," in McKim, ed., *Major Themes,* 108–16.

17. Cocceius speaks of two covenants, a "covenant of works" with Adam and the "covenant of grace" with Christ, the new Adam (1 Cor. 15:22). While this distinction follows a phrase of Paul's in one way and is used by a number of federal thinkers, it both understates the grace of creation and overstates the freedom of Adam before the Fall to fulfill the covenant by works alone. This exacerbated no small number of debates about the depravity of fallen creation and the nature of God's will in predestination, which have plagued parts of the Reformed tradition since.

18. D. A. Weir, *The Origins of the Federal Theology in Sixteenth-Century Reformation Thought* (Oxford: Clarendon Press, 1990), 155.

19. See Miller, "Creation and Covenant," 161–63.

20. See J. Wayne Baker, *Heinrich Bullinger and the Covenant: The Other Reformed Tradition* (Athens: Ohio University Press, 1980).

21. See Presbyterian Church (U.S.A.), *The Book of Confessions* (Louisville, Ky.: Office of the General Assembly, 1994), 53–119, esp. 115–19, articles 28–30.

22. The Dutch Calvinist tradition, under the influence of Abram Kuyper, is especially famous for its treatment of the "spheres," but Emil Brunner continues the use of the concept of "orders." Karl Barth, while disagreeing in many respects with Brunner, adopts a parallel conceptuality in his famous *Church Dogmatics,* vol. 3, part 4. Other parts of the Reformed tradition influenced the development of sociological theory and borrow from it when they refer to various "departments of life" or "sectors of society." See Max Stackhouse, "Religion, Society and the Independent Sector: Key Elements of a General Theory," in *Religion, the Independent Sector, and American Culture,* ed. C. Cherry and R. A. Sherrill (Atlanta: Scholars Press, 1992), 11–30. The idea of *federal-covenantal thought* thus may appear even where the term is not used.

23. PC(USA), *Book of Confessions,* 124–258.

24. See Williston Walker, *The Creeds and Platforms of Congregationalism* (Boston: Pilgrim Press, 1960), 157–237.

25. The relationship of the Puritan and covenantal traditions to those of classical "liberal" theories is presently under intense investigation. See, e.g., E. Clinton Gardner, "John Locke, Justice and the Social Compact," *Journal of Law and Religion* 9, 2 (1992): 347–72. The use of the term *free church* in this connection can be confusing to Catholic natural law theorists or An-

abaptist advocates, both of whom remain doubtful or ill-informed about the Reformed heritage. These Catholic and Anabaptist theorists apparently influenced some formulations in Michael L. Westmoreland-White's otherwise excellent summary of much current scholarship, "Setting the Record Straight: Christian Faith, Human Rights, and the Enlightenment," *Annual of the Society of Christian Ethics* (1995): 76–96, esp. 81.

26. H. Richard Niebuhr draws the contrast between "covenant" and "contract" rather sharply in his often quoted "The Idea of Covenant and American Democracy," *Church History* 23 (June 1954): 126–35. The idea that covenantal thinking turns inevitably into contractual practice is suggested by James B. Torrence, "Covenant or Contract," *Scottish Journal of Theology* 23 (1970): 59. However, as Klempa acknowledges, this tends to apply only to some, such as Hermann Witsius in his *De Œconomia Foederum* (Amsterdam, 1677), 102.

27. Ernst Troeltsch, *The Social Teachings of the Christian Churches,* trans. O. Wyon (New York: Harper & Brothers, 1932).

28. Weir, *Origins of the Federal Theology,* 154. Weir, however, in his eagerness to show that these developments derive from only one theological concern, simply overstates the case when he concludes that "the seeds of the federal theology are not to be found in ethics or moral; it only affected these areas" and has "nothing to do with, sacramental theology, the theology of Church and State and their internal and external relationships . . . [etc.]" (154, 156).

29. See James Hastings Nichols, *Democracy and the Churches* (Philadelphia: Westminster Press, 1961); John F. A. Taylor, *The Masks of Society: An In quiry into the Covenants of Civilization* (New York: Appleton-Century-Crofts, 1966); Robert Bellah, *The Broken Covenant: American Civil Religion in a Time of Trial* (New York: Seabury Press, 1975); Joseph L. Allen, *Love and Conflict: A Covenantal Model of Christian Ethics* (Nashville: Abingdon Press, 1984); and Douglas Sturm, *Community and Alienation* (Notre Dame, Ind.: Notre Dame University Press, 1988), esp. part 2.

30. Jon D. Levenson, "Covenant and Consent: Biblical Reflections on the United States Constitution," *Religion & Values in Public Life* 3, 3 (spring 1995): 1ff.

31. The emphasis on "family values," articulated in Victorian theological terms by the Speaker of the House, is quite well known, but the president's views on this matter are less so. In a 1993 speech to the fall convocation of the Church of God in Christ, however, Bill Clinton stressed the crisis of the family and called for a new cooperation between government and church to overcome the breakdown of the family. See "Excerpts from Clinton's Speech to Black Ministers," *New York Times,* November 14, 1993, sec. A, 24.

32. Recovery from the damage to the Reformed and ecumenical heritage by these inclusions is discussed by Max Stackhouse, Peter Berger, Dennis McCann, and Douglas Meeks in *Christian Social Ethics in a Global Era* (Nashville: Abingdon Press, 1995).

33. Key examples that draw on ideas from the covenantal, pluralistic tradition include John Witte, Jr., ed., *Christianity and Democracy in a Global Context* (Boulder, Colo.: Westview Press, 1993); José Casanova, *Public Religions in the Modern World* (Chicago: University of Chicago Press, 1994); and Luis E. Lugo, *Religion, Public Life and the American Polity* (Knoxville: University of Tennessee Press, 1994).

34. Indeed, in a new phase of research, Robert D. Putnam, a Harvard professor of political science who gained considerable attention with his "Bowling Alone: America's Declining Social Capital," *Journal of Democracy* (January 1995), 65–78, suggests that television, more than any other factor, is decisive in the decline of civil society; see his "The Strange Disappearance of Civic America," *American Prospect* (winter 1966): 34–48. If he means media communication of all sorts, he may have isolated at least one contributor to the changes, but his short-term sense of history, his nonglobal focus, and his neglect of theological matters as potentially causative make one doubtful of the long-term cogency of his argument.

35. These developments have been at the center of my research for more than a decade and need not be reviewed here. Two recent works, however, summarize my views: Max Stackhouse et al., *Christian Social Ethics in a Global Era* (Nashville: Abingdon Press, 1995); and Max Stackhouse, "Theology and the Economic Life of Society in a Global Era," in *Policy Reform and Moral Grounding,* ed. T. W. Boxx and G. Quinlivan (Latrobe, Pa.: Center for Economic and Policy Education, 1996).

36. I do not here take up the problems of that portion of the population who are on welfare, but the most substantive recent review of the issues can, in my view, be found in the remarkable collection by Stanley W. Carlson-Thies and James W. Skillen, eds., *Welfare in America: Christian Perspectives on a Policy in Crisis* (Grand Rapids: Wm. B. Eerdmans Publishing Co., 1995). Their book proposes a new form of cooperation between religious, community, voluntary, and governmental institutions to aid excluded or socially incompetent people in becoming participants in civil society.

37. See William R. Garrett, "The Protestant Ethic and the Spirit of the Modern Family," *Association for the Sociology of Religion* (August 1994).

38. See Lake Lambert, "The Concept of Vocation in Contemporary Economic Life" (Ph.D. diss., Princeton Theological Seminary, forthcoming).

39. Several recent studies touch on these delicate connections and insist on their indispensability and the need for justice in them. See, especially, Lisa Sowle Cahill, *Between the Sexes: Foundations for a Christian Ethics of Sexuality* (Philadelphia: Fortress Press, 1985); Susan Moller Okin, *Justice, Gender and the Family* (New York: Basic Books, 1989); and Stephen G. Post, *Spheres of Love: Toward a New Ethics of the Family* (Dallas: Southern Methodist University Press, 1994).

40. I have argued this position on the grounds of cross-cultural studies in my *Creeds, Society and Human Rights.* Cf. H. Dooyeweerd, *A Christian Theory of Social Institutions,* trans. M. Verbrugge, ed. J. Witte (La Jolla, Calif.:

Dooyeweerd Foundation, 1986); Michael Walzer, *Spheres of Justice* (Princeton, N.J.: Princeton University Press, 1983).

41. This point not only has been explicitly recognized by theologians for more than half a century (see Emil Brunner,"The Community of Love: Marriage and the Family," in *The Divine Imperative* [London: Lutherworth Press, 1937]) but has been a part of social-scientific theories for a generation (see E. M. Schur, *The Family and the Sexual Revolution* [Bloomington: Indiana University Press, 1964]) and of political debate for a decade (see Daniel P. Moynihan, *Family and Nation* [New York: Harcourt Brace Jovanovich, 1986]).

Index of Names and Subjects